WINE COUNTRY EUROPE

ORNELLA D'ALESSIO

MARCO SANTINI

WINE COUNTRY EUROPE

TOURING, TASTING, AND BUYING
IN THE MOST BEAUTIFUL WINE REGIONS

RIZZOLI
NEW YORK

EDITORIAL DIRECTOR: Valeria Camaschella
EDITORIAL COORDINATOR: Davide Bernardini
GRAPHIC COORDINATOR: Marco Santini
TECHNICAL COORDINATOR: Roberto Ghidoli
EDITORIAL PRODUCTION: Studio Selmi, Milano
DESIGN AND TYPESETTING, ITALIAN EDITION: Twister, Milano
TRANSLATOR, ENGLISH EDITION: Marguerite Shore
EDITORIAL COORDINATOR, ENGLISH EDITION: Christopher Steighner
DESIGN AND TYPESETTING, ENGLISH EDITION: Sara E. Stemen
PRINTING: Deaprinting Officine Grafiche
SEPARATIONS: Legatoria del Verbano

ISBN 0-8478-2770-4
LIBRARY OF CONGRESS CONTROL NUMBER: 2005929097

© 2005 Istituto Geografico De Agostini, Novara
© 2005 Rizzoli International Publications, English-language translation

First published in the United States of America in 2005
by Rizzoli International Publications, Inc.
300 Park Avenue South
New York, NY 10010
www.rizzoliusa.com

2005 2006 2007 2008 / 10 9 8 7 6 5 4 3 2 1

Distributed in the U.S. trade by Random House, New York

Printed in Italy

CONTENTS

INTRODUCTION

WINE IS NOT only something to drink. Over time, it has become a means to learn about the lands of its origin, and the people who produce it. Wine devotees today are not content to know the best vintages and producers; they want to get to know the places where the grapes are grown, and the land whose characteristics make the wine unique. Every year this trend is prompting a growing number of people to travel off the beaten path to experience their favorite wines combined with traditional regional dishes—in other words, to discover everything that a wine region can offer: culture, landscape, and the environment.

And so wine becomes the leitmotif for this fascinating journey through the most beautiful regions of Europe. There are twenty wine routes, chosen for their historical value, the quality of the wines, and the interest of the itinerary itself. From Champagne to Chianti, from the Douro to the Rhine, from Slovenian Collio to Andalusia, this is a continuous and passionate pursuit carried out against the backdrop of timeless landscapes. Each itinerary combines the beauty of the iconography with an interest in content; the enjoyable and engaging text accompanies this trip, while the spectacular images of these regions tell their own story, stirring us to dream of making the trip.

The pages that follow contain twenty itineraries by the author, to be followed in their entirety or in part. You only have to choose your route and then set out, in a virtual fashion if you like, toward these regions of wine cellars, vineyards, and ancient villages . . . where there are always delightful discoveries to be made.

PORTUGAL

 THIS IS THE far western boundary of Europe, looking out over the infinite expanse of the Atlantic Ocean, which for centuries signified the edge of the world. If Portugal today can boast utterly unique wines, this is due precisely to its historical and geographic isolation. In addition to port—or decades synonymous with Portuguese wine—there are over five hundred indigenous grape varieties in this small country.

It is a land rich in climatic contrasts. The Atlantic regions, where ocean breezes create cool temperatures, produce light wines characterized by a vibrant acidity, such as Vinho Verde. In contrast, the continental climate that dominates the inland area, with cold winters and often torrid summers, produces strong wines of great character, such as port.

Vines were introduced to the region by the Phoenicians, who had a commercial base where the Spanish city of Cádiz now stands, and from there they settled present-day Algarve. With the arrival of the Romans at the end of the second century BC, the cultivation of vines greatly increased and became a form of specialized agriculture. New winegrowing areas were found toward the north, subsequent to the Roman conquests. A sarcophagus dated between the first and third centuries AD, discovered in Alentejo (now on display in the Museo Nacional Soares dos Reis, in Porto), shows two young men dancing while pressing grapes.

Beginning in the second century the Christian influence brought new developments to viticulture in this western portion of the Iberian Peninsula, promoting its progressive spread until the arrival of the Moors in 711. The emir of Cordoba proved to be tolerant with regard to the cultivation of vines, but this was not the case in the

RIGHT: a selection of prestigious bottles of port.
OPPOSITE PAGE: the Douro River valley at sunset.

late eleventh century with the new Almoravides rulers. The Christian "reconquest" brought a return of the vine. By 1139, when Alfonso Henriques became the first to assume the title of king of Portugal in Guimaraes, the city was already surrounded by vineyards.

In the fourteenth century Portugal became a naval power, and dried cod, imported principally from the British Isles, became a staple of the Portuguese diet on both sailing vessels as well as on land. The trading currency for this flourishing market was Vinho Verde, from the region of Minho. Thus by the late sixteenth century, Portugal was the principal market for English fish, and England was the main market for Portuguese wine. This narrowly defined trade agreement laid the foundation for the explosion of the phenomenon of port, the "wine for the English." After the grave economic and agriculture crisis following the Spanish occupation of Portugal in the first half of the seventeenth century, which led to the near abandonment of the vineyards, it was English merchants who gave new impetus to Portuguese viticulture and wine production, with their search for new sources of supply. This period saw the development of the Douro region and the birth (the story of which lies somewhere between reality and legend) of the fortified wine that was destined to become first a passion for the English and then one of the most famous wines in the world.

Present-day Portugal, however, is not only about port. In addition to widely disseminated wines such as Mateus, Lancers, or Vinho Verde, dry red wines of notable structure are produced in the Douro region, particularly Barca Velha, which is considered the best Portuguese red wine. The Bairrada region, around the city of Agueda, produces important red wines, tannic and long-lived, based on the Baga grape, and a robust white wine of limited acidity, made from Bical grapes. The Dão region, northeast of Lisbon, produces dry red wines that are increasingly fine and elegant, based on Touriga Nacional, Tempranillo (or Tinta Roriz), Bastardo, and Jaen grapes. Other Portuguese wine areas include Carcavelos, Bucelas, Ribatejo, and Colares.

THE ITINERARY

But it is the Douro region, with its hundred miles of rough hills and seductive vineyards behind the city of Porto, that remains the hub for the country's oenological culture, and port is still the king of Portuguese wines. And so the itinerary goes from Piñhao, in the heart of the wine-producing region, along the historical path of the *rabelos* (the brightly colored boats that transported the young wine along the river, and which are anchored today at the mouth of the Douro River), passing through the most spectacular wineries and the most beautiful vineyards, through the city of Porto, with its bridges and *azulejos* tilework, to arrive at the famous cellars in Vila Nova de Gaia.

PORTO

WINE TRAIL *Itinerary*

ITINERARY LENGTH
100 miles / 160 kilometers

BEST TIME TO GO
April to late October

TIME TO SPEND
Five to six days

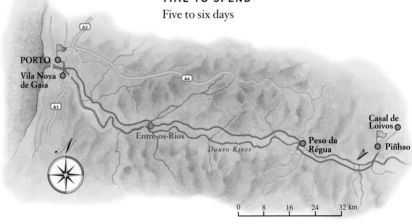

USEFUL ADDRESSES
Tourist Information Office
Rua Clube dos Fenianos 25,
Porto
Tel. 00351.223393470,
www.portoturismo.pt
Istituto do Vinho do Porto,
Rua Ferreira Borges, Porto,
Tel. 00351.22.006522

ON A CRUISE TO PORTO
An evocative day cruise along the Douro River allows the traveler to retrace the historic route used to transport barrels of young port, which the brightly colored boats known as *rabelos* carried down the river as far as Vila Nova de Gaia, where the barrels were left to age. (For more information, visit Douro Cruises at www.douroazul.com.)

LEAVING SPAIN AND crossing the border into Portugal, the Duero River changes its name and becomes the Douro. Along the banks, one can see the first vineyards of Touriga Nacional, Tinta Amarena, and Touriga Francesa vines and other indigenous varieties that are used for making port, the famed Portuguese wine that owes its success to the embargo between France and England at the end of the seventeenth century.

In the late 1600s, due to growing difficulties in importing French wines, English merchants began looking for alternatives. Two Londoners traveling up the Douro arrived at the Baroque sanctuary of Nossa Senhora dos Remédios in Lamego. Tasting the monks' wine, they discovered that it was delicious. They also learned something else: it was fortified with the addition of *aguardiente,* a practice vital for the essence of port, which now is carried out directly on the must. In addition to defining the character of the wine, the alcohol made it possible to preserve its quality during long sea voyages. The success of port among Charles

OPPOSITE PAGE, FROM THE TOP: a vine branch against the backdrop of the Douro valley; towers and crenellations of the Castello di Penedono; the Sandeman cellar in Vila Nova de Gaia; a *rabelo* on the Douro River in Porto.

RIGHT: a spectacular aerial view of the Douro valley, with the terraced hills and vineyards.

CITIES *Porto*

Located between the last curves of the Douro River and the Atlantic Ocean, Porto, Portugal's second largest city, is charming and atmospheric. Typical tall, narrow houses covered with majolica tiles and embellished with wrought-iron balconies mingle with priceless monuments. The church of São Francisco, whose simple Gothic lines contrast with its sumptuous interior, has a high altar, pillars, and a ceiling decorated in pure gold, while the majestic and austere cathedral of Sé preserves the spare lines of its Romanesque origins. The Palacio da Bolsa boasts opulently decorated interiors, and the railroad station of São Bento proves one of the city's grandest buildings. In the old city, it is possible to climb the Baroque Clerigos tower, which for a time was the tallest in Portugal. It provides a beautiful view of the city, which stretches out toward the south, and beyond the river as far as Vila Nova de Gaia; on clear days, it is possible to see the mouth of the Douro and the coast.

A nighttime view of the cathedral in Porto.

II's subjects was immediate: By 1728 more than a million and a half crates of port were being exported per year, and in 1799 the number exceeded three million. Many English merchants moved to the city of Porto or along the banks of the Douro so that they could begin producing their own wine, and many of the most prestigious labels still bear English names today.

In England, to meet the growing demand for port, they began to adulterate the product. The wine's image risked being seriously compromised, and the Marquês de Pombal, the strong-willed Portuguese prime minister, made a revolutionary decision. In 1756, he decided to use great granite markers to delimit the region that produced the best wines and introduced a series of precise laws that regulated wine production, shipping, and prices. Thus this patch of land—barely 1,000 square miles (2,500 square kilometers) in area—became the first wine-growing region with guaranteed control of origin, nearly two centuries before this was introduced in the rest of the world.

THE WINE ROUTE
ALONG THE DOURO VALLEY

Leaving Spain, the spectacular broad valleys narrow and give way to more impressive and majestic hills, and the view grows more dramatic until one reaches **PINHÃO**, heart of the wine region. Numerous detours along the route lead to lookout points from which one can admire the orderly expanse of vineyards. The rows of vines disappear into the distance,

following the gentle curves of the terrain like waves in an emerald sea. Pinhão, located on the bank of the river, is the hub for this itinerary and merits a visit, most of all for the station embellished with *azulejos*, the white and blue tiles typical of the region, and for the Vintage House, an old manor house overlooking the Douro that has been restored and transformed into a hotel. Here, the opening of a vintage bottle of wine becomes a spectacle. In the *di la tenaz* ritual, red-hot tongs are held around the neck of the bottle at the height of the cork until the glass is well heated. Then the tongs are removed and an ice cube is placed against the hot surface. The resulting jolt in temperature creates a precise cut through the bottle neck, without chipping the glass — a trick that avoids demolishing the old cork with a corkscrew.

WHERE PORT WAS BORN

To fully experience the atmosphere at the heart of the land of port, one has to visit the *quintas*, or wineries, where often it is possible to stop for dinner. The Quinta Do Noval, in **CASAL DE LOIVOS**, has one of the few parcels of land in Europe with indigenous vines that survived the phylloxera blight; everywhere else the original vines have been replaced by American vines, which are coarser but resistant to the disease. Five original acres have endured, from which 3,000 liters of

The orderly expanse of vineyards that blanket the hills of the Douro valley.

Vintage Nacional Quinta do Noval are produced every year (*Wine Spectator* named the 1931 production one of the ten best wines in the world, and it has fetched a price of 6,000 euro, or $7,300, at auction).

Toward **PESO DA RÉGUA**, the route continues along the sinuous edge of the river, caressing the steepest and most spectacular slopes and traversing the most prized wine-producing regions. In the morning, the sun's rays gild the mist that rises from the water and cause the ripe clusters of grapes to gleam. The lovely Pousada Solar da Rede, an eighteenth-century house, sits halfway up the hill amid the vineyards, with a commanding view of the river. Then the road to the sanctuary of **LAMEGO** leads to Quinta da Pacheca, one of the oldest wineries in the country, where one can taste a port that has been aged for sixty years.

HARVEST AND TRADITION

The harvest is an important time in the creation of port, and it is accompanied by an explosion of folkloric ritual. The grapes are transported to the *lagar*—where occasionally they are still pressed by foot—and are scrupulously chosen one by one. The fermentation begins with the must to transform the sugar into alcohol. The process is interrupted by the addition of 75 percent *aguardiente*, obtained from the distillation of wine produced in the Alto Douro region.

The journey continues along the banks of the river following the same path as the *rabelos*, the sail-boats that until a few decades ago transported the barrels of young port to the great cellars in **VILA NOVA DE GAIA**. Here the port was left to age anywhere from two to one hundred years before being sold. The route remains unchanged but the colorful vessels have given way to trucks. The worn-out *rabelos* remain moored on the left bank of the river, which at this point mingles with the ocean waters. Before disappearing, the Douro is transformed into a border that divides Vila Nova de Gaia from **PORTO**.

AMONG THE BARRELS, AT THE EDGE OF THE SEA

To experience the exhilaration of walking among the centuries-old barrels, a visit to some of the old wineries is a must. The first of these is Sandeman, which merits a visit more for the beauty of its properties and its port museum than for the quality of its wine; then there are Taylors, Ferreira, Cockburn Smithes, Fonseca, and Adriano Ramos Pinto. In the latter's cellar, in addition to the wines, visitors can enjoy listening to the warm notes of a grand piano being played in the sancta sanctorum, where the most valuable and ancient bottles rest. The only thing left to do is to cross the Dom Luis I bridge, designed by Gustave Eiffel, and enter **PORTO**. The town includes monu-

An evocative nocturnal view of the Dom Luis I bridge in Porto.

RIGHT, ABOVE: Eduardo Pimentel, winemaker and owner of the ancient Quinta da Pacheca winery. *BELOW:* view of the Sandeman cellar in Porto.

WINES FROM RUBY TO COLHEITA

The world of port is complex, and it is difficult to orient oneself in the maze of definitions, labels, blends, vintages, families, and colors. Here is a concise guide to the eight basic types of port.

WHITE
A mix of wines with the addition of brandy, aged for a few years in the barrel. Ideal as an aperitif.

UNDATED REDS
Ruby, a young and fruity blend, is the least prized. Fine as a dessert wine.

Vintage character, a mix of young port, aged for three to four years, complex and full-bodied. Fine as an aperitif, as a complement to medium-aged cheeses, or as a dessert wine.

Tawny, an amber-colored mix of wines aged for a few years in oak barrels. A perfect accompaniment to dry pastries.

Aged tawny, a blend of different vintages that remain in wood barrels for ten, twenty, thirty, or forty years or more, the average age of which is indicated on the label. Complements very aged cheeses.

DATED REDS
LBV (Late-Bottled Vintage), like the vintage, is produced only in exceptional years but remains in the barrel for five to seven years. Complements green-veined cheeses or can also be a wine for meditation.

Vintage must remain in the barrel for two years and rest in the bottle for at least fifteen to twenty years. A vintage year is stated when the harvest has superb characteristics. Complements green-veined cheeses, chocolate, or can also be a wine for meditation.

Colheita is made from a single harvest and remains in the barrel for a minimum of seven years, and from then on is bottled when the market requires. Can complement a variety of dishes, depending on the vintage and length of aging.

ments decorated with scrollwork, *azulejos*, and old grocery shops, along with wine shops selling extremely rare bottles, such as Garrafeira Tio Pepe (at Rua Eng. Ferreira Dias 51), or Livraria Lello (at Rua das Carmelitas 144), an Art Deco-style bookstore with an interesting cafe-wine shop on the second floor that holds the "jewels" of the city. And to conclude the trip, nothing could be better than a dinner of *bacalhau*, a cod dish prepared according to one of 365 existing recipes.

A view of Porto from the waters of the Douro, with the closely packed façades of the tall, narrow buildings; in the foreground is one of the typical *rabelos*, used for transporting barrels of wine.

TAKE A BREAK

LODGING

Pinhão: **LUGAR DA PONTE**
Note: Closed from January to March.
Vintage House, an old manor house overlooking the Douro, has been transformed into a pleasant and romantic hotel, which in addition to an excellent restaurant boasts a superb cellar of port.

Lung oil Douro: **MESAO FRIO**
Pousada Solar da Rede, a splendid house located halfway up the hill, has a wonderful view of the Douro River and a swimming pool amid the vine-yards. Period furnishings and an excellent restaurant that serves typical dishes, from *pasties de bacalhau* to *queijadinhas*, along with cheese, almonds, eggs, and fruit, and *favas quisadas com chouriço*.

DINING

Porto: **RESTAURANTE PORTUCALE**
In its dominant post overlooking the entire city, this restaurant serves traditional cuisine accompanied by an excellent wine list, with a splendid selection of port.

RIGHT: Solpicaõ ao vinho do Porto.

W. & J. GRAHAM'S

Vila Nova de Gaia, tel. 00351.22.3776300
www.symington.com

Founded: 1820
Production region: Douro valley
Wines and grape varieties: 95% reds, 5% whites; Touriga Nacional, Tinta Roriz, Tinta Barroca, Tinta Cão, Touriga Francesa

GREAT WINES

Graham's 2000 Vintage Port
Made from grapes from old vines on the Quinta dos Malvedos, Quinta da Vila Velha, Quinta do Vale de Malhadas, and Quinta das Lages properties. Deep violet color, full-bodied to the nose, complex and very persistent, with hints of wild fruit and violet. Robust and velvety taste of great body and harmony, with notes of raspberry. Can be aged at length, for up to fifty years, and complements chocolate.

Graham's 40 Year Old Tawny
A blend of wines fermented with natural leavens and aged on average forty years in large wooden vats in Vila Nova de Gaia. Amber color with bits of greenish reflections. A rich, elegant, complex, and rather persistent bouquet, with hints of walnut and caramelized orange. The taste is powerful, warm, and full-bodied, with notes of dry fruit and caramel. Ready to drink, complements aged cheeses and dry fruit.

Visits and tastings: yes

SANDEMAN

Largo Miguel Bombarda 3,
Vila Nova de Gaia, tel. 00351.22.3740500
www.sandeman.com

Founded: 1790
Production region: Douro valley
Wines and grape varieties: 90% reds, 10% whites; Touriga Nacional, Tinta Roriz, Tinta Barroca, Tinta Cão, Touriga Francesa

GREAT WINES

Vau Vintage 2000
Made from highly selected grapes from the most prized vineyards on the property. The 2000 vintage, considered exceptional in quality, produced a wine of great class, complexity, and structure. Intense ruby-red and violet color, full, complex, fruity, and very persistent to the nose, Powerful, harmonious, velvety taste, with notes of red berry, plum, and licorice. Should be drunk after five to fifteen years of aging, complements chocolate-based desserts.

40 Years Old
Aged in wood and bottled in 1999. Dark amber color with reflections tending to oil. Full, complex, harmonious, and persistent bouquet, with hints of date, dry fig, and almond. Powerful, rich, and balanced taste. Long aftertaste with notes of caramel and licorice. Ready to drink by itself or as a complement to vanilla ice cream.

Visits and tastings: yes

RAMOS PINTO

Avenida de Ramos Pinto 380,
Vila Nova de Gaia, tel. 00351.22.3707000
www.ramospinto.pt

Founded: 1880
Production region: Cima Corgo, Alto Douro
Wines and grape varieties: 95% reds, 5% whites; Touriga Nacional, Tinta Roriz, Tinta Barroca, Tinta Cão, Touriga Francesa

GREAT WINES

Porto Vintage 2000
Aged for twenty years in oak, chestnut, and mahogany barrels. Deep red-violet color with bluish reflections. Complex bouquet with hints of ripe plum, pepper, and cocoa. Powerful, concentrated, and voluptuous taste with great body. Long and velvety finish. Should be aged for up to thirty years, and complements green-veined cheeses or chocolate.

Porto 20 Years Quinta do Bom Retiro
Made from a blend of Touriga Nacional, Tinta Roriz, Tinta Barroca, Tinta Cão, and Touriga Francesa grapes, aged for an average of twenty years in large wooden barrels. Amber color with yellowish reflections. Full nose, with hints of grapefruit, apricot, almond, hazelnut, vanilla, and cocoa. Warm and velvety taste, good body, with almond, exotic fruit, dried figs and dates. Ready to drink, complements sweets made with melted chocolate.

Visits and tastings: yes

FERREIRA

Rua da Carvalhosa 19, Vila Nova de Gaia,
tel. 00351.22.3745292/3746100

Founded: 1751
Production region: Douro valley
Wines and grape varieties: 100% reds; Touriga Nacional, Tinta Roriz, Tinta Barroca, Tinta Cão, Touriga Francesa

GREAT WINES

Ferreira Vintage 2000
Made from highly selected grapes, this vintage shows the great character of the best wines of Porto. Dark purplish-blue color. Intense, complex, and very persistent to the nose, with hints of woods and plum. Concentrated taste, excellent structure, velvety, with notes of preserves and chocolate. Capable of excellent aging, complements tarts and chocolate-based sauces.

Ferreira Duque de Bragança 20 Years
Blend made from mixing different wines aged on average for twenty years in large oak barrels. Brilliant amber color with brass reflections. Complex and concentrated bouquet, with hints of pipe tobacco, almond, and leather. Powerful and balanced taste, good structure with notes of dry fruit and caramel. Ready to drink, and complements dry pastries.

Visits and tastings: yes, by appointment

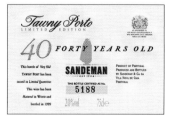

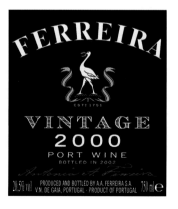

COCKBURN SMITHES

Rua das Corados 13, Vila Nova de Gaia, tel. 00351.22.3776500

Founded: 1815
Production region: Upper Douro valley
Wines and grape varieties: 100% reds; Touriga Nacional, Tinta Roriz, Tinta Barroca, Tinta Cão, Touriga Francesa

GREAT WINES

Quinta dos Canais Single Quinta Vintage 2000
Extremely restricted selection of the best grapes from the Quinta dos Canais. Vinified in traditional *lagares* and aged for two years in large oak barrels. Intense violet color tending to black. Full, intense, and persistent bouquet, with hints of wild fruit. Velvety, warm taste, great body and harmony, with notes of ripe fruit, licorice, and chocolate. Should be aged ten to twenty years, and complements Stilton cheese or fresh hazelnuts.

Cockburn's Special Reserve Port
Made from selected grapes from the Quinta do Atayde and from certain outside suppliers, it is the result of a blend of various ruby ports of an average age between four to five years. Aged in old oak barrels of various sizes. Deep ruby-red color, tending to violet. Full and persistent bouquet, with hints of strawberry, raspberry, and plum. Rich, soft taste, with good structure and balance, long aftertaste with notes of chocolate. Should be drunk young, and complements green-veined cheeses or chocolate-based desserts.

Visits and tastings: yes, by appointment

TAYLOR FLADGATE & YEATMAN

Rua do Choupelo 250, Vila Nova de Gaia, tel. 00351.22.3742800
www.taylor.pt

Founded: 1692
Production region: Upper Douro valley, Moselle, Saar
Wines and grape varieties: 95% reds, 5% whites; Touriga Nacional, Tinta Roriz, Tinta Barroca, Tinta Cão, Touriga Francesa, Tinta Amarela

GREAT WINES

Quinta de Vargellas 2001
Quinta de Vargellas was the first "single quinta" vintage port to be sold, in 1958. The 2001 has a dark inky color with violet reflections. Full, very complex, and persistent bouquet, with hints of cherry and ripe wild fruit. Velvety taste with great body and structure, and notes of blueberry and plum accompanied in the aftertaste by coffee and chocolate. Can be aged at length, complements sweets based on melted chocolate or, once aged, can be a wine for meditation.

40 Year Old Tawny
A blend of port aged in large oak barrels, with an average age around forty years. Amber color with greenish reflections and a full, complex, fine, and very persistent bouquet, with hints of almond and rare wood. Powerful taste, balanced, of notable structure, with notes of coffee and chocolate. Extremely long aftertaste. Ready to drink, and complements dry pastry.

Visits and tastings: yes

FONSECA

Rua Barrão de Forrester 404, Vila Nova de Gaia, tel. 00351.22.3719999
www.fonseca.pt

Founded: 1822
Production region: Douro Valley.
Wines and grape varieties: 90% reds, 10% whites; Touriga Nacional, Tinta Roriz, Tinta Barroca, Tinta Cão, Touriga Francesa

GREAT WINES

Fonseca Vintage 1985
Made from selected grapes from the San Antonio, Cruzeiro, and Panascal estates. Vinified in traditional *lagares*, where the grapes are pressed by foot. Intense ruby-red color tending to violet. Elegant, complex, and very persistent bouquet, with hints of spices. Harmonious and velvety taste, great body and concentration, with notes of raisin and leather. Should be aged at length, and complements chocolate.

Fonseca BIN 27
Created over a century ago as a private wine of the Guimaraens family, now the standby of the Fonseca winery. A blend from vineyards on the property, aged four years in wooden barrels before being bottled. Deep ruby-red color with purplish-blue reflections. Complex and persistent bouquet, with hints of blueberry and cassis. Soft and velvety taste, with notes of plum and chocolate. Ready to drink, and excellent after a meal.

Visits and tastings: yes

MARTINEZ

Rua das Coradas 13, Vila Nova de Gaia, tel. 00351.22.3776500
www.martinez.pt

Founded: 1790
Production region:
Cima Corgo, Upper Douro, Vilarica
Wines and grape varieties: 100% reds; Touriga Nacional, Tinta Roriz, Tinta Barroca, Tinta Cão, Touriga Francesa

GREAT WINES

Porto Vintage 2000
Vinified in traditional granite *lagares* and aged two years in old oak barrels before being bottled. Intense red, purplish-blue color with slight blue reflections. Concentrated and persistent bouquet, with hints of violet, plum, dog rose, and wild fruit. Full and velvety taste, notable structure with notes of ripe fruit and plum. Should be drunk young or aged for perhaps twenty to thirty years, and complements toasted hazelnuts or green-veined cheeses.

Porto 10 Years
After vinification in traditional granite *lagares* and fortification, it is aged in small, 600-liter oak barrels. A mix of wines of different ages. Amber color with brilliant ruby reflections. Full, intense, and fine to the nose, with hints of walnuts and almonds, raisins, and rare wood. Complex, vigorous, and balanced to the palate, with notes of dry fruit and a long, clean aftertaste. Should be consumed in the first years after bottling, and complements aged cheeses or dry pastry.

Visits and tastings: yes

SPAIN

SPAIN IS ONE country in the western world where the changes of recent decades have taken on an urgent, profound, inexorable rhythm, from the economy to the culture, and from services to lifestyle. This is also true of wine production in the Iberian Peninsula: There is a long history, going back centuries; the more recent past, characterized by immobility and backwardness; and a present in full development, rich in possibility.

Grapevines probably arrived with the Phoenicians in the area of present-day Cádiz and took root on the hills that surround the modern "city of light," before spreading throughout Spain and Portugal. It is believed that the first wines in the region were sweet and oxidized, true precursors to today's sherry, which originates just a short distance from Cádiz.

The long Moorish domination (from the eighth to the fifteenth century) halted the development of viticulture in much of Spain, although the vineyards were never truly wiped out. The Moors consumed fresh grapes as a fruit, and raisins were used as a garnish in many recipes; they also drank unfermented grape juice. Wine appeared, with discretion, only on the tables of the highest classes: the nobles, those in power, and the intellectuals.

The return to the culture of wine had to await the "reconquest" of Spain from the Moors in the late fifteenth century. Curiously, during those years the Spaniards turned their attention not only to the rediscovery of wine in their own country, but also with the export of vines and winemaking techniques to the New World,

RIGHT: a view of the Alion cellar in Peñafiel, along the Ribera del Duero.
OPPOSITE: Sherry ages in bottles at the Domecq cellars, in Jerez de La Frontera.

thereby unwittingly laying the foundations for competition and a catchment area (the United States as a whole) that today is a driving force for the international wine market.

From the eighteenth to nineteenth century, commercial wine production was in the hands of the Spanish noble families and large landowners—people who could allow themselves the luxury of aging wine in their cellars before selling it. The foundations for traditional high-quality Iberian wine include aging for long periods in barrels of American oak, after which it is bottled and sold once it is ready for drinking.

Alongside this niche market, which has persisted over the centuries, a mass-production wine industry has developed, particularly in the twentieth century. In the 1970s and 1980s, hundreds upon hundreds of liters of low-quality wine, in large part destined for export, risked bringing the entire Spanish wine sector to the point of collapse. The traditional style of winemaking had been dormant too long, and there was an ocean of wine that was increasingly difficult to sell on the international market.

The turning point came in the 1990s, with the awareness that quality could not get any worse (while in many other countries, the wine business was experiencing tremendous growth). At the same time new, large amounts of capital were becoming available, communications were being modernized (opening up previously remote areas), and more modern and efficient vinification techniques were being disseminated.

SPANISH WINES TODAY

Today the Spanish wine scene has changed drastically and is showing exciting vitality, with possibilities for development that can put Spain at the center of the international stage.

The areas that traditionally produced the major Iberian wines (particularly the Rioja region) are witnessing enormous capital investment, construction or renovation of immense cellars, and the excavation of entire mountains to create cellars in the subsoil. These are temples of wine-production technology, designed by some of the world's most famous architects. New

wine-producing regions are also emerging—from Priorato to Toro (along the Duero, toward Portugal), from Penedés to Somontano, and from Mancha to Navarra—where wines of modern inspiration are being created, in response to ever-younger but demanding tastes.

Today in Spanish wine country, quality is of the utmost importance. This is expressed in greater care given to the vines, in a focus on indigenous varieties, especially Tempranillo, in the effort given to imbue red wines—traditionally rather rough—with greater refinement; it is also evident in the birth of a new generation of wines, so-called wines of "high expression" in which an international style, rich in hints of wood and vanilla, is combined with an explosion of fruit. The latter wines, meant to be drunk young, are accessible but not banal.

A brilliant example of this can be found in the Ribera del Duero region. Along with the Vega Sicilia estate, which pioneered the present-day search for quality, and its wines of wonderful refinement and elegance, there are newer names—Alejándro Fernández, Aalto, Pingus, Bodega Valduero—all growers of indigenous vines that can produce wines of great class and personality.

The Jerez de La Frontera region merits a discussion all its own. This is the land of sherry and the birthplace of vines in the Iberian Peninsula. Located in the far corner of Andalusia, it produces wines with extraordinary characteristics, wines that breathe in the ocean while they age and absorb the brilliant sun from nearby Africa. These wines also are subject to the caprices of climate, in open-air cellars where the wind and birds come and go at will. The development of these wines is antithetical to all modern trends, which impose climate control and hygienic regimes in the workplace, but the result is wines that are absolutely original: clean, almost cutting when they are young, opulent and reflective when they are aged. Sherry not only is affected by the ocean, but also has a fascinating

history populated by voyagers and merchants, visionaries and warriors, great families and multinationals. The world of sherry must be discovered slowly to appreciate its special characteristics.

THE ITINERARIES

Just one glance at a cellar will suffice to understand that Spain is a land with astounding potential for viticulture. Much of the region is made up of a plateau, and 90 percent of the vines are found at an ideal altitude. Hot summers and stern winters, scant precipitation, and long hours in the sun force the vines into a daily struggle that results in concentrated fruit, rich in extract. The abundance of microclimates and the relative geographic isolation have protected indigenous species, with the result that this land can offer tremendous surprises to those who want to discover them.

The pages that follow propose a long dash across the Iberian Peninsula. The journey is divided into three large stages—Andalusia, Ribera del Duero, and Rioja—conceived so the traveler can experience the world of Spanish wine in a single great voyage.

A landscape of vineyards, hills, and castles in the Rioja region, along the Ebro River valley.

RIBERA DEL DUERO

WINE TRAIL *Itinerary*

ITINERARY LENGTH
270 miles / 430 kilometers

BEST TIME TO GO
April to late October

TIME TO SPEND
Four to five days

Map labels:
VALLADOLID
Valbuena de Duero
Quintanilla de Onésimo
Pesquera de Duero
Roa
Peñafiel
Aranda de Duero
Peñaranda de Duero
Gumiel de Mercado
Soria
Quéllar
Segovia
AVILA DE LOS CABALLEROS
El Escorial
MADRID

N

0   8   16   24   32 km

USEFUL ADDRESSES
Patronato Provincial de
Turismo de Soria
Avenida de la Victoria 5
Soria
Tel: 0034.975.220511
www.sorianitelaimaginas.com

THE TYPICAL OCHER color of the Iberian plateau—immense highlands in the heart of Spain that fade into the gentle hills of Ribera del Duero—along with skies streaked with clouds as in the paintings of El Greco, and hilltop castles and fortifications characterize a trip through the countryside of the Castile y León region, where one discovers true architectural marvels and the great red wines made from the Tempranillo grape. This region led the revival of Spanish oenology with the development of wines marked by full body and complexity, which in only a few years have achieved recognition on the international market, following in the steps of the mythic Bodega Vega Sicilia.

THE WINE ROUTE
AVILA AND SEGOVIA,
THE CHARM OF SPAIN

AVILA DE LOS CABALLEROS is a walled city like Carcassonne in France or Lucca in Italy, but there is something even more magical about it. This might be because of its eighty-eight perfectly preserved

OPPOSITE PAGE, FROM THE TOP: the vocabulary and geometries of Ribera del Duero—bottles in the modern Bodega Valduero, in Gumiel de Mercado; bunches of grapes and rows of sunflowers; piles of casks on the Torremilanos estate, home of Bodega Peñalba Lopez.
RIGHT: the ancient castle of Peñafiel, keeping watch over the Castilian plain.

Rows of vines in a perfectly ordered vineyard stretch out along the Ribera del Duero.

watchtowers or its eight gates, or its impregnability—it is surrounded by a steep, craggy hill on three sides—or the storks that nest there every year and fly around the crenellated walls. Whatever the reason, this town, recognized by UNESCO as a world heritage site and known as the "city of singing and saints," casts its own distinctive spell. One can wander through the alleyways of the historic center or along the terraces of the eleventh-century walls, look out over the green lands that stretch as far as the eye can see, and surrender to the charms of the surround-

ings. It is a privilege that few get to enjoy. Avila lies between the Sierra de Gredos and the Sierra de Avila mountains, northwest of Madrid, and if the walled city presents an evocative view by day, at night the superbly illuminated fortifications seem almost surreal. The stones, if they could, would speak of Saint Theresa, whose memory is everywhere, even in the town's distinctive sweets: *yemas de Santa Teresa*, pastries made with eggs and sugar.

Before entering the wine-producing periphery of Ribera del Duero, this splendid journey through

the history and heart of Spain continues north of Sierra de Guadarrama, through spectacular landscapes and distant horizons to **SEGOVIA**, loftily set at the summit of a hill between the Eresma and Clamores rivers. Because of its position and its distinctive form, it almost looks like a ship, with the Alcázar castle looming over the bluff like the prow of a vessel and the pointed tips of the Renaissance cathedral resembling masts. To fully enjoy the city's impressive beauty, it is not enough to visit the monuments; one has to explore on foot, following the

crests of the hills that surround it, particularly to the west, from where there are exceptional views of the entire fortified complex.

The aqueduct from the times of Trajan, still perfectly preserved, is one of the finest existing examples of Roman architecture. The granite blocks, superimposed using a dry-stone technique, with a double-story, forty-three-arch arcade overlooking the main piazza, jut nearly 100 feet (30 meters) above the ground, imbuing the site with a mysterious sense of softness and lightness, in contrast with the work's

FOLLOWING PAGES: bottles in the Bodega Emilio Moro in Pesquera de Duero, where prestigious red wines are aged.

titanic proportions. It calls out to the visitor to stop and admire its majesty and elegance, to follow the enchanting play of light and shadow that the aqueduct's vaults cast over the city and onto the tiny human figures below.

Leaving Segovia, the traveler is confronted by the immobile immensity of the central plateau, traversed by long, straight, deserted roads. Especially at dusk, when the hot, oblique light creates a suspended atmosphere, there is the feeling of having stepped outside time, into a new dimension.

ALONG THE DUERO, AMID VINEYARDS AND VILLAGES

Just a little over 60 miles (100 kilometers) farther lies **VALLADOLID**, capital of Castile y León, once an Arabic city called Belad-Walid ("City of the Governor"). Christopher Columbus died here, alone and forgotten, in 1506. Hidden amid the ruins of the industrial era, there are gleaming monuments that are worth a visit, such as the cathedral, the Colegio de San Gregorio with its famous late-Gothic façade by Gil de Siloé, or the Palacio Vivero where King Ferdinand married Queen Isabella in 1469. After the reconquest of the city by Spain in 1492, the royal couple made Valladolid their capital. A tour of the city can end with a quick visit to the modest dwelling, now a museum, where Miguel de Cervantes, author of *Don Quixote*, spent his final years.

Back on the road, it is only some 12 miles (19 kilometers) to Ribera del Duero itself, a long stretch of ancient, noble vineyards amid mountains and clay plains, at an average altitude of 2,600 feet (800 meters). This rolling valley, Miocenic in origin, stretches 70 miles (115 kilometers), with some hundred or so towns. Its continental climate is characterized by moderate rainfall and dry summers.

The gentle, flat landscape of the plateau is broken by a 20-mile (35-kilometer) cut in the land that was carved out by a river, and is covered almost entirely by vineyards planted with the Tinto Fino grape, a clone of the Tempranillo della Rioja. The walls of the valley are steeply sloped, their straight edges dotted with castles and fortifications.

Along the slow course of the Duero, vineyards are followed by lovely little towns full of history, where some of the best-known cellars are found. **QUINTANILLA DE ONÉSIMO**, a center for one of the largest concentrations of great wines, is where Pingus, one of the most expensive wines in Spain, is produced. A bit farther along, in **VALBUENA DE DUERO**, are the highly prized cellars of Bodega Vega Sicilia, a name recognized throughout the world for the extremely high quality of its aged products.

Gleaming barrels in the Bodega Vega Sicilia; some of its wines are shown in the text box to the right. These wines are among oenology's elite, and not only in Spain.

On the other side of the river, in **PESQUERA DE DUERO**, lies the Bodega Tinto Pesquera of the Alejandro Fernández family, an important name in the country's oenological history. The Bodegas Emilio Moro, also in Pesquera, is equally important, and its Maleolus de Valderramiro, a red with purplish-blue reflections, has won many international prizes.

Rising up from the valley, the road leads to **PEÑAFIEL**, with its extremely beautiful tenth-century stone castle, twelve cylindrical and crenellated towers, and masonry enclosing wall that is still intact. It stands erect on a hill that overlooks the Castilian plain. The Peñafiel fortress also recalls the shape of a ship, and in the evening, when it is illuminated, a strange play of lights makes it seem to almost dissolve into the hillside. The single, solitary keep, 80 feet (25 meters) high, houses an interesting and modern museum of regional wine.

Along the Duero river, toward **SORIA**, there are other important cellars. **ROA**, known for the Collegiale di Santa Maria, a triumph of the Gothic style built in the sixteenth century, is home to the Bodega Aalto. Here two leading figures in Spanish oenology, Mariano Garcia and Javier Zaccagnini, joined forces to create Aalto PS, one of the so-called high-expression wines known for their structure and formidable concentration.

Just before arriving at **GUMIEL DE MERCADO**, another historic village made up of noble houses clustered around two fortified church-

PERSONALITIES *Vega Sicilia*

Unico: The name of this wine means unique, and it summarizes the philosophy of Vega Sicilia. Great care is taken in tending the vineyards and harvesting the grapes and in the controlled and pruned layout of the vines, so there is never more than 3/4 pound (two kilos) of yield per vine, resulting in the greatest possible concentration of minerals and nutrients from the soil. The commitment to limit the maximum yield per hectare to 580 gallons (20 hectoliters) and the profound respect for regional characteristics are fundamental to the enormous success of this bodega, which is modern yet mindful of tradition. Now a legend, it was founded in 1864. Its wines age in the cellar longer than usual to obtain Vega Sicilia's distinctive character, elegance, and exclusive aromas. The aging occurs in air-conditioned rooms, where technology is at the service of the wine. The aging period varies, depending on the type of bottle, but it is usually around ten years before a wine is placed on the market. The cellar's motto is: "There is no hurry." These are the most prized wines in Spain because of their complexity and long duration over time. Elegant and intricate, they are refined to the taste rather than muscular, and can remain in the cellar for twenty to thirty years. Vega Sicilia is owned by the Alvarez family, who are part of the international wine-producing aristocracy comprising the small circle of *primae familiae vini*, or "First Families of Wine" association.

es from the fifteenth century, is the Bodega Valduero with its striking modern architecture. Three cement tunnels—260, 330, and 395 feet long (80, 100, and 120 meters), respectively—have been covered with earth and recently planted vineyards. The first is for wine production, the second is for wine preservation, and the third functions as storage. A different climate is maintained inside each of the three tunnels, depending on the needs and the stage of development of the wine.

In **ARANDA DE DUERO**, capital of this wine denomination and home of the finest Spanish *lechazo asado* (milk-fed lamb), the Bodegas Peñalba Lopez can be glimpsed amid the vines. In the property's large cellar, wine ages in barrels produced on-site by master coopers.

A few miles farther lies one of the ancient bridges that span the river, followed by **PEÑARANDA DE DUERO**, with its astounding fifteenth-century castle built after the Castilians had cast out the Moors south of Duero, and the remains of the medieval walls. The manor house literally leans out over the edge of the cliff and dominates both the town and the surrounding landscape. It is an evocative site, beaten by the wind, the sky marked by the fighting of hawks. At dusk, particularly in summer, these ancient fortified villages on the hilltops take on a vivid hue, nearly blending in with the rest of the parched and silent countryside.

The trip culminates in **SORIA**, with a walk in the shady park that extends along the banks of the Duero and a visit to the ruins of the monastery of San Juan de Duero. This Romanesque cloister with obvious Arabic influences is a unique triumph, with interlaced marble arches sculpted in the thirteenth century.

OPPOSITE PAGE, ABOVE: the landscape of Pesquera de Duero.

RIGHT: Merlot vines of the Torremilanos estate.

TINTO PESQUERA

Real 2, Pesquera de Duero,
tel. 0034.98.3870037

Founded: 1975
Production region: Pesquera de Duero
Wines and grape varieties: 100% reds;
Tempranillo

GREAT WINES

Janus Tinto Pesquera Gran Reserva 1995
Made from pure Tempranillo grapes from
the Vigna Alta vineyard. Aged thirty-six
months in American oak barrels. Intense
ruby-red color with garnet reflections.
Full and elegant bouquet, with notes of
blackberry preserves, cocoa, and toasted
wood. Full bodied in the mouth, velvety,
warm, with the wood well integrated and
soft tannins. Good, persistent aftertaste,
with a memory of vanilla. Complements
game dishes and grilled red meat.

Tinto Pesquera Millenium 1996
Made from pure Tempranillo grapes from
the Vigna Alta vineyard. Aged twenty-six
months in barrels of French oak and ten
months in the bottle. Intense ruby-red
color. Full and complex nose, with hints of
wild berries, new wood, and roasted coffee. An elegant, well-balanced flavor, silky
on the palate, with vanilla on the long finish. Complements game dishes or can be a
wine for meditation.

Visits and tastings: yes, by appointment

BODEGAS CONDADO DE HAZA

Carrettera Roa-La Horra, Burgos
tel. 0034.947.525254

Founded: 1988
Production region: Roa de Duero
Wines and grape varieties: 100% reds;
Tempranillo

GREAT WINES

Alenza 95
Made from 100 percent Tempranillo
grapes. Aged twenty-three months in barrels of American oak. Complex, intense,
and very persistent on the nose. Notes of
raspberry, ripe fruit, and minerals.
Intense, potent flavor, concentrated and
rich in fine tannins. Complements game
and medium-aged cheeses.

Condado de Haza 2000
Made from 100 percent Tempranillo
grapes. Aged sixteen months in barrels of
American oak. Intense ruby-red color.
Strong and persistent bouquet, with hints
of ripe red fruit, cocoa, and vanilla. Fresh
in the mouth, with a vibrant and well-
balanced acidity. Complements grilled
meats.

Visits and tastings: yes, by appointment

BODEGAS EMILIO MORO

Carrettera Peñafiel-Valoria,
Pesquera de Duero
tel. 0034.983.878400
www.emiliomoro.com

Founded: 1988
Production region: Pesquera de Duero, Roa
de Duero
Wines and grape varieties: 100% reds;
Tempranillo, Tinto Fino

GREAT WINES

Malleolus 2000
Made from pure Tempranillo grapes, aged
eighteen months in new barrels of French
oak. Intense ruby-red color with purplish-
blue reflections. Intense and lingering
bouquet, with hints of ripe wild fruit. Full
and potent on the palate, fine tannins
properly balanced with ripe fruit and
notes of spices. Complements grilled red
meat or roasts.

Visits and tastings: yes, by appointment

BODEGAS PEÑALBA LÓPEZ

Jardines de Don Diego 4,
Aranda de Duero
tel. 0034.947.501381

Founded: 1903
Production region: Aranda de Duero
Wines and grape varieties: 100% reds;
Tempranillo, Cabernet Sauvignon, Merlot

GREAT WINES

Torremilanos Crianza 2000
Made from pure Tempranillo grapes, aged
thirteen months in small barrels of French
oak. Intense ruby-red color, with purplish-blue reflections. Hints of new wood
and wild fruit. Full taste with young, elegant tannins and cinnamon. Long, clean
finish. Complements roasts and stews.

Torre Albéniz Riserva 1997
Made from Tempranillo, Cabernet
Sauvignon, and Merlot. Aged twenty-
three months in small barrels of French
oak. Intense ruby-red color with garnet
reflections. Full and complex bouquet,
with hints of spice, ripe fruit, moss, and
leather. Smooth, complex, and earthy,
with notes of citrus, cinnamon, pepper,
leather, and wood. Complements roasted
milk-fed lamb and traditional rustic fare.

Visits and tastings: yes, by appointment

AALTO

Quintanilla de Arriba
tel. 0034.947.540781

Founded: 1998
Production region: Quintanilla de Arriba
Wines and grape varieties: 100% reds;
Tempranillo

GREAT WINES

Aalto 2000
Pure Tempranillo grapes, from vineyards
that are up to sixty years old. Aged twenty-
four months in small French and American
oak barrels. Intense ruby color. Complex,
aromatic bouquet of red berries and spice.
Concentrated, full-bodied on the palate,
with firm structure and elegant tannins.
Complements grilled red meat and pork.

Aalto PS 1999
Made from pure Tempranillo grapes, from
vineyards that are over fifty years old.
Aged twenty-five months in small barrels
of French and American oak. Deep ruby-
red color with purplish-blue reflections.
Concentrated and complex nose, with
hints of blackberry preserves, spices, and
fine wood. Powerful mouthfeel, with fine
structure and depth. Complements roasts
and grilled or smoked meats.

Visits and tastings: yes, by appointment

BODEGAS Y VIGNEDOS VALDUERO

Gumiel de Mercado, Burgos
tel. 0034.947.545459
www.bodegasvalduero.com

Founded: 1982
Production region: Gumiel de Mercado,
Villanueva de Gumiel
Wines and grape varieties: 100% reds;
Tempranillo

GREAT WINES

Valduero Gran Reserva 95
Made from pure Tempranillo grapes from
select vineyards. Aged forty-two months
in barrels of American oak. Ruby-red
color with garnet reflections. Full, complex bouquet, with lush notes of jammy
fruit, leather, and toasted wood. Potent
and velvety on the palate, with hints of
wood and toasted bread, and smooth tannins. Complements game and lamb.

Valduero Reserva Special Premium 96
Made from pure Tempranillo grapes from
select vineyards. Aged twenty-six months
in barrels of American oak. Intense ruby-
red color with purplish-blue reflections.
Fruity nose, with black olives and toasted
wood. Full, balanced flavor, smooth tannins and caramel on the long finish.
Complements roasts and grilled meats.

Visits and tastings: yes, by appointment

BODEGAS Y VIGNEDOS ALION

Carretera Nacional 122, Peñafiel
tel. 0034.983.881236

Founded: 1981
Production region: Peñafiel, Valbuena de
Duero
Wines and grape varieties: 100% reds;
Tempranillo

GREAT WINES

Alion 2000
Made from pure Tempranillo grapes, vinified in wood, and aged fourteen months in
oak barrels. Intense ruby-red color with
purplish-blue reflections. Full, complex,
and elegant on the nose, with wild fruit
and cherry perfectly integrated with the
wood. Rich in fine tannins, harmonious,
with notes of cherry and vanilla. Long,
rich finish. Complements roasted lamb
and should be drunk young in order to
enjoy its explosive vibrancy.

Visits and tastings: no

FINCA VEGA SICILIA

Carretera Nacional 122, km 323,
Valbuena de Duero
tel. 0034.983.680147
www.vegasicilia.com

Founded: 1864
Production region: Valbuena de Duero,
Quintanilla de Onésimo
Wines and grape varieties: 100% reds;
Tempranillo, Cabernet Sauvignon, Merlot

GREAT WINES

Único 1991
Made from 85 percent Tempranillo and 15
percent Cabernet Sauvignon grapes, first
aged in new barrels and then transferred
to old barrels for a long period of refinement, before resting for three years in
large barrels of oak. Intense and brilliant
ruby-red color. Incredibly complex on the
nose, with hints of wild fruit, stewed cherries, and spices. Full, potent, and velvety
mouthfeel with both fresh and jammy
fruit early, and then wood, chocolate, and
licorice. Fine tannins with a clean finish.
Complements red meat or hard, medium-
aged cheeses, it can also be drunk by itself
to appreciate its elegant purity.

Visits and tastings: no

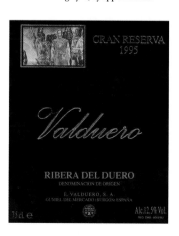

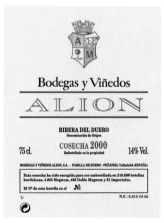

RIOJA

WINE TRAIL *Itinerary*

ITINERARY LENGTH
250 miles / 400 kilometers

BEST TIME TO GO
April to late October

TIME TO SPEND
Five to six days

USEFUL ADDRESSES
Dirección General de Turismo
de la Rioja
Prado Viejo 62 bis
Logroño
Tel: 0034.941.291230
www.larioja.org/turismo

OPPOSITE PAGE, FROM THE TOP: in Zaragoza, a club and the Plaza del Pilar, with the domes and bell towers of the cathedral of Nuestra Señora; a view of Lerma; the Lopez de Heredia Viña Tondonia cellar, in Haro.

ABOVE: landscapes and vineyards of Rioja.

THE ROMANS WERE fascinated by this countryside, bathed by the Ebro River, and Benedictine monks embellished its valleys with sacred buildings and abbeys, elegantly beautifying the land before it became famous for its deep, spicy red wines. Rioja has long been home to the most prestigious Spanish wines, traditionally characterized by their passage in wood and capacity to age for long periods, thanks in part to the influence of the Bordeaux winemaking style and technique, which reached the banks of the Ebro during the phylloxera blight in France in the nineteenth century. Today local producers in Rioja also take into consideration the emerging wine-producing areas in Spain, and efforts are made to combine tradition with new technologies, resulting in wines of great concentration and extract, rich in fruit and tannins.

THE WINE ROUTE
FROM SANTO DOMINGO DE SILOS TO BURGOS

This itinerary is the ideal continuation of the wine trail through Ribera del Duero. Leaving ancient Soria, in a few miles one comes upon one of the most remarkable buildings constructed by the Benedictine monks in this region: the **MONASTERY OF SANTO DOMINGO DE SILOS**, a place of contemplation and quiet, rare beauty and graceful architecture. The Romanesque cloister is unequalled: a two-story rectangle from the eleventh and twelfth centuries, built with great attention to proportion, its capitals sculpted into different shapes both symbolic and realistic, and above a coffered ceiling in the Mudéjar style. In the refined and spiritual atmos-

41

Fields of lavender in the countryside around Burgos, an ancient city of Castile.

phere of the monastery, likely founded in 593 by the Visigoth king Recare, one can hear Gregorian chants by the Benedictine monks.

There is a strong contrast between the tranquility of the monastery and the spectacular whimsy of nature in the Yecla pass, a deep, narrow gorge carved into the rock by the Cauce, a tributary of the Mataviejas River. The lapping of its waters provides a soundtrack along the aerial path of walkways and bridges that cuts through the high, rocky walls of the gorge. Toward **BURGOS**, the landscape fades into golden fields of wheat, undulating expanses of lavender, meadows, and olive groves. Walnut and cherry trees and vines encircle **COVARRUBÍAS**, a village

enclosed by medieval walls, along the Arlanza River. Downtown, the Collegiate Church of San Cosme and San Damián houses the tomb of Count Fernán Gonzáles, who in the tenth century was instrumental in gaining Castile's independence from León.

Climbing along the path of the Arlanza, the road leads to **LERMA**. The majesty of its palaces reflect the ambitions of the Duke of Lerma, a favorite of Philip III and his minister from 1598 to 1618, who spent enormous sums to beautify his native city. Among the monuments, the Palacio Ducal stands out; the statesman's residence beginning in 1605, it is now a *parador*, or government-run hotel. The best overall view of the valley can be

Titanium, stone, and glass: These are the elements that American architect Frank Gehry has brought together in the spectacular Guggenheim Bilbao, an audacious example of the most avant-garde architecture of the twentieth century, for which the city center acts as a stage. The building—an enormous metal structure that brings to mind the gleaming scales of a fish—changes color with each blink of the eye, depending on the season, the time of day, and the atmospheric conditions. It is made up of a series of interconnected volumes, in which octagonal forms clad in limestone and round forms covered in titanium "skins" are combined with glass walls. Inside, the visitor is even more astonished by the sensational play of space, light, and artwork on display. The aesthetic offerings include an important selection of works by the most significant artists from the Guggenheim museums in New York, Venice, and Berlin, as well as temporary exhibitions. In short, the museum presents the multiple visions of art in our time. For more information, go to the web site: www.guggenheim-bilbao.es

enjoyed from the colonnade near the Convent of Santa Clara.

After traveling over a bucolic stretch of road among the fertile highlands, the crenellated spires of a Gothic cathedral announce the presence of **BURGOS**, city of El Cid Campeador and the former capital of Castile. The cathedral, built of white limestone similar to marble, is one of Spain's most impressive churches, rich in works of art. Its construction, which began in 1221 and ended in the mid-eighteenth century, involved the most famous artists and architects in Europe.

CELLARS AND WINES
IN THE BENDS OF THE EBRO

A few miles farther is the geographic region of
RIOJA, which doesn't coincide precisely with the
wine region of the same name that encompasses Rioja
itself, Navarra, and the Basque region. Highway 120
toward Logroño winds through the heart of the wine
region. There are nearly 125,000 acres of vines divided
into three subregions with different characteristics:
Rioja Alavesa, the northernmost area, with vineyards
at altitudes of up to nearly 2,000 feet (600 meters);
Rioja Alta, on the southern bank of the river; and
Rioja Baja, at a lower altitude, warmer, and with clay
terrain. The Ebro, which traces the boundary
between Rioja Alavesa and Rioja Alta and constitutes
the backbone of the official Rioja wine region, winds
like a snake, offering new views at every turn and gen-
erating specific microclimates. The spectacle is continuous and ever-changing—gentle slopes covered
with vineyards, orchards, and golden fields of wheat,
punctuated by old *pueblos*. Although in the past the
red wine that was produced here was made from
grapes from all three regions, today there is an
increasing tendency to emphasize the typical characteristics of each region.

Travelers who enter the region along the Oja
River arrive at the gleaming town of **SANTO
DOMINGO DE LA CALZADA**, one of the most
important way stations for pilgrims going to Santiago
de Compostelo. In the twelfth century, besides devot-

ing himself to prayer, the saint built a church, a bridge, and a hospital for pilgrims (now transformed into a *parador*). The cathedral, part Romanesque and part Gothic, has been embellished over the centuries with decorative and sculptural elements.

Throughout the region, rustic villages alternate with stone cottages, ancient monasteries, and rows of vines. Perhaps this is why, even before arriving in **HARO**, the wine capital of Rioja Alta, there is a strong temptation to stop in one of the many *bodegas* to taste the wine. The town boasts some of the most famous names in Spanish wine, such as the Lopez de Heredia Viña Tondonia cellar, founded in 1877, as well as the historic buildings of Cune (1879), a true colossus of Spanish oenology that recently introduced a new immense production and storage facility designed by architect Philippe Mazieres and carved into the heart of a mountain near Laguardia. On the three floors of the Museum of Rioja Wine in Estación Enológica in Haro, the story and culture of wine are told in a new and original fashion, with explanatory panels, work tools, and photos. The sense of just how precious wine is in this region is symbolized by a small strongbox in the first room of the museum, which contains old bottles.

The Bodega Granja Nuestra Señora de Remelluri in **LABASTIDA** is unusual and extremely beautiful. Located in the extreme west of Rioja Alavesa and battered by the semi-humid Atlantic climate, this previously was the farm of the Toloño monastery. Written

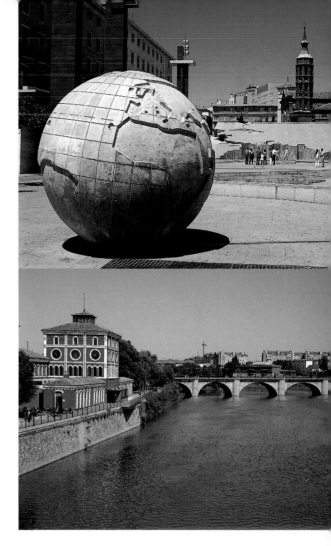

testimony reveals that wine was being produced there as far back as the fifteenth century. The property is endowed with a necropolis from the early Middle Ages, made up of tombs excavated into the rock and only partially uncovered. Since 1968 Jaime Rodriguez Salís, the current owner, has devoted himself to becoming one of the first to produce a *vino de finca*, or wine from estate-grown grapes, in a quest to celebrate the distinctive characteristics of his land. In addition to great reds, his white wine is outstanding, with its

The famous Herederos del Marqués de Riscal wine cellar in Elciego.

blend of Garnacha Blanca, Malvasia, Moscatel, Sauvignon Blanc, and Petite Corvue grapes.

Wandering about the vineyards of Rioja, the visitor can understand the region's geology: a plateau, long ago submerged by the sea, full of rocky spurs. Postcard landscapes are set in mountains that protect them from the ocean winds. The Bodega Sierra Cantabria and Il Señorio de San Vicente, located at the foot of the Sierra Cantabria mountains in **SAN VICENTE DE LA SONSIERRA**, provide an opportunity to delve into the nature of Riojan reds. Taking a lovely road through the vineyards, against the backdrop of the hermitage of San Assension, it is possible

to follow the Ebro as far as **CENICERO**, the site of one of the best-known cellars: Marqués de Cáceres, founded in 1980 by Enrique Forner, who had already spent a good deal of time working in the industry in France, particularly in Bordeaux. He is one of the first to produce Rioja wine in the modern style. A bit further on, in **ELCIEGO**, is the famous Herederos del Marqués de Riscal wine cellar, which for years has been in the forefront of high-quality wine production. A visit there requires some time, since the property is a labyrinth where old restored buildings alternate with new structures, including a cellar designed by Frank Gehry, audacious architect of the

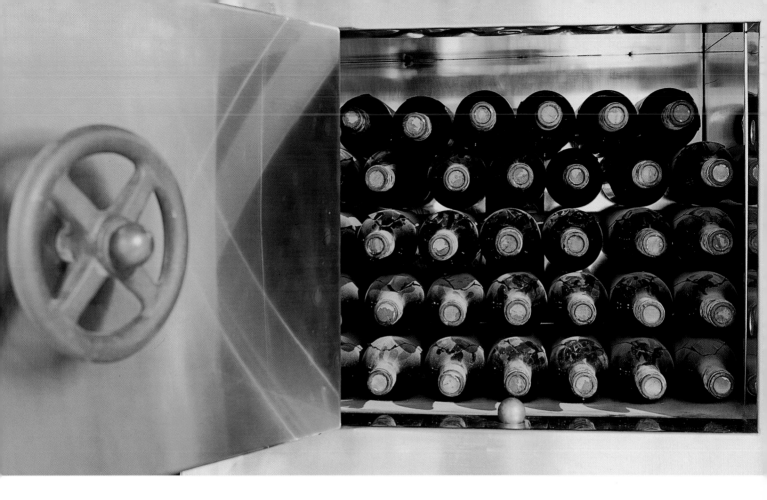

Guggenheim Bilbao. In **LASERNA**, also in Rioja Alavesa, a bend of the Ebro embraces the vineyards of Tempranillo, Graciano e Mazuelo del Viñedos del Contino, one of the historic names of the region.

In Rioja Alta, at the level of **FUENMAYOR**, the Valpiedra estate is located in an area that opens up, sheltered from the Atlantic winds and the hot breezes of Africa. The Martinez Bujanda family is one of the few to possess over 400 hectares (990 acres) of vineyards, and has been connected to wine production in this region for over one hundred years. They recently opened a modern *bodega* that is fully integrated with the surrounding vineyards—which is particularly evi-

dent in the autumn, when the leaves turn red and more fully conceal the building's red roof. Inside, there is a spectacular aging room, with dozens of tall columns and hundreds of small oak barrels. It is considered one of the most technologically advanced wine production facilities in the region.

Gently cradled along the Ebro among the vineyards, tilled fields, and fruit trees lies the ancient Roman settlement of **LOGROÑO**, now the capital of the autonomous region of Rioja. Hidden among the alleyways, churches, and splendid cathedrals in the historic center is an important neighborhood for *tapas*, with clubs and bars that serve typical Riojan products.

ABOVE: wine in a safe, in the first room of the Museum of Rioja wine in Haro, oenological capital of Rioja Alta.

FOLLOWING PAGES, LEFT: old bottles stacked up to age in the Herederos del Marqués de Riscal wine cellar in Elciego.

47

Roughly 25 miles (40 kilometers) of vineyards separate **LOGROÑO** from the monasteries of **SAN MILLÁN DE LA COGOLLA**, on the northern slopes of the Sierra de la Demanda mountains. The monastery of Suso astonishes with its small mozarabic church dating from 984, carved into the pink sandstone and rich in Romanesque elements; the monastery of Yuso, set farther into the green Cárdenas valley, has a church, partially Renaissance, with gilded entrance doors in the Baroque style.

Continuing southward, the landscape stretches out, and hundreds of energy-producing windmills appear; then the land fades into the plain that surrounds **ZARAGOZA**, the cheerful and lively capital of Aragon, overlooking the Ebro. This former Roman settlement was the starting point for the Latinization of the Iberian region. The Roman, Islamic, and Christian past and Gothic-Muegar, Renaissance, Baroque, and neoclassical architecture coexist harmoniously and help to make this a city full of surprises. The city's tangle of narrow streets house an infinite number of little restaurants, where the ambiance and kitchen aromas beckon to the visitor to stop and try the *tapas*, accompanied by sangria or the wines of Rioja.

La Republica wine shop in Zaragoza, right, and a view of the Viñedos del Contino, in Laserna, far right.

TAKE A BREAK

LODGING

Lerma: **PARADOR DE LERMA**
Plaza Mayor 1
Tel: 0034.947.177110
www.parador.es
This monumental seventeenth-century building that dominates Lerma was only recently turned into a *parador*. The light-filled central courtyard is surrounded by a double colonnade. Many of the sumptuous rooms overlook the city and the valley. The excellent restaurant serves a tasty cold almond soup and has a good wine selection.

Santo Domingo de la Calzada:
PARADOR DE SANTO DOMINGO DE LA CALZADA
Plaza del Santo 3
Tel: 0034.941.340300
www.parador.es
This ancient twelfth-century building next to the cathedral was built to accommodate pilgrims on their way to Santiago and boasts majestic parlors, Gothic arches, and antique furniture. At the noteworthy restaurant, guests can sample stuffed *piquillo* peppers and Rioja-style salted cod.

DINING

Ezcaray: **ECHAURREN**
Calle Héroes del Alcázar 2
Tel: 0034.941.354047
www.echaurren.com
South of Santo Domingo de la Calzada, this is one of the most typical restaurants in Rioja, run by the Paniego family. The chef is young Francis, who brings a modern touch based on regional ingredients to his mother's more traditional cooking. The specialties include chickpea soup with monkfish and clams and Navaz pigeon with dried pear sauce. Francis's father runs the dining room and oversees the wines, with over three hundred labels.

HEREDEROS DEL MARQUÉS DE RISCAL

Torrea 1, Elciego
tel. 0034.941.606000
www.marquesderiscal.com

Founded: 1858
Production region: Rioja Alaveza
Wines and grape varieties: 98% reds and 2% rosés; Tempranillo, Graciano, Mazuelo, Cabernet Sauvignon

GREAT WINES

Marqués de Riscal Gran Reserva 1996
Made from 65 percent Tempranillo, 10 percent Graciano, and 25 percent Cabernet Sauvignon grapes from over thirty-year-old vineyards. Aged thirty-two months in American oak barrels, then three years in bottles before being sold. Intense ruby-red color with coppery reflections. Full nose, with wild raspberry, blackberry, ripe banana, and cinnamon. Smooth and velvety on the palate, with elegant tannins and a long finish. Complements roasts and grilled meat.

Baron de Chirel Reserva 1996
Made from 54 percent Tempranillo and 46 percent Cabernet Sauvignon grapes hand-selected from old vineyards. Aged twenty-six months in American oak barrels, then three years in bottles before being sold. Deep ruby-red color. Complex bouquet, with hints of cherries in brandy, ripe fruit, and old wood. Velvety and warm on the palate, with notes of vanilla, toasted bread, and rare wood. Complements game, lamb, and hard cheeses.

Visits and tastings: yes, by appointment

VIÑEDOS DEL CONTINO

Finca San Gregorio, Laserna
tel. 0034.945.600201
www.cune.com

Founded: 1973
Production region: Finca San Gregorio a Laserna
Wines and grape varieties: 100% reds; Tempranillo, Graciano, Mazuelo, Garnacha

GREAT WINES

Contino Gran Reserva 1996
Made from 85 percent Tempranillo, 10 percent Graciano, and 5 percent Mazuelo grapes. Aged thirty months in barrels of American and French oak, then thirty months in the bottle before being sold. Intense ruby-red color. Powerful and lingering bouquet, with notes of carnations, ripe fruit, spices, and tobacco. Full, structured taste, with sweet tannins that balance the fruit. Long and clean finish. Excellent for aging, goes particularly well with roasted and grilled lamb.

Contino Viña del Olivo 2000
Made from 90 percent Tempranillo and 10 percent Graciano grapes, aged eighteen months in small oak barrels. Intense ruby-red color with purplish-blue reflections. Fresh bouquet with wild fruit, almond, and notes of balsamic vinegar. Full and structured taste, with a balanced and elegant body, and a long, fruity aftertaste. Should be drunk young or aged five to seven years. Complements game in sauce.

Visits and tastings: yes, by appointment

BODEGAS SIERRA CANTABRIA SEÑORIO DE SAN VICENTE

Los Remedios 27,
San Vicente de La Sonsierra
tel. 0034.941.334080
www.sierracantabria.com

Founded: 1985
Production region: San Vicente de La Sonsierra
Wines and grape varieties: 100% reds; Tempranillo Peludo

GREAT WINES

San Vicente 2000
Clusters of this indigenous Tempranillo clone are selected by hand and aged twenty months in small oak barrels. Intense ruby-red color. Full and complex bouquet, with notes of wild fruit and spices. Smooth and velvety flavor, full of red fruit and cherries in brandy, soft tannins, and a long finish. Goes particularly well with wild boar and game.

Visits and tastings: yes, by appointment

CUNE

B. de la Estación, Haro
tel. 0034.941.304800
www.cune.com

Founded: 1879
Production region: Rioja
Wines and grape varieties: 90% reds, 10% whites; Tempranillo, Graciano, Mazuelo, Garnacha Tinta, Garnacha Blanco, Viura, Malvasía

GREAT WINES

Viña Real Gran Reserva 1994
Made from Tempranillo grapes with 5 percent Graciano. Aged four years in large barrels of French oak. Intense ruby-red color with cherry reflections. Full and elegant bouquet, with vegetables, spices, and leather. Powerful taste, with balanced acidity and smooth tannins. Should be aged at length, and complements roasts and medium-aged cheeses.

Imperial Gran Reserva Tinto 1995
Made from 85 percent Tempranillo, 10 percent Graciano, and 5 percent Mazuelo grapes, harvested and selected by hand. After a particularly long maceration, the wine ages in wood for over two years. Intense ruby-red color. Powerful bouquet, with wild fruit and licorice. Dry and potent, with great structure. Long, spicy finish. Should be aged at length. An ideal complement to grilled meat and game.

Visits and tastings: yes, by appointment

BODEGAS MARTINEZ BUJANDA
Camino Viejo, Oyón
tel. 0034.945.622188
www.martinezbujanda.com

Founded: 1889
Production region: Rioja Alavesa
Wines and grape varieties: 90% reds and 10% whites; Tempranillo, Graciano, Mazuelo, Cabernet Sauvignon, Garnacha Tinta, Viura, Malvasía

GREAT WINES
Conde de Valdemar Gran Reserva 1996
A wine with 13.5° alcoholic content, made from 85 percent Tempranillo and 15 percent Mazuelo grapes. Aged forty months in barrels of French and American oak. Intense ruby-red color with garnet reflections. Full and complex to the nose, with notes of ripe fruit and oak. Fresh in the mouth, with still evident acidity, rich in fruit and well-integrated tannins. Complements medium-aged cheeses.

Conde de Valdemar Gran Reserva Vindimia Seleccionada 1995
Made from 50 percent Tempranillo and 50 percent Cabernet Sauvignon grapes, the clusters selected by hand. Intense ruby-red color. Full, harmonious bouquet, with hints of ripe fruit, spices (particularly cinnamon), and leather. Velvety and potent to the palate, rich in fine tannins and ripe fruit, spices, and green pepper. Pair with game in sauce.

Visits and tastings: yes, by appointment

FINCA VALPIEDRA
Finca Valpiedra, Cenicero
tel. 0034.945.622188
www.martinezbujanda.com

Founded: 1994
Production region: Finca Valpiedra, Rioja Alta
Wines and grape varieties: 100% reds; Tempranillo, Graciano, Mazuelo, and Cabernet Sauvignon

GREAT WINES
Finca Valpiedra Reserva 1998
Made from 70 percent Tempranillo grapes with the remaining 30 percent Graciano, Mazuelo, and Cabernet Sauvignon. Intense ruby-red color. Elegant and complex bouquet, rich in ripe fruit, spices, and rare wood. Full, velvety taste, with a persistent and pleasantly spicy aftertaste. Should be aged for an average length of time. Complements medium-aged cheeses.

Visits and tastings: yes, by appointment

GRANJA NUESTRA SEÑORA DE REMELLURI
Labastida de Alava, Logroño
tel. 0034.945.331801

Founded: 1967
Production region: Labastida, Rioja Alavesa
Wines and grape varieties: 96% reds and 4% whites; Tempranillo, Graciano, Garnacha Tinta, Garnacha Blanca, Moscatel, and Malvasía

GREAT WINES
Remelluri Blanco 2001
Made from Garnacha Blanca, Malvasía, Moscatel, Sauvignon, and Petite Corvue grapes. Fermented and aged in the barrel. Straw-yellow color with golden reflections. Complex bouquet, with fruity hints of pear, apricot, peach, and pineapple. Full and sumptuous taste, with mineral notes and a clean, elegant finish. An excellent aperitif and with foie gras.

Remelluri Coleccion Jaime Rodríguez 2000
Made from Tempranillo, Graciano, Garnacha, and Mazuelo grapes from very old vineyards (some Garnacha vines date back to 1875). Aged twenty-two months in small barrels of French oak. Intense ruby-red color with carmine reflections. Elegant, complex bouquet with floral notes and those of ripe fruit, cinnamon, and minerals. Fresh and potent on the palate, rather structured with sweet tannins and hints of rare wood. Persistent and clean finish. Complements fine game.

Visits and tastings: yes, by appointment

MARQUÉS DE CÁCERES
Carretera Logroño, Cenicero
tel. 0034.941.454000

Founded: 1970
Production region: Rioja Alta and Alavesa
Wines and grape varieties: 65% reds, 10% whites, 25% rosés; Tempranillo, Graciano, Garnacha, Viura, Malvasía

GREAT WINES
Gaudium 1996
Made from Tempranillo, Garnacha, and Graciano grapes from vineyards that are over seventy years old. Aged eighteen months in French oak barrels and then another two years in the bottle before being sold. Intense ruby-red color, with purplish-blue reflections. Intense, persistent bouquet, with notes of wild fruit, spices, and oak. Full, rich, velvety taste. Well structured with soft tannins. Complements large roasts and grilled red meat.

M C 2001
Made from pure Tempranillo grapes from an extremely select harvest. Dark ruby-red color, with purplish-blue reflections. Surprising, intense, and profound to the nose, with notes of blackberry, ripe fruit, fruit preserves, and old wood. Full, velvety, smooth, harmonious, and sumptuous taste. A potent wine, both elegant and fruity. Extremely long finish, with hints of dry fig and date. A wonderful wine for meditation, or as a complement to soft, well-aged cheeses.

Visits and tastings: yes, by appointment

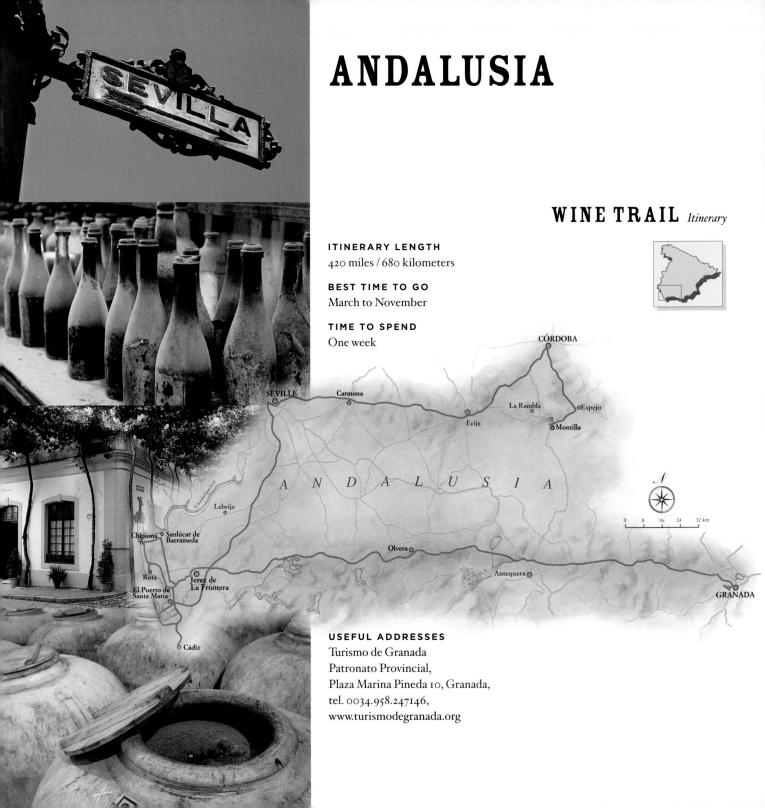

ANDALUSIA

WINE TRAIL *Itinerary*

ITINERARY LENGTH
420 miles / 680 kilometers

BEST TIME TO GO
March to November

TIME TO SPEND
One week

USEFUL ADDRESSES
Turismo de Granada
Patronato Provincial,
Plaza Marina Pineda 10, Granada,
tel. 0034.958.247146,
www.turismodegranada.org

OPPOSITE PAGE, FROM THE TOP: the road to Seville, from Jerez de la Frontera; old bottles of Tio Pepe in the Bodega Gonzalez Byass in Jerez, and the exterior of the wine cellar; a detail of the Bodega Pérez Barquero in Montilla.

ABOVE: the fortified walls of Carmona, at the edge of the Guadalquivir plain.

ANDALUSIA, THE SOUTHERNMOST

region of Iberian Spain at the edge of Europe, gracefully combines suggestive contrasts of snowy peaks, immense landscapes, and luminous coastlines with extraordinary monuments from the past: the Córdoba mosque's forest of columns, the Alhambra in Granada, the Giralda minaret in Seville. This cradle of Moorish culture, Christianized with ferocity, is also known for its *pueblos blancos*, the "white villages" that for centuries have marked the border between the Arab and Christian worlds, as well as its bullrings and endless beaches. It is the home of the mythic wine of Jerez, which we know as sherry, produced in the far southern triangle of Andalusia—a fragment of land along the ocean with rows of vines that brush up against the sea, a land of infinite horizons.

THE WINE ROUTE
FROM THE ALHAMBRA TO
THE ATLANTIC

In Andalusia the landscape changes continuously. Along the slopes of the Sierra Nevada range the uninterrupted sequence of barren hills, almost like dunes, evolves into a panorama of canyons, peaks, and large rock formations with unusual shapes, leading up to the ancient Moorish stronghold of **GRANADA**, one of the most fascinating cities in Spain. Its period of greatest prosperity was under the Nasrid dynasty,

between the thirteenth and fifteenth centuries, when Arabs transformed it into a Muslim bastion of defense against the Christians. When the Moors were cast out in 1492, it came under the rule of the Catholic kings. Walking through the narrow alleyways, steps, and patios of the Albaicín quarter with its small artisan workshops, the visitor can grasp the Arabic essence of the city; but it is the Alhambra, the fabulous fortified residence on the red Sabika hill, that most fully expresses this culture. One of the most spectacular views of the fortress, against the backdrop of the Sierra Nevadas, can be enjoyed at dusk from the tower opposite the church of St. Nicolas in Albaicín.

This renowned complex dominates the city, casting a spell with its architecture, its magical use of space and light, the sculpted tracery of its interior halls, and the exceptionally rich and infinitely varied decoration of the patios, palaces, and gardens of the Generalife. This true masterpiece of Moorish art, visited every year by two million people, was built at the behest of the Nasrid caliphs who, to conceal the decline of their power, wanted a grandiose undertaking—putting into concrete form the concept of an earthly paradise. The Alhambra, which survived pillaging and an attempt by the Napoleonic troops to blow it up, was restored to reveal and emphasize the delicate mastery of its architecture.

Leaving Granada, the road traverses the undulating country landscape that uninterruptedly delineates

the horizon, hiding from view other hills that rise one after another. Neat, orderly olive groves fade into immense expanses of sunflowers, white fields of wheat, and the occasional dazzling country estate. Then, beyond the Ronda mountains, the Ruta de los Pueblos Blancos de la Frontera, or "Route of White Frontier Villages," appears—sun-drenched, white-washed rural villages that for centuries have marked the border between the Arab and Christian worlds. From a distance they look the same, with only certain details differentiating them: a church, a bell tower, a small fortress. **OLIVERA**, a protected collection of white houses on a hill, with a crenellated castle and a neoclassical church, all surrounded by olive groves, is emblematic. The road weaves its way through a sea of hills, yielding glimpses of other *pueblos blancos*: **ALGODONALES**, **VILLAMARTÍN**, **BORNOS**, and finally **ARCOS DE LA FRONTERA**, with its labyrinthine old quarter. Then the highlands vanish into the coastline, turning into the calcareous promontory at the end of a 6-mile-long (10-kilometer) spit of land between Bahia de Cádiz and the Atlantic Ocean.

THE JEREZ REGION

CÁDIZ is an odd city that at first glance might leave the visitor questioning the decision to have traveled there, but within a few hours it casts its spell. There are many reasons: the incredible light, strong and clear, which cheers the intricate labyrinth of alleyways in the historic center; the frescoes of Francisco de Goya and the canvases of Francisco de Zurbaran, Bartolome Murillo, El Greco, and Rubens; the comings and goings of large ships on the glassy sea that the city overlooks; the first-rate seafood dishes. According to legend, Cádiz was founded by Hercules, but history explains that it was the Phoenicians who settled Gadir ("fortress" in Arabic) in 1100 BC. And it was here, in 1812, that the country's first constitution was formally proclaimed.

OPPOSITE PAGE: the interior of the Córdoba mosque, a splendid legacy of Islamic culture in Spain.

ABOVE: contrasting Andalusian images and colors: the Atlantic coast in Cádiz, above, and, below, the massive structure of the Alhambra in Granada at sunset.

WINE *The sherry families*

Every cellar of *jerez*, or sherry as it is known, preserves authentic oenological treasures. Whether in immense cathedral-like cellars or in more intimate spaces, sherry is matured in *soleras*—casks close to the ground—an ancient method marked by organized systems of barrels that date back as far as the eighteenth century. Only the *catadores*, or tasters, disturb the quiet of the cellars, to carefully follow the progress of each barrel. They select the wines for the most special casks. To identify the most prized selections, the regulatory council for the guarantee of origin for sherry has created two special categories of aged wines: V.O.S. (Vinum Optimum Signatum), which is aged for more than twenty years, and V.O.R.S. (Vinum Optimum Rarum Signatum), aged for more than thirty years.

Essential to sherry's nature is its fortification, the addition of natural alcohol to elevate the alcoholic content. Every winter the *catadores* classify the new wine into two categories: *finos*, paler and lighter, and *olorosos*, which have more structure and color. At this point the distillate is added, ranging from 12 to 15 percent for the *finos* and up to 17 or 18 percent for the *olorosos*. The 15 percent alcohol content for the *finos* allows the development of *flor*, a natural yeast that gives the wine its unmistakable taste, and prevents oxidation. With *olorosos*, the 18 percent alcohol content kills the *flor* and the protective skin does not form. Thus the wine comes into contact with the air and begins an irreversible process of oxidation. Sherry is divided into eight types, based on five great families:

Fino: Straw-yellow in color, dry, aging protected by the veil of *flor* for approximately three years, with an alcohol content of 12 to 15 percent.

Manzanilla: Like the *fino*, but produced only in Sanlúcar de Barrameda.

Amontillado: Amber in color, this is a *fino* that continues to age in the cask, even after having lost its *flor*. It has an alcohol content of approximately 17.5 percent.

Oloroso: Usually dry, its color ranges from amber to mahogany. A full-bodied wine, with an alcohol content of about 18 percent.

Palo Cortado: This wine has the delicacy and cleanness of the *amontillado* but the structure and complexity of an *oloroso*. Its alcohol content is about 18 percent and its color is a light mahogany.

Pale Cream: A velvety wine with a light golden color and sweet aroma, its alcohol content is about 17.5 percent.

Cream Vino: A sweet wine obtained from *oloroso*, dark mahogany in color, full-bodied, with an alcohol content of about 17.5 percent.

Pedro Ximénez: A dense, very sweet, almost syrupy wine, with hints of dried fruit. Very full-bodied and complex, it has a dark mahogany color and an alcohol content of about 17 percent.

Precious bottlings from Bodega Pérez Barquero, in Montilla.

PREVIOUS PAGES, LEFT: the brilliant green of the vineyards around Jerez de La Frontera, in the land of the region's celebrated wine.

ABOVE: barrels in the Bodega Sánchez Romate Hermanos cellar in Jerez.

OPPOSITE: the art of the *catador*, the expert who watches over the selection and aging of jerez, or sherry as it is called in English.

In the extreme south of Andalusia, moving up the Costa de la Luz, which stretches from Portugal to the Strait of Gibraltar, the golden triangle of Jerez—also known as Xérès, or Sherry, opens out. The region's renowned fortified white wine attained its greatest popularity in the eighteenth and nineteenth centuries, when the English discovered it and began exporting it. Even Shakespeare mentions it in *Henry IV*. Sherry is produced only in this small triangle of Andalusia, which is buffeted by the hot winds of Africa and the humid Atlantic breezes. It owes its special qualities to a fortuitous combination of conditions: the special terrain called *albariza* (capable of absorbing the scant rainfall and then becoming compact, to limit evaporation) and the climate, which favors the growth of a microflora of the Palomino

grape known as *flor,* without which the quintessential sherry, or *fino*, would not be possible. To control, defend, and promote this fortified wine, whose name was long used to designate wines coming from and produced in other places, in 1933 the Consejo Regulador de Vino de Jerez-Xérès-Sherry y Manzanilla-Sanlúcar de Barrameda (the oldest such council in Spain) was established. Since 1999, sherry, scrupulously made from Palomino, Pedro Ximénez, and Moscatel grapes, has regained possession of the exclusive use of the name.

The first stop in the universe of this wine that boasts three names in three different languages is **EL PUERTO DE SANTA MARIA**, at the mouth of the Guadalete River. Founded by the Phoenicians and later a Roman port, in the fifteenth and sixteenth centuries its visitors included Christopher Columbus and Amerigo Vespucci. It also drew the Osborne wine merchants, a firm that has been in the same family since 772 (and is a member of the extremely select group of *primae familiae vini* that make up the oldest family-owned wine-producing companies in the world). Like many other companies, they also produce brandy in addition to sherry. Their logo, the silhouette of a black bull, stands out clearly at the highest points of all the main streets that traverse the town. A tour of the city can begin with the immense sherry cellars, which, along with the Marsala cellars in Sicily, are the most scenic in the world. To facilitate the ventilation that is necessary for the aging of the wine, the cellars must be spacious and large, with high ceilings, floors of clay to preserve a high level of humidity (the floors are wet down very frequently during the summer), and, if possible, oriented toward the west to take advantage of the natural Atlantic breeze. The largest companies seem like small towns within themselves, with buildings, streets, vines on arbors going from one cottage to another, and an endless stream of people who are involved with the winemaking process.

A lovely road parallel to the ocean leads to **SANLÚCAR DE BARRAMEDA**, a fishing village at the mouth of the Guadalquivir, across from the Doñana park. In 1498 Christopher Columbus departed from here on his third voyage to the new world, and in 1519 Magellan began his expedition to circumnavigate

the world here. The itinerary then continues through **CHIPIONA**, where for centuries the lighthouse at the mouth of the Guadalquivir has guided sailors transporting sherry to Great Britain; the road then proceeds to **ROTA**, renowned for its beaches.

The intoxicating trail moves through the low vineyards that graze the water and the river, ending in the snow-white town of **JEREZ DE LA FRONTERA**, the true and aristocratic capital of sherry wine, equestrian arts, and flamenco. In 711, the region between Jerez and Cape Trafalgar was the site of a great battle between the Visigoths and the Moors, after which for centuries Christian Spain was dominated by the Arabs. For this reason Jerez is included in the *pueblos blancos*, those villages that until

the reconquest by Spain marked the boundary between the Christian and Arab worlds. Another battle took place here in 1340, which concluded with the victory of the Christian troops and prevented the final invasion from North Africa.

There are wine shops everywhere in Jerez, but at least five should not be missed. Gonzalez Byass is known throughout the world for Tio Pepe (distributed in one hundred countries), a *fino* white wine that should be drunk extremely cold as an aperitif; in Italy it is usually served mistakenly at room temperature with dessert, which spoils it, and it is consequently unappreciated. A visit to this historic winery is extremely fascinating and requires time. La Concha, one of the many wine cellars on the property, and a patio were built by

famed architect Gustave Eiffel; in Cuarto de Muestras, there are casks signed by kings and queens and a tiny anteroom where the oldest bottles are displayed.

An equally complex realm belongs to Allied Domecq, another world-famous name for sherry and for Fundador brandy. The wine cellar inspired by the Mezquita mosque in Córdoba is spectacular, with 1,100 columns and 40,000 500-liter casks. Tastings are unforgettable.

Smaller compared to the two huge wineries mentioned above but no less important is Bodega Sánchez Romate Hermanos. In Italy its brandy, Cardinal Mendoza, is more famous than its wines, which have such a distinctive character in the glass that they are enchanting. The Bodega Lustau ages wines, vinegar,

and brandy in its typical cathedral-like cellars, and finally there is the Bodega Williams & Humbert, founded in 1877.

Sherry's unique taste is produced by the *solera* system, whereby wines from different barrels and different years are mixed. Unlike with other wines, the trick lies in exposing the barrels to the sun and the elements for at least three hundred days a year. One curious fact: the navigator Sir Francis Drake, after sacking this little corner of Spain, took away three thousand wineskins of sherry.

IN ANDALUS: BETWEEN SEVILLE AND CÓRDOBA

Jerez is surrounded by gentle, green land that offers lovely excursions among the vines and fantastic views. Just a few miles away lies the romantic Andalusian capital: **SEVILLE**, city of love, home of the opera figures Don Giovanni, Carmen, and Figaro, and "pleasant for its oranges and women," as the poet Byron wrote in the nineteenth century. But it is also known for Alcázar Palace, with its light, refined architecture and beautiful gardens; its immense cathedral (approximately 380 feet long by 250 feet wide, with five naves) and the twelfth-century Giralda bell tower, over 300 feet high (100 meters); the enormous Plaza de España; the Guadalquivir River and its many elegant bridges; and unforgettable bullfights (which everyone must see at least once). It is an extremely rich city and must be experienced slowly if one is to truly get to know it.

An infinite expanse of vineyards, sloping down into a hilly plateau, announce **CARMONA**, a former Carthaginian colony and one of the oldest human settlements in this part of Europe. Today it is a lovely little town that clings to a hill overlooking the fertile Guadalquivir plain. The blue-and-white tile bell towers of the churches of San Pedro and Santa Maria la Mayor stand out from the fortified walls that encircle the dazzling little white houses built in the Muslim style.

Continuing eastward, rows of vines stretch as far as **CÓRDOBA**, a city that is reserved and cool, shadowy and alluring. In the tenth century it was one of the most important cities in the West, and it still preserves much of its former grandeur. The Mezquita—the mosque begun by the Emir Omayyade Abd al-Rahman I in the eighth century—leaves the visitor breathless with the almost dreamlike beauty of its obsessive sequence of hundreds of columns, pillars, and capitals. The great mosque fully expresses the splendor of Islamic culture in Spain, and it represents the most important creation of Arabic architecture in the country. The royal residence of Al-Zahra, which Abd al-Rahman III had built in 936 and which was later completely destroyed, is considered the Versailles of the Córdoba caliphate.

The complex world of *fino* extends as far as the outskirts of Córdoba, specifically to **MONTILLA**, native land of Gonzalo Fernández de Córdoba, a brilliant strategist to the Catholic kings (1453–1515). The wines produced here, based on the Pedro Ximénez grape, attain a 15 percent alcohol content by natural means, thanks to the climate; in the golden triangle of Jerez the Palomino grape dominates and the wines are fortified to raise the alcoholic strength, but the system for aging is the same. At tastings, the Montilla-Moriles wines, which benefit from Mediterranean and continental climatic conditions, seem quite similar to those from the coastal area. The historic Bodega Pérez Barquero offers wine tastings and visits to the property.

TAKE A BREAK

LODGING

Carmona: **CASA PALACIO DE CARMONA**
Plaza de Lasso 1
Tel: 0034.954.191000
www.casadecarmona.com
Instead of sleeping in fascinating but chaotic Seville, one can stay in Carmona in one of the loveliest hotels in Spain. A sixteenth-century building that belonged to the Lasso de La Vega family, members of the Andalusian nobility, it was respectfully renovated and decorated by the current owner, Doña Marta Medina. This Madrid architect and author has given new life to the structure, once in utter disrepair. She has introduced technological improvements while preserving the dimensions and elements of the original design. The result is an elegant country house, variously Andalusian, English, and French. Every room has different colors, curtains, and textiles. There are original parquet floors throughout, English antiques, and precious Spanish furniture; each room has a canopy bed. The building has been transformed into a truly special hotel that welcomes guests rather than customers. The peaceful atmosphere seems like that of nineteenth-century mansion, updated with modern comforts. In the shadow of the porticos, in the winter garden, and in the reading rooms, romantic silence reigns.

DINING

Córdoba: **EL CABALLO ROJO**
Cardenal Herrero 28
Tel: 0034.957.475375
This was one of the first restaurants that began to offer authentic dishes tied to the country's Arabic, Christian, and North African past, readapting those cuisines to current tastes without distorting them—from *bacalà* (salt cod) to cinnamon- and honey-flavored lamb, from soups to sweets with Egyptian origins. Try dining on the terrace.

GONZALEZ BYASS

Calle Manuel Maria Gonzalez 12,
Jerez de La Frontera
Tel. 0034.956.357000
www.gonzalezbyass.es

Founded: 1835
Production region: Jerez, El Puerto de Santa
Maria, Sanlúcar de Barrameda
Wines and grape varieties: 100% whites;
Palomino and Pedro Ximénez

GREAT WINES

Tio Pepe
This is a traditional Fino, aged five to
seven years using the solera method, in
500-liter barrels of American oak. Made
from pure Palomino grapes, gathered by
hand in the winery's vineyards. Delicate
straw-yellow color. Pungent, intense, and
persistent to the nose, with hints of wood,
yeast, and bread crust. Potent, almost
explosive in the mouth, with hints of
wood and honey. Long, persistent aftertaste that leaves a flavorful taste in the
mouth. Should be drunk cold, as an aperitif, or as a complement to shellfish.

Apostoles
Made from Palomino grapes with a small
percentage (18 percent) of Pedro
Ximénez. Aged thirty years in barrels of
American oak. It starts out as a Fino, then
after aging becomes an Amontillado but
has the body of an Oloroso. A very complex wine with an intense amber color,
hints of wood, licorice, and dry fruit. Full
and sumptuous in the mouth.
Complements foie gras.

Visits and tastings: yes

DOMECQ

San Idelfonso 3, Jerez de La Frontera
Tel. 0034.956.151500

Founded: 1730
Production region: Jerez, El Puerto de Santa
Maria, Sanlúcar de Barrameda
Wines and grape varieties: 100% whites;
Palomino and Pedro Ximénez

GREAT WINES

Amontillado 51-1a
Aging for over thirty years in a solera system from 1830 produces this Amontillado
of great elegance. Amber color with bur-
nished reflections. Complex and harmonious bouquet, with notes of wood and
hazelnut. Taste structured by great aging,
potent and velvety. Very persistent with
an aftertaste of hazelnut. Complements
game and hard cheeses.

Sibarita
An Oloroso wine made from Palomino
grapes with 2 percent Pedro Ximénez
aged at least thirty years in a historic solera system put in place by Pedro Domecq
in 1792. Intense and brilliant topaz color.
Rather complex and profound to the
nose, with hints of dry fruit, spices, and
oak. Smooth to the palate, large body, velvety and very persistent. Should be drunk
by itself, or as a complement to fine
cheeses and dry fruit.

Visits and tastings: yes

SÁNCHEZ ROMATE

Lealas 26, Jerez de La Frontera
Tel. 0034.956.182212
www.romate.com

Founded: 1781
Production region: Pago Balbaina (between
Jerez, El Puerto de Santa Maria, and
Sanlúcar de Barrameda)
Wines and grape varieties: 100% whites;
Palomino Fino, Moscatel, and Pedro
Ximénez

GREAT WINES

NPU (non plus ultra)
Amontillado made from 100 percent
Palomino Fino grapes, solera-aged for
more than thirty years. Elegant, with brilliant amber color. Deep, refined bouquet
with almond notes. Dry and balanced
with a long finish. A perfect aperitif, or
pair with meat tapas.

Moscatel Ambrosia
Made from 100 percent Moscatel grapes,
solera-aged for more than thirty years. A
dark, elegant wine, fruity and very sweet,
perfect with blue cheese or sweets. A
dessert wine or a wine for meditation.

Cardenal Cisneros
Made from 100 percent Pedro Ximénez
grapes, using the solera system. A very
sweet, dense, velvety wine, with a strong
finish of raisins. After eight to twelve years
the barrels are reused for aging Cardinal
Mendoza brandy.

Visits and tastings: yes

OSBORNE

Calle Los Moros, El Puerto de Santa
Maria
Tel. 0034.956.869100
www.osborne.es

Founded: 1772
Production region: Jerez, El Puerto de Santa
Maria, and Sanlúcar de Barrameda
Wines and grape varieties: 100% whites;
Palomino Fino and Pedro Ximénez

GREAT WINES

Oloroso BC 200
Made from Palomino grapes with 5 percent Pedro Ximénez grapes. Comes from
the Osbornes' oldest solera system, in
operation since 1864. Aged forty-two
years, with 22 percent alcoholic content
and a considerable sugary residue (45
grams per liter). Dark amber color tending to mahogany. Bouquet of old wood,
with hints of oak, velvety and persistent.
Smooth in the mouth, large body, with
hints of caramel, bitter almond, and
toasted bread. An extremely long aftertaste. A meditation wine par excellence.

Oloroso Solera India
Comes from a solera system set up in
1922. Palomino grapes with 6 percent
Pedro Ximénez passito. Aged thirty-five
years, it is an unusual wine that falls outside the usual Jerez categories. Dark,
dense mahogany color. A profound bouquet to the nose, with hints of toast and
burned rubber. Intense, sumptuous, spicy
in the mouth, with a marked presence of
vulcanized rubber. A wine for meditation.

Visits and tastings: yes

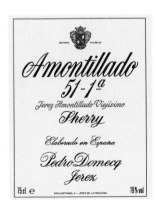

LUSTAU

Arcos 53, Jerez de La Frontera
Tel. 0034.956.341597
www.emilio-lustau.com

Founded: 1896
Production region
Jerez, El Puerto de Santa Maria, and
Sanlúcar de Barrameda
Wines and grape varieties
100% whites; Palomino Fino, Moscatel,
and Pedro Ximénez

GREAT WINES

East India Sherry
Made from Palomino grapes with a small
percentage of Pedro Ximénez; the two
wines are aged separately. After blending,
the sherry is left to age in American oak
barrels. The resulting wine is aged approximately twelve years on average. Dark
mahogany color. Very concentrated bouquet with dry fruit and smoke. Complex,
even and velvety on the palate; rich with a
persistent presence of dried figs. Perfect
for milk-based sweets or chocolate cake.

Riserva Moscatel Emilín
An elegant dessert wine made from pure
Moscatel grapes, aged in wood for seven
years. Dark mahogany color with yellowish reflections. Intense floral and fruity
aromas, typical of Moscatel. Sweet and
spicy taste, with aromas of dried fruit.
Should be drunk by itself or as a complement to rich desserts.

Visits and tastings: yes

PÉREZ BARQUERO

Avenida Andalucía 27, Montilla
Tel. 0034.3957.650500
www.perezbarquero.com

Founded: 1905
Production region: Montilla-Moriles
Wines and grape varieties: 100% whites;
Pedro Ximénez

GREAT WINES

Fino Gran Barquero
Average aging of ten years in the solera
system. Pure Pedro Ximénez grapes.
Brilliant straw-yellow color. Pungent, harmonious, and intense aroma, with hints of
wood and dry fruit. Slightly aromatic, dry,
with memories of bitter almond, very persistent. Should be drunk as an aperitif or
as a complement to shellfish.

1905 Pedro Ximénez
Pure Pedro Ximénez aged over seventy
years in a solera system set up in 1905
(which means that most of the wine is
from 1905, with a percentage of younger
wine). Dark mahogany color with garnet
reflections. Intense, profound, and persistent bouquet, with hints of date, dry
fig, honey, and caramel. Sweet in the
mouth, with enormous body, hints of date
and dry fig, licorice, and chocolate. A wine
for meditation or a complement to chocolate-based dishes.

Visits and tastings: yes

FRANCE

FRANCE AND WINE—it is a combination of legend and a grand reality. French wines such as Burgundy, Alsace, Champagne, and Bordeaux can be found in every corner of the world. France is the principal stage for the history of wine, a long history beginning on the coasts of the Mediterranean at the time of the Greek and Phoenician settlements, and gaining importance under the Roman Empire. The Romans were the first to view wine as a commodity and manage its production with commercial criteria. Twenty centuries ago Bordeaux was one of the main trading destinations for wine that came from Pompeii. When that city was destroyed by the eruption of Vesuvius in 79 AD, the Romans understood how important it was to spread the cultivation of vines in order to guarantee the supply to their garrisons and settlements in the farthest reaches of their empire. France and the entire ancient world owe the origin of much of their winegrowing regions to this decision. By the Roman Empire's decline, the landscape of areas such as Bordeaux, Burgundy, and the Rhine valley was already profoundly marked by the layout of vineyards, and there was a significant wine economy. But the end of Roman rule left a void that was detrimental to French viticulture, and barbarian invasions caused enormous damage, bringing an abrupt halt to the development of winegrowing techniques and production.

The rebirth of viticulture in Europe began in France and in the Rhine valley in Germany. During the Middle Ages, first Charlemagne and then the Benedictine and Cistercian monks once again oversaw the cultivation of vines, particularly in

RIGHT: bottles from the Maison Dappier in Urville, in the Champagne region.
OPPOSITE PAGE: Château de Brissac in the Loire Valley.

66

Burgundy. In the centuries that followed Bordeaux consolidated its role as a center of wine exports to the Anglo-Saxon world, and around the end of the eighteenth century became the driving economic force for the wine industry worldwide.

The nineteenth century was crucial for French wine. Following the example of Riesling in Germany, French winemakers made their first serious attempts to analyze grapevines, which led to the successful development of certain varieties that are now considered international, such as Cabernet Sauvignon, Merlot, and Chardonnay. The evolution of taste, which demanded more full-bodied and complex wines, the introduction of increasingly complicated vinification techniques, and the invention in the Champagne region of the modern glass bottle used with natural cork stoppers created the basis for aging, a concept that is inextricably linked to a wine's quality. The French wine industry demonstrated fantastic vitality, perhaps unique for the time, and this was expressed through significant innovations, economic power, and attention to promotion. Changes occurred across the board, from agriculture to marketing, and from technology to image. The golden age of French wine began with the classification of the great Bordeaux châteaux at the International Fair of 1855. But the industry immediately had to contend with an unexpected disaster in the form of phylloxera, a deadly grapevine pest. In the late nineteenth century more than six million grapevines were destroyed, and French production fell by two-thirds. Once again the French winemakers acted to save their way of life.

THE FRENCH WINE WORLD TODAY
Although the quality of wine has improved everywhere and there has been a proliferation of new production regions, often in countries with strong economies such as the United States, French wine has been and remains the world epitome of quality and image. This success is due to the ability of French producers to express their regional qualities, their diversity, their typical characteristics, in clear contrast to the prevailing tendency in the New World toward homogenization of taste and product.

France and wine combine to create a profound relationship, rooted in custom and tradition, as in no other part of the world. Indeed, in 1999 a diplomatic incident was caused by a dinner and the wine that was to have accompanied it. An official visit of the president of Iran was planned for October and, in keeping with protocol, called for a state dinner. The Iranian authorities, invoking Islamic law, asked that wine not be served. The French responded that an official dinner was inconceivable without wine. The dinner was canceled and the state visit downgraded to a simple official visit, a situation that would be unimaginable in any other country.

In addition to France's long history and profound cultural ties to wine production, its geological and climatic diversity have helped make the country an ideal temple of viticulture. The Atlantic Ocean and the Mediterranean Sea affect conditions far inland, while the mountain chains and massifs of central France act as a climatic barrier. The result is a great variety of microclimates and varying terrains, creating a significant number of winegrowing regions and an exciting oenological panorama.

ITINERARIES

More than a world, realm of French wine is an entire universe, multifaceted and brilliant; it is difficult to summarize and impossible to catalogue. This universe can be discovered region by region, encountering the local people, seeing the hands that work the earth, understanding the deep ties between wine and culture. The wine routes suggested here meander through old vineyards, lead to the most wonderful wine cellars, and stop at the finest restaurants, so the traveler can grasp the essence of the flavors of each individual region.

In France, contiguous vineyards express regional variations. Burgundy offers the most dramatic example. Here, in this most traditional of territories, winegrowers must contend with high rainfall and the frequent risk of frost. Often austere environments, where cellars are frequently bare and reduced to essentials, have given birth to some of the finest Pinot Noir and Chardonnay wines.

Champagne, the northernmost wine region in France, is located in the farthest reaches of the latitudes where grapes can ripen. Visitors can move among the mazelike cellars carved into tufa stone and visit opulent residences, and then go on to discover that there is an entire parallel world of small producers that create astonishingly wonderful champagnes.

Alsace, despite its continental position, protected from ocean storms by the Vosges Mountains, is known for a winemaking technique featuring overripe grapes. The hilly vineyards of this region bordering Germany produces Gewürztraminer, Pinot Grigio, and Riesling wines that combine elegance and sensuality.

On its long path to the sea, the Loire valley traverses climate zones that range from the continental to regions that grow increasingly humid as the river gradually nears the estuary, and the vineyards located along the banks reflect these differing conditions. In turn this variety is expressed in the character of the wines, from the dry, mineral Sauvignon Blancs of Sancerre to the full-bodied and velvety Cabernet Francs of Chinon.

The Mediterranean coast varies from the almost torrid climate on the Spanish border to the beginning of the Alps on the Italian frontier, where icy winds encounter the sea. The route goes from the terraced vineyards of Banyuls, birthplace of the marvelous wine of the same name that goes perfectly with chocolate, to the Côte d'Azur and the brusque, muscular red wines of Bandol. In Avignon and Châteauneuf du Pape, the perfectly balanced climatic elements influence the ripening of the grapes and result in wines of unbeatable personality, made from indigenous varieties such as Grenache, Mourvèdre, and Viognier.

In the Bordeaux region, the pebbly terrain, rivers, and ocean conspire to produce the conditions for the creation of legendary wines. Our journey makes stops in Saint-Émilion, Sauternes, Graves, and Médoc, sampling wines that include Figeac, Rothschild, Yquem, Haut-Brion, and Margaux; it is a parade of French grandeur that makes its way among the most celebrated wines in the world.

Six itineraries travel through an equal number of regions, traversing the beauty of widely varying landscapes, getting lost in a sea of indigenous grape varieties; these are only a few of French wine's many faces.

Bottles and wine culture at the Athenaeum de la Vigne et du Vin in Beaune, Burgundy.

THE LOIRE

ITINERARY LENGTH
300 miles / 480 kilometers

BEST TIME TO GO
May to October

TIME TO SPEND
One week

WINE TRAIL *Itinerary*

USEFUL ADDRESSES
Comité Regional du Tourisme Centre
Val-de-Loire
Avenue de Paris 37, Orléans
Tel: 0033.2.38799528
Fax: 0033.2.38799510
www.visaloire.com

**DISCOVERING CASTLES
FROM ABOVE**
In a hot-air balloon: France Montgolfières
Loire Valley, La Riboulière,
www.franceballoons.com
In a helicopter: Jet Systems,
www.jet-systems.fr

THE HEART OF France has a winding strip of vineyards that follow the path of the Loire, river of kings. Located on sunny slopes that run from the central massif to the Atlantic Ocean, orderly and precise rows of vines extend as far as the eye can see. The serpentine watercourse crawls through different terrains, vineyards, and climates, touching upon approximately fifty AOC (*appellation d'origine controlée*, a guarantee of origin) zones, which mirror the wide range of wines produced.

Over the centuries, the Loire valley has acted as a large stage on which sovereigns and princes, queens and dukes, courtesans and singers have all played a role, seduced by the beauty of the setting. After King Charles VII moved his court to this region during the first half of the fifteenth century, his successors and their retinues of aristocrats and the bourgeoisie chose it as a place to make their homes. They began restoring old manor houses and building new and sumptuous dwellings that still reflect their former glory days of amorous intrigues,

OPPOSITE PAGE, FROM TOP: Vines along the Loire; the "album" of labels at the Bouvet-Ladubay cellar in Saumur; the canal bridge in Briare; bottles aging in the Gaec Allias cellar in Vouvray.

ABOVE: a Loire valley landscape.

71

celebrations, and grand balls. It is a land that visitors should discover bit by bit, entertained by literary recollections — François Rabelais, Honoré de Balzac, and Henri Alain Fournier were born here — and surrendering to the allure of the region's landscapes and great wines.

THE JOURNEY
FROM BOURGES TO ORLÉANS, AMID ART AND WINE

The gateway to the Loire valley is **BOURGES**, an impressive historic city that boasts an extraordinary artistic patrimony. The grand cathedral of Saint-Etienne dates from the thirteenth century; with 28,000 square feet (2,600 square meters) of stained glass, it keeps a close vigil over downtown's narrow lanes, thatched houses, and Gothic palaces. From May to September, expert set designers searching for locations scan the city at night, the most fascinating time to visit it, particularly the medieval quarter. In the darkness, a trail of blue lights lead toward the historic sites, from the cathedral to the noble houses, enveloping the streets in iridescent beams that enhance even the smallest architectural detail. This is an excursion for those who enjoy walking in complete freedom, without haste and without crowds.

OPPOSITE: a mosaic of tilled fields and the sky above the Loire valley, looking toward Sancerre.

RIGHT: Château d'Artigny, not far from Tours.

The journey continues for approximately 25 miles (40 kilometers) through vineyards of Sauvignon grapes, which achieve the highest levels of excellence in this region, to reach **SANCERRE**, land of great white wines. The tiny streets of this village perched on a rocky hill are dominated by the medieval tower of the Château de Sancerre, owned by Marnier Lapostolle (which, in addition to wine, produces the famous orange liqueur Grand Marnier). For gourmands, this is the place to try the winning combination of a glass of Sancerre (the white is best) and the renowned goat cheese, *crottin de Chavignol*. Farther along, on the slopes of the left bank of the river facing the vineyards of **POUILLY-SUR-LOIRE**, the Bourgeois family has been producing excellent wines for ten generations. The commitment and care that Jean-Marie Bourgeois gives to the different geological

characteristics of the soil are reflected in the uniqueness of his Sancerre wines. The wines of Daniel Chotard, a modest producer in **CRÉZANCY-EN-SANCERRE**, are also appealing.

Continuing on toward Orléans, a series of villages overlooking the river testify to the historical importance of the Loire as a means of communication and transport. At **BRIARE**, the imposing profile of the canal bridge stands out against the river, a masterpiece of hydraulic engineering on whose design Gustave Eiffel also worked. A bit farther, in the village of **GIEN**, which is known for its ceramics, is a striking stone bridge with thirteen spans that was restored at the time of Anne de Beaujeu, daughter of Louis XI. In **SULLY-SUR-LOIRE**, on the left bank of the river, the extremely beautiful and irregular medieval tower heralds the splendor of the journey to come, as does

the grand Benedictine abbey of **SAINT-BENOÎT-SUR-LOIRE**, which stands out among the old fishermen's houses lining the riverbank. The placid waters of the Loire then traverse **ORLÉANS**, a city inextricably bound to the memory of the heroic acts of Joan of Arc (1412–31), who entered the city victorious after freeing it from English rule in 1429.

PLACES OF KINGS

BLOIS, native city of Louis XII, is the starting point for our tour of the strong and romantic heart of the luminous valley that won over the French Renaissance kings and their courts. A succession of prized vineyards, golden fields of wheat, gentle slopes and verdant plains combine harmoniously with the network of tributaries that feed into the Loire. The palace of **CHAMBORD** appears quite suddenly,

OPPOSITE PAGE, LEFT: an aerial view of one of the castles in the Loire valley.

ABOVE: the splendors of art in Bourges.

PERSONALITIES *Jean-Marie Bourgeois*

To make the most of his grapes, Jean-Marie Bourgeois is scrupulous, methodical, and attentive to every speck of earth in his vineyards outside Sancerre, and he is one of the strongest supporters of the region's importance in wine production. "Information about the terrain," he says, "should always be indicated and should be in accordance with the information on the grape variety, to allow one to understand how the composition of the soil influences the grape. But to do serious work is not enough. One has to take care with the selection on the vine, the transport, and during the various phases of work." Bourgeois's exuberance is reflected in the dynamism of his business, as evidenced by the huge number of young people who flock here from all over, above all during the harvest, to learn. There are also long-term plans to plant new vineyards in Marlborough, New Zealand. The young plants will be cultivated in three different types of soil: the rocky soil of Renwick, and the clay soil of Broadbridge and Wither, in an area that is still underutilized.

OPPOSITE: a luxurious view of wines in the famous cellar of the Château de Brissac, near Agnes.

FOLLOWING PAGES: Chambord castle.

enhanced by a forest of stone pinnacles and chimneys (385 in all). Built from 1519 to 1537 at the behest of King Francis I, it is the largest castle along the Loire with 440 rooms, 500 feet (160 meters) long, 380 feet (120 meters) wide, and 185 feet (60 meters) high. A progression of splendid manor houses follows in a Rossinian crescendo, all different, all beautiful. There is one in **AMBOISE**, where the great Leonardo da Vinci spent the last three years of his life as the guest of Francis I; a pagoda in **CHANTELOUP**, built by Le Camus (1775–78), sits on the edge of the Amboise forest. **CHENONCEAUX**, on the waters of the Cher River, holds the secrets of four centuries of court intrigues: Henry II gave it to his favorite, Diana de Poitiers; upon the death of her powerful rival, Queen Catherine de Medici, she was banished to the castle of **CHAUMONT** (the same place where Madame de Staël took refuge in 1810, when Napoleon forbade her to reside within 25 miles [40 kilometers] of Paris), which she transformed into a scene of opulent celebrations, with costumes in the latest fashion.

In the summer almost all the castles of the Loire are animated by the thrilling *Son et Lumiere* (Sound and Light) spectacles, a series of outdoor events that bring to life the history of these manor houses.

TOURAINE AND ANJOU

The vineyards that surround **TOURS** and its castles are part of the Touraine AOC, which borders those of Anjou and Saumur. For over a millennium until the

The historic wine cellar of Maison Couly-Dutheil in Chinon, birthplace of Cabernet Franc.

late nineteenth century, the tufa extracted from this area was used for the construction of French monuments, villas in the Loire valley, and even part of Westminster Abbey in London. Many of the former quarries have been transformed into wine cellars, making ideal places for aging wine in darkness at a cool, constant temperature.

In the village of **VOUVRAY**, the versatility of the Chenin Blanc grape variety can be fully appreciated by tasting it in the calcareous tufa grottoes of Gaec Allias where wines rest, often made from late harvests; even after years they maintain their rich characteristics. In the subterranean tasting room a decorative hearth has been carved out, a showcase

displaying fossils, shells, and pieces of petrified wood found in the tunnels. One wall is devoted to samples of all the wines produced until 1893, the last harvest before the vines were attacked by phylloxera, and those after 1915, the year they began harvesting grapes from transplanted American vines.

After Tours, Balzac's native city, the itinerary continues into the homeland of Chinon. During the Hundred Years' War, the castle of the town of **CHINON** was one of the last bastions of the French crown. In this triangle at the confluence of the Vienne and the Loire, Cabernet Franc finds one of its finest expressions—the Clos de l'Echo of Maison Couly-

Dutheil. Once again, to better understand the allure and culture of these wines, a visit to the cellars is a must: go inside and breathe in the calm, cool atmosphere of the tenth-century tunnels. When these tufa grottoes were excavated, the material that was extracted was used for the construction of Chinon castle. Darkness and silence protect the precious bottles, while in the vineyards, the warmth and light of the sun ripen grapes for future harvests.

The flat, solemn landscape of the Saumur Champigny grape region is a checkerboard of fields, vineyards, and small watercourses, where in the twelfth century a hectare of vineyard cost 30 percent more than that in Champagne. Our route continues as far as the castle of **SAUMUR**, which dominates the Loire with broad towers topped with conical roofs. A Protestant stronghold in the seventeenth century, then a prison and barracks, since the early twentieth century the castle has housed a museum dedicated to medieval decorative arts, toy figurines (about twenty thousand pieces), and horses (the collection includes harnesses and saddles from all over the world). The stony, calcareous lands around the castle are cultivated with Cabernet Sauvignon and Cabernet Franc grapes, which yield velvety reds capable of great aging, and Chenin Blanc grapes, which produce ele-

The barrels of Château La Varière in Vauchrétien, in Anjou, not far from Brissac-Quincé.

gant whites. At the Château de Targé, a beautiful property on the left bank of the river, some of the best wines in the region can be tasted, including the Cuvée Ferry, a red of great structure and personality. The Bouvet-Ladubay winery also is surprising and a veritable temple of bubbles: *grand cru* whites, rosés, or reds, sweet or dry, made according to traditional methods and aged in the labyrinthine *caves*, where artist Philippe Cormand has sculpted his *Cathedrale engloutie*, or "sunken cathedral," into the tufa. It is an underground oenological-theatrical world, which winds for over 1,300 feet (400 meters) among bottles, music, and the play of light.

In **ANJOU**, between Saumur and **ANGERS**, there are extremely ancient tufa quarries that the French call "troglo," hidden troglodytic sites that have been converted into mushroom beds and sometimes informal restaurants. Artist Jacques Warminski has carved out spectacular gigantic sculptures in the subsoil with an original arrangement of concave and convex spaces in **SAINT-GEORGES-DES-SEPT-VOIES**. Between 1990 and 1994 he mined over 4,400

ABOVE: detail of a capital in the Bouvet-Ladubay cellar in Saumur.

LEFT: bottles of Domaine de Beauvois.

tons of material, which he reused outdoors, giving the material in positive form the same shapes that now exist in the negative within his monumental underground work, *Hélice terrestre*.

On the road again, embankments are flanked by rows of plane trees and poplars as far as **BRISSAC-QUINCÉ**, in the Aubance hills. The town has a monumental castle dating from 1502 that has been inhabited by the dukes of Brissac for over five hundred years. It boasts ceilings painted in gold leaf, a lovely theater, and a famous wine cellar, and if you are lucky, you may get to meet the thirteenth Duke of Brissac himself. The journey through the vineyards leads to Château la Varière, in **VAUCHRÉTIEN**, and a hayloft transformed into a tasting room for sampling excellent reds from Anjou and the prized late-harvest white wines, golden in color and deliciously sweet and elegant. They are perfect as a complement to foie gras or green-veined cheeses.

The journey ends in **ANGERS**, former stronghold of the Dukes of Anjou, which is reflected on the placid waters of the Maine, 5 miles (8 kilometers) from where it merges with the Loire. The buildings of Anger combine dark slate with the light tones of tufa, as in the impressive fortress flanked by seventeen inner towers that hold the largest tapestry in the world: the *Tapisserie de l'Apocalypse*, the "Tapestry of the Apocalypse," almost 330 feet (100 meters) long and more than 13 feet (4 meters) high. It remains one of the symbols of the grandeur of France.

TAKE A BREAK

LODGING

Amboise: **LE CHOISEUL**
Tel: 0033.2.47304545
www.le-choiseul.com
Now part of the Grandes Etapes Françaises chain, this lovely hotel is near Amboise castle.

Beauvois: **DOMAINE DE BEAUVOIS**
Tel: 0033.2.47555011
www.beauvois.com
A sumptuous manor house exudes an intimate, luxurious atmosphere, and is surrounded by a 146-acre (140-hectare) park.

Artigny: **CHÂTEAU D'ARTIGNY**
Tel: 0033.2.47343030
www.artigny.com
Overlooking the valley of the Indre, built by perfumer François Coty as a majestic copy of the Château de Champlatreux, with interiors inspired by Versailles.

Noirieux: **CHÂTEAU DE NOIRIEUX**
Tel: 0033.2.41425005
www.chateaudenoirieux.com
Welcoming and exclusive, this luxurious resort is immersed in the quiet Angers countryside.

DINING

Montlouis-sur-Loire: **RESTAURANT LA TOURANGELLE**
Tel: 0033.2.47509735
Full of regional flavors, with outstanding homemade foie gras, and a good wine list.

A dish at Restaurant La Tourangelle; the interior at Domaine de Beauvois.

HENRI BOURGEOIS

Chavignol, Sancerre
Tel: 0033.2.48785320
www.bourgeois-sancerre.com

Founded: 1950
Production region: Sancerre, Chavignol, Saint-Satur, Amigny, Saint-Laurent l'Abbaye
Wines and grape varieties: 80% whites, 20% reds; Sauvignon Blanc, Pinot Noir

GREAT WINES

Sancerre Blanc-La Bourgeoise 2001
Made from pure Sauvignon Blanc grapes from vineyards in the Saint-Satur region on land rich in silicon. Vinified partially in steel and partially in chestnut barrels, fermented on its own leavens for seven to eight months. Brilliant straw-yellow color, full and persistent to the nose, with hints of flint and spices. Dry taste, of great refinement and balance, with notes of flowers, vine sap, and spices. Should be aged four to five years, and complements shellfish and grilled fish.

Sancerre Blanc — Sancerre d'Antan 1998
Made from an extreme selection of pure Sauvignon Blanc grapes vinified according to the most traditional methods. Fermented on its own leavens in barrels and bottled without filtering. Brilliant straw-yellow color with golden reflections. It has a full, complex bouquet, elegant and aromatic, with hints of minerals, fresh fruit, and ripe grapes. Dry, clear taste, clean and refined, with a cloudy concentration. Should be aged six to eight years and complements shellfish or white meat.

Visits and tastings: yes

DANIEL CHOTARD

Crézancy-en-Sancerre
Tel: 0033.2.48790812
www.chotard-sancerre.com

Founded: Seventeenth century
Production region: Sancerre, Crézancy
Wines and grape varieties: 60% whites, 20% rosés, 20% reds; Sauvignon Blanc, Pinot Noir

GREAT WINES

Sancerre Blanc—Cuvée "Marcel Henri" 2000
Made from the best grapes on the property, selected on the vine, fermented at length on its own leavens. Brilliant straw-yellow color, full, complex, and persistent to the nose, with hints of white flowers and linden. Dry, concentrated taste, good structure. Ages well, and a good complement to asparagus, white meat, and fish.

Sancerre Rouge—Cuvée "Champ de l'Archer" 2000
Made from pure, selected Pinot Noir grapes, aged in chestnut barrels. Intense ruby-red color with violet reflections. Full, complex bouquet with good persistence. Rich in floral hints, particularly violet, sweet pepper, and spices. Dry, balanced, soft taste, with sweet and well-integrated tannins. Can be drunk young and served cool, or can be aged five to six years. Complements baked fish, pork, or medium-aged cheeses.

Visits and tastings: yes

CHÂTEAU DE SANCERRE

Sancerre
Tel: 0033.2.48785152
www.grandmarnier.com

Founded: 1919
Production region: Sancerre
Wines and grape varieties: 100% whites; Sauvignon Blanc

GREAT WINES

Château de Sancerre 2001
Made from pure Sauvignon Blanc grapes from vines with an average age of twenty-five years. Brilliant straw-yellow color with golden reflections. Full, fine, and persistent bouquet, with hints of orange, peach, and vanilla. Dry, decisive, elegant taste, good structure, with notes of citrus and peach. Long, clean aftertaste. A wine of good longevity. Complements fish with sauce, white meat, or the famous *crottin de Chavignol* goat cheese.

Visits and tastings: yes, by appointment

GAEC ALLIAS

Rue de la Vallée Moquette 106
Vouvray
Tel: 0033.2.47527495
www.tours-online.com/allias

Founded: Nineteenth century
Production region: AOC Vouvray
Wines and grape varieties: 100 % whites; Chenin Blanc

GREAT WINES

Vouvray Moelleux Réserve 1990
Made from pure Chenin Blanc grapes, selected and harvested by hand. First aged in wooden barrels and then in the bottle in the centuries-old tufa cellars. Brilliant yellow color with golden reflections. Full, complex, and very persistent bouquet, with hints of ripe fruit, honey, and tobacco. Velvety taste, oily, sumptuous, and harmonious, of notable structure, with notes of vanilla, green tea, honey, and caramel. Can be aged at length, and complements goat cheeses.

Visits and tastings: yes, by appointment

COULY-DUTHEIL

Rue Diderot 12
Chinon
Tel: 0033-2-47972020
www.coulydutheil-chinon.com

Founded: 1921
Production region: Chinon
Wines and grape varieties: 5% whites, 10% rosés, 85% reds; Cabernet Franc, Cabernet Sauvignon, Chenin Blanc

GREAT WINES

Chinon-Clos de l'Olive 1995
Made from pure Cabernet Franc grapes from centuries-old vines. Vinified in steel, aged in chestnut barrels for eighteen to twenty-four months. Intense ruby-red color with garnet reflections. Potent and very persistent bouquet, with hints of wild fruit, cherries in brandy, plum, licorice, and spices. Long finish, with notes of licorice and coffee. Can be aged considerably, up to fifteen to twenty years, and complements white meat, grilled beef, or pheasant.

Chinon—Clos de l'Echo Cuvée Crescendo 1997
Made from pure Cabernet Franc grapes harvested by hand. Vinified in steel, aged in chestnut barrels for twenty-four months. Deep ruby-red color with garnet reflections. Full, complex, and very persistent bouquet, with hints of cooked fruit, spices, and rare wood. Dry, concentrated, harmonious, and velvety taste, with fine and well-integrated tannins. Can be aged for up to twenty-five to thirty years, and complements roast lamb, grilled meats, and pheasant.

Visits and tastings: yes, by appointment

CHÂTEAU DE TARGÉ

Parnay
Tel: 0033.2.41381150
www.chateaudetarge.com

Founded: 1655
Production region: Chinon and environs
Wines and grape varieties: 95% reds, 5% whites; Cabernet Franc, Cabernet Sauvignon, Chenin Blanc

GREAT WINES

Blanc de Targé— Saumur 2001
Made from pure Chenin Blanc grapes. Slow fermentation on its own leavens with batonnage. Brilliant straw-yellow, with golden reflections. Intense, complex, fruity, and persistent bouquet, with hints of citrus and honey. Dry, full, warm, and velvety taste. Long aftertaste, with notes of ripe fruit and green tea. Can be aged for up to ten years, and complements fish or green-veined cheeses.

Saumur Champigny—Cuvée Ferry 2000
Made from 100 percent Cabernet Franc grapes from old vines, selected by hand and vinified in the traditional fashion and aged in the barrel, resulting in a wine of great balance and elegance. Intense ruby-red color with garnet reflections. Full, potent, and rather persistent bouquet, with pleasant hints of red berry. Dry, rich taste of excellent balance and elegance. Long and clean aftertaste, with mentholated notes. Should be aged five to ten years. Ideal complement to large roasts.

Visits and tastings: yes, by appointment

BOUVET-LADUBAY

Rue de l'Abbaye,
Saint-Hilaire-Saint-Florent
Saumur
Tel: 0033.2.41838383
www.bouvet-ladubay.fr

Founded: 1851
Production region: Saumur, Touraine, Anjou
Wines and grape varieties: 80% whites, 10% rosés, 10% reds; Chenin Blanc, Chardonnay, Cabernet Franc

GREAT WINES

Bouvet-Ladubay Tresor 1984
Made from 80 percent Chenin Blanc and 20 percent Chardonnay grapes. Vinified in traditional fashion, with first fermentation in cherry vats and second fermentation in the bottle for twenty-four to thirty-six months. Straw-yellow color, with amber reflections, fine and persistent perlage. Fruity bouquet, with notes of strawberry and honey. Dry, clean, fresh taste, with good structure and balance. Excellent aperitif or an elegant complement to smoked salmon.

Cuvée Rubis Excellence 2002
Made from pure Cabernet Franc grapes, vinified in the traditional fashion. The first fermentation is in wood and the second in the bottle for eighteen to twenty-four months. Brilliant ruby-red color, fine and persistent perlage. Full and complex bouquet, with hints of red berry. Mellow, fresh taste, with an explosion of fruit aromas—blackberry, cassis, strawberry, and raspberry. Clean aftertaste. An ideal complement to cold cut hors d'oeuvres or risottos, or can be drunk as an aperitif.

Visits and tastings: yes, by appointment

CHÂTEAU LA VARIÈRE

Brissac-Quincé
Tel: 0033.2.41912264

Production region: Brissac, Anjou
Wines and grape varieties: 25% whites, 5% rosés, 70% reds; Chenin Blanc, Cabernet Sauvignon, Cabernet Franc, Gamay

GREAT WINES

Anjou Villages Brissac "La Grande Chevalerie" 1999
Made from pure Cabernet Sauvignon grapes, selected and gathered by hand once they are completely ripe, in mid-October. Aged in new barrels for fourteen to sixteen months and bottled without filtering. Ruby-red color, tending to garnet. Full, complex, and very persistent to the nose, with hints of wild fruit, licorice, truffles, leather, and coffee. Dry, rather structured, robust, almost opulent taste. Long aftertaste, with notes of licorice. Can be aged considerably. Ideal complement to game.

Château la Varière - Bonnezeaux 1997
Made from pure Chenin grapes, completely botrytized, harvested in several stages. Aged eighteen months in barrels. Golden yellow color with topaz reflections, of extraordinary vitality. Full, sumptuous to the nose, with great aromatic complexity, with hints of acacia honey, orange flowers, and apricot preserves. Sweet, oily, balanced taste with a lively acidity, notable richness and elegance. Ages exceptionally well, superb with foie gras or green-veined cheeses, or as a wine for meditation.

Visits and tastings: yes, by appointment

BORDEAUX

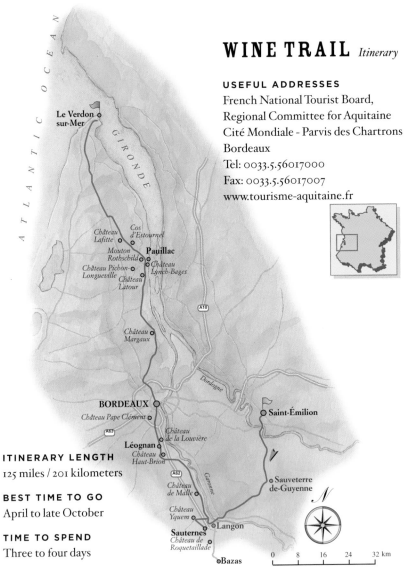

WINE TRAIL *Itinerary*

USEFUL ADDRESSES

French National Tourist Board,
Regional Committee for Aquitaine
Cité Mondiale - Parvis des Chartrons
Bordeaux
Tel: 0033.5.56017000
Fax: 0033.5.56017007
www.tourisme-aquitaine.fr

ITINERARY LENGTH
125 miles / 201 kilometers

BEST TIME TO GO
April to late October

TIME TO SPEND
Three to four days

MARGAUX, MOUTON ROTHSCHILD,
Latour, Lafitte, Haut-Brion, Yquem—these magical
names evoke color, intensity, and substance of myth
and imbue with legend the nearly 300,000 acres
(120,000 hectares) located along the estuary of the
Gironde, in southwestern France. This unique place
has ever-changing microclimates, which vary from
castle to castle. The panorama is gentle and the soil
diverse, ready to welcome the skillful labor of
humankind; together, labor and land have allowed

Bordeaux's vineyards to fully express their quality and
elegance. Here everything is unique, and each bottle
bears the name of a château. The wine cellars are not
referred to as *caves*, as in the rest of the France, but
instead are known as *chais*, and barrels are called *bar-
riques*, not *tonneaux*. Everything is extraordinary.
When, in the twinkling of an eye, the wind blows
away the Atlantic turbulences, a clear, boundless sky
remains, revealing the landscape in all its gentle,
immutable beauty: dunes, pinewoods, rivers, the

OPPOSITE PAGE, FROM TOP:
keys to the wine cellar in
Sauternes; Médoc grapes;
a sculptural detail of the
Château de Malle; selec-
tion of grapes at the
Château Pape-Clément,
near Bordeaux.

ABOVE: a fishing hut along
the Gironde.

87

Geometric configurations of vines and bands of sky in the land of Sauternes, a small production region known for great wines.

ocean, orderly and well-tended vineyards, impressive castles and châteaus. In this section of France, when they say *château*, they mean something specific— namely the residence of the winemaker, the cellar, the rows of vines, and everything that revolves around this world.

The manor houses are not terribly old—only a few have been built atop medieval remains—but this does not rob them of their charm and enchantment. The local Bordeaux stone tinges the buildings with shades of ocher and honey. The lines of these grand architectural works make them seem light, almost as if they were floating in the air, like hot-air balloons.

THE WINE ROUTE
FROM SAINT-ÉMILION
TO SAUTERNES

If the left bank of the Garonne is considered to be the side of the elite lords of wine, the right claims an irreplaceable role in the region's wine history. It is here that **SAINT-ÉMILION** holds court. Its roots are long, dating back to the time of the Roman consul Ausonius in the fourth century, who was known as the poet of *Burdigala* (Bordeaux) and loved tending his vineyards and producing wine. In the Middle Ages the village, enclosed by thirteenth-century walls (with a parapet walk and brackets added in the fourteenth

and fifteenth centuries), passed under the rule of the kings of England, who granted it privileges and gave the local red wines, then reserved for the palates of aristocrats and sovereigns, the title of *vins honorifiques,* or "royal wines." Rule over Aquitaine did not return to France until the fifteenth century, at the end of the Hundred Years' War, but the change of crown did not distract the inhabitants' attention away from their wine.

Today Saint-Émilion proudly displays its history and art and shows surprising architectural harmony. In addition to houses made of warm, luminous stone and red terra-cotta roofs, a monolithic church carved into the rock, and a solitary bell tower surmounted by a sixteenth-century spire, the town also features a castle, a grotto that was inhabited by the Breton hermit Saint Émilion, and the Romanesque-Gothic cloister of the collegiate church. The delight continues in the network of *tertres* and *escalettes,* an interweaving of narrow, paved streets, steep and contorted in a manner typical of an old French village. Flights of steps disappear into the greenery of the vines, the most luminous part of the landscape.

Saint-Émilion is known as the hill of a thousand vineyards, and in reality there are 1,200 covering 13,300 acres (5,400 hectares). This small *appellation* (the gov-

ernment designation guaranteeing the quality of wine from a specific area) comprises thirteen *premier grands crus classés*, eleven of which are grown in the calcareous soil of the steep slope around the town. Powerful, elegant, and complex like the territory that yields it, the wine of Château Figeac, considered to be the most Medoc-like of the Saint-Émilion wines, stands out because it is made from 70 percent Cabernet (a mix of half Cabernet Sauvignon and half Cabernet Franc) and only 30 percent Merlot grapes. Merlot is the most widespread grape variety in the *appellation*, with Cabernet Franc the second most common.

Green, gentle hills dot the Entre-Deux-Mers, the vast region surrounded by the broad and majestic Dordogne and Garonne rivers. This triangle of country-side is filled with valleys blanketed with chestnut and elm trees. Amid the rows of vines are fortified mills from the fourteenth century, prestigious abbeys, châteaus, and *bastides*—small villages built in the Middle Ages along the border between the domains of the king of France and the king of England.

This is the *Rive Gauche*, or the left bank. In the vicinity of Bazas, **ROQUETAILLADE** stands proudly on a green knoll. It has an enclosing wall, two

OPPOSITE: tidy rows of vines in Saint-Émilion.
RIGHT: Cos d'Estournel in the Médoc.
FOLLOWING PAGES: Château Yquem.

WINES   *Bordeaux: A true riddle*

With nearly 250,000 acres (nearly 100,000 hectares) of land and 500 million bottles produced annually, the vineyards of the Gironde constitute the largest in the world. Adding the diverse grapevine technology to the geological and climatic diversity, one can understand why the oenological panorama of this region is so complex. The first attempt to catalogue the region's wines dates back to 1855, when on the occasion of the World's Fair in Paris, Emperor Napoleon III commissioned what was then commonly called a *classement,* or classifying of wines, divided into whites and reds. Aimed principally at production in the Médoc, thanks to few modifications over the years it is still a valid tool for finding one's way around this complex region. The current *classement* for red wines are:

MÉDOC
Five premiers crus (Château Lafitte, Château Latour, Château Margaux, Château Mouton Rothschild, Château Haut-Brion in the region of Graves)

Second crus (14 châteaus)
Third crus (14 châteaus)
Fourth crus (10 châteaus)
Fifth crus (18 châteaus)
Crus bourgeois (230 producers)

SAINT-ÉMILION
Premiers crus classés, classe A (Château Ausone, Château Cheval Blanc)
Premiers crus classés, classe B (Château Beauséjour, Château Belair, Château Canon, Château Figeac, Château La Gaffelière, Château Magdelaine, Château Pavie, Château Trottevielle, Château Clos Fourtet)
Grands crus classés (62 châteaus)

The Pomerol *appellation* merits a separate discussion. It has no classification but includes top names such as Château Petrus and Château Yquem in the Sauternes region, which since 1855 has been the only *premier cru supérieur* in the classification of white wines from the Gironde.

castles that date from the twelfth and the fourteenth centuries, and a legend. It is a unique example of feudal architecture in France. Eugene Viollet-le-Duc, the architect linked to the new look of the cathedral of Notre Dame in Paris, participated in its restoration in the nineteenth century.

The itinerary continues toward **SAUTERNES** and its small region of sweet, voluptuous, and sensual wines of extraordinary complexity. This area of only about 5,000 acres (2,000 hectares) is traversed by the Ciron, a small river that creates an ideal microclimate for producing this delightful wine. In the autumn, the

changes from morning mist to the heat of the day and then the humidity of the night favor the proliferation of *Botrytis cinerea*, the noble rot that works on the grape clusters still on the vine. The growth of this fungus is neither regular nor predictable, and so the late harvest can extend for weeks, with the velvety grapes being collected in various stages (known as *trie*, or pickings). The yield is extremely low.

Château d'Yquem, *premier cru supérieur classé* in 1855, represents the quintessence of Sauternes. The castle is surrounded by perfect vineyards, tended and pampered as in no other part of the world. Among these elegant rows of vines, which bring to mind more a garden than a country vineyard, the few grapes at just the right point of moldiness are collected with almost obsessive care and selection to create the king of sweet wines and a champion of sublime pairings (it is a perfect complement to foie gras and green-veined cheeses); it can age without losing its edge. In every corner of the world, gourmands and collectors know the legends and stories of this wine.

The design of the Château de Malle is splendid, elegant, and original, and its horseshoe shape hides an appealing architectural extravagance, with unusual

OPPOSITE PAGE: a spiral envelops the visitor to the L'Intendant wine shop in Bordeaux.

ABOVE: straight lines and steel in the prestigious cellar of the Château Haut-Brion in the Médoc.

and harmonious decor tempered by the sobriety of the building. The superb residence is surrounded by a resplendent Italianate garden. In addition to tasting the wine from an amber chalice (its Sauternes has been a *grand cru classé* since 1855), preferably in the cellar, it is lovely to walk around inside the castle to appreciate its two façades—classical in front and Renaissance in the back—along with the library, the chapel, and the grand entranceway. Throughout the region, vineyards as far as the eye can see come right up to the dwellings. Rows of vines, like brushstrokes of color, vary in shade from green to red, depending on the season. No two journeys through this land are ever the same.

FROM CASTLE TO CASTLE, TOWARD BORDEAUX

The journey recommences in the direction of Bordeaux, passing through the celebrated lands of Graves, whose wine was the first to be appreciated by the English in the Middle Ages. Known at that time as *Clairet*, it was the only wine considered worthy of interest, guaranteed by the council of Bordeaux.

Along the left bank of the Garonne, woods alternate with vineyards that embrace lavish residences.

OPPOSITE: A view of Saint-Émilion, dominated by the church's impressive bell tower.

RIGHT: A dish at the Château Cordeillan Bages, and a kitchen in Roquetaillade, near Bazas.

TAKE A BREAK

LODGING

Saint-Émilion: **HOSTELLERIE PLAISANCE**
Place du Clocher; Tel: 0033.5.57550755
www.hostellerie_plaisance.com
Twelve of this hotel's rooms look out over the village of Saint-Émilion and its vineyards.

Saint-Émilion: **HÔTEL CHÂTEAU GRAND BARRAIL**
Route de Libourne; Tel: 0033.5.57553700
www.grand-barrail.com
Elegant and refined, this hotel sits amid a 7-acre park with orderly rows of vines of the *appellation* Saint-Émilion. In addition to the good restaurant, there is also a wellness center.

DINING

Bordeaux: **RESTAURANT LE CHAPON FIN**
Rue Montesquieu 5; Tel: 0033.5.56791010
In the early twentieth century, the prestigious clientele of the Café Anglais would gather here, including artists, dignitaries, and royals. With three Michelin stars, Le Chapon Fin now draws gourmands. Amid lavish Belle Epoque decor, one can eat and drink like a king.

Pauillac: **CHÂTEAU CORDEILLAN BAGES**
Route des Châteaux; Tel: 0033.5.56592424
www.cordeillanbages.com
In the heart of the most prestigious vineyards in the world, this historical dwelling stands out for its warm hospitality and for the quality of the ingredient-driven, regional dishes created by chef Thierry Marx.

On sunny days the soil gleams—rich in quartzes, the stones act like small mirrors and reflect the sunlight that ripens the grapes. The sense of peace and wonder generated by this land is magnified as one approaches the neoclassical Château de la Louvière, built according to the design of Parisian architect Victor Louis. Here one can taste a great red wine and visit the estate. The dreamlike backdrop of the castle is reflected proudly in the small lake circled by tall trees.

Leaving behind the town of **LÉOGNAN** and continuing northward in the Pessac-Léognan *appellation*, just outside of Bordeaux, there are two other great regional names: Château Haut-Brion (*premier grand cru classé*), which was acquired in 1801 by Charles-Maurice de Tayllerand, the foreign affairs minister for Napoleon, and Château Pape-Clément (*grand cru classé de Graves*), which owes its name to its most celebrated owner—Clement V, the pope who moved the Holy See to France in 1309.

A few miles away lies **BORDEAUX**, the "holy city" of wine. Arrogant and refined, "bord d'eau" is inextricably linked to two fundamental elements: water, from the Garonne, the Dordogne, the Gironde, and the Atlantic Ocean; and wine, the

LEFT: Château Lynch-Bages in the Médoc.
OPPOSITE: harvesting (with style) in the vineyards of Sauternes.

supreme expression of this region's earth. From the eighteenth century onward, the city has prospered from the wealth accumulated when it was the first port of France, a wealth written in the lofty architecture and on the opulent building façades. Today it has been reborn and is open and joyous as never before. "The beautiful Italian lost in the Gironde," as Michel de Montaigne called it, has had a profound face-lift, and today it is possible to agree with Victor Hugo: "Take Versailles, add in Antwerp, and you will have Bordeaux."

Visitors can enjoy themselves along the riverbanks, walking in the Chartrons district among the antique stores and secondhand shops, and admiring the shop windows on the Place des Grands Hommes. Prized bottles can be bought in the L'Intendant wine shop and the senses stimulated by the cheeses at Jean d'Alos or at the restaurant Le Chapon Fin, with its Belle Epoque decor.

The historic center of Bordeaux is best experienced on foot: the Place de la Bourse, alongside the Garonne, the Saint-Pierre district with its picturesque, narrow medieval streets, and the Esplanade de Quinconces, one of the broadest such walkways in Europe. A few hours will suffice for a casual knowledge of the "port of the Moon," as the Celts called Bordeaux, but to more profoundly understand its spirit, one needs to stay for several days.

THE MÉDOC: PART OENOLOGY, PART LEGEND

The most prestigious red wines in the world are produced northeast of Bordeaux, on the long, narrow strip of land wedged between the Atlantic and the Gironde. Rows of vines of Cabernet Sauvignon, Cabernet Franc, Merlot, and Petit Verdot color the landscape along the estuary. Due to its proximity to the ocean, the light changes constantly and becomes clearer and more crystalline.

Getting to know the Médoc region (in Latin, *in medio aquae*, or "amid the waters") means alternating visits to famous châteaus with brief incursions into the wetlands. Here one can discover ports where flat-bottomed boats are moored and corridors that the water run between the reeds as it makes its way to the Gironde. The oenological and naturalistic journeys are interwoven, wedding wild wetlands with the harmonious lines of grapevines.

Château Margaux, the Versailles of the Médoc, is the birthplace of one of the most elegant reds, a milestone in the history of wine—a *premier grand cru classé* that weds strength and refinement, longevity and complexity. The voyage into legend is only beginning. A bit farther along is Château Latour, with its unmistakable tower that keeps watch over the solemn and austere property. As if in a film, one draws near Château Cos d'Estournel, an exotic locale within the panorama built in 1830 by a wine merchant from the Middle East, and the Château Lynch-Bages (*cru classé* in 1855) and the Château Pichon-Longueville (*grand cru classé* in 1855).

Toward the north lie the placid waters of the estuary. It is not difficult to imagine the great sailing ships of the past, which departed laden with wine for distant ports. In **PAUILLAC**, one can glimpse Château Mouton Rothschild and Château Lafitte, whose *premier grand cru classé* have always been in the elite of French oenology. The bottles of Château Mouton Rothschild are embellished with labels by the great twentieth-century artists Pablo Picasso, Georges Braque, and Joan Miró. Here, there is cellar after cellar, and legend after legend. The grape varieties are the same and there are similar climates in adjacent properties, but the wines are diverse because the characteristics of the terrain change.

After more châteaus, rows of vines, modest villages, and ports, the landscape gradually changes and the land becomes silent, uninhabited, off the beaten track. This is a different Médoc, frozen in the time that preceded the wine colonization of the eighteenth century. There are the sweet, hazy tints of the estuary of the Gironde, occasional platform fishing huts, boats, and labyrinths of reeds. The enchantment ends at **LE VERDON-SUR-MER**, and the visitor is brought back to reality. The continuous passage of large cargo boats is a reminder that this is the port of entry to Bordeaux—the port of access to the Olympus of wines.

Vineyards in Médoc, one of the largest wine-producing regions in France and in the world.

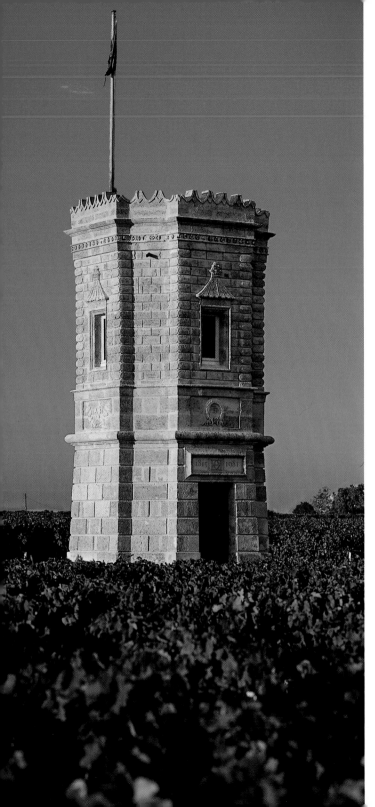

LABELS TO LOOK FOR

CHÂTEAU FIGEAC

Château de Figeac
Saint-Émilion
Tel: 0033.5.57247226
www.chateau-figeac.com

Founded: Twelfth century
Production region: Figeac
Wines and grape varieties: 100% reds; 70%
Cabernet Franc, 35% Cabernet Sauvignon,
30% Merlot

GREAT WINES

Château Figeac 1988
Made from the vinification in large
wooden vats of Cabernet Sauvignon (35
percent), Cabernet Franc (35 percent), and
Merlot (30 percent) grapes (unusual for
Saint-Émilion, where normally there is a
predominance of Merlot), and subsequent
aging for sixteen months in new barrels of
French oak. Intense ruby-red color, tending to garnet. Full, complex, fine, and very
persistent bouquet, spicy, with delicate
hints of animal, mint, and red berry, elderberry, licorice, sandalwood, and leather.
Dry, powerful, but velvety taste, with
sweet tannins and notes of cinnamon,
chocolate, coffee, and licorice. A wine of
great elegance and character, it should be
aged twenty to thirty years, and complements grilled rack of lamb or pheasant.

Visits and tastings: yes, by reservation

CHÂTEAU YQUEM

Sauternes
Tel: 0033.5.57980707
www.chateau-yquem.fr

Founded: 1666
Production region: Sauternes
Wines and grape varieties: 100% whites;
Semillon, Sauvignon Blanc

GREAT WINES

Château d'Yquem 1998
Made from 80 percent Semillon and 20
percent Sauvignon Blanc grapes, gathered
by hand in five or six passes in the vineyard. Vinified and aged in new barrels of
French oak for three-and-a-half years,
then refined in the bottle for one-and-a-
half years before being sold. Brilliant
golden-yellow color. Full, complex, and
persistent bouquet, of great refinement.
Hints of acacia flowers, peach, apricot,
candied fruit, and acacia honey. Sweet,
velvety, voluptuous taste, of notable harmony and elegance. Notes of citrus,
honey, fig, and caramel. Extremely long,
fresh, and clean aftertaste. Should be aged
at length, and complements foie gras,
green-veined cheeses, and roast chicken,
or can be served cold as an aperitif.

Visits and tastings: yes, by reservation

CHÂTEAU DE MALLE

Preignac
Tel: 0033.5.56623686
www.chateau-de-malle.fr

Founded: Early seventeenth century
Production region: Preignac
Wines and grape varieties: 60% whites, 40% reds; Semillon, Sauvignon Blanc, Muscadelle, Cabernet Sauvignon, Merlot

GREAT WINES

Château de Malle 1998
Made from completely botrytized Semillon (78 percent), Sauvignon Blanc (20 percent), and Muscadelle (2 percent) grapes, vinified in wood. Aged in French oak for eighteen months. Brilliant golden-yellow color. Full, complex, and persistent nose with hints of jasmine, exotic fruit, apricot, and tobacco. Sweet, velvety taste, great balance, and notes of green tea. Long, clean finish of quince.

Château de Malle 1991
Made from completely botrytized Semillon (80 percent), Sauvignon Blanc (18 percent), and Muscadelle (2 percent) grapes vinified in wood. Aged in barrels of French oak for eighteen months. Golden-yellow color with amber reflections. Full, complex, and refined nose, with hints of jasmine, exotic fruit, apricot, tobacco, minerals, and smoke. Sweet, velvety taste, with great balance, and notes of caramel and green tea. Long, clean finish.

Visits and tastings: yes

CHÂTEAU HAUT-BRION

Pessac
Tel: 0033.5.56002930
www.haut-brion.com

Founded: 1525
Production region: Pessac
Wines and grape varieties: 5% whites, 95% reds; Sauvignon Blanc, Semillon, Cabernet Franc, Cabernet Sauvignon, Merlot

GREAT WINES

Château Haut-Brion 1998 (white)
Made from Semillon (60 percent) and Sauvignon Blanc (40 percent) grapes, vinified and aged in new barrels of French oak. Brilliant straw-yellow color, with golden reflections. Full, complex, and very persistent bouquet. Hints of pineapple, ripe banana, and vanilla to the nose. Dry and powerful taste, of great body and harmony, with toasted almond, honey, and caramel. Of superb character, it should be drunk young, as a complement to white fish in sauce, or aged for ten to fifteen years and served with foie gras.

Château Haut-Brion 2001 (red)
Tasted before being bottled. Made from Merlot (52 percent), Cabernet Sauvignon (36 percent), and Cabernet Franc (12 percent) grapes, vinified in special steel fermentation vats, where malolactic fermentation occurs without decanting. Aged eighteen months in small French oak barrels. Intense ruby-red color with purplish-blue reflections and a full, fruity bouquet with hints of strawberry, raspberry, spice, tobacco, and sandalwood. Dry, powerful, complex, and elegant with a long finish. Age at least fifteen to twenty years, and pour with poultry and roasts.

Visits and tastings: yes, by appointment

CHÂTEAU LA LOUVIÈRE

Grezillac
Tel: 0033.5.57255858
www.andrelurton.com

Founded: Mid-fourteenth century
Production region: Léognan
Wines and grape varieties: 35% whites, 65% reds; Sauvignon Blanc, Semillon, Cabernet Sauvignon, Merlot

GREAT WINES

Château La Louvière 1998 (red)
Made from Cabernet Sauvignon and Merlot grapes, with some Cabernet Franc and Petit Verdot. Fermented in steel and aged for fifteen months in French oak barrels. Garnet-red color with purplish-blue reflections. Full and persistent nose, with hints of animal, red fruit, and wood. Good structure, with dry, powerful flavors of plum, chocolate, licorice, and tannins. Age at least ten to fifteen years, and pair with large roasts.

Château La Louvière 1996 (white)
Made from Sauvignon Blanc (85 percent) and Semillon (15 percent) grapes, fermented and aged for one year in French oak barrels. Intense straw-yellow color. Full, aromatic, and floral, with exotic fruit and elderberry. Dry, fresh taste, good structure and elegant acidity. Age for up to ten years, complements fish dishes in sauce and poultry.

Visits and tastings: yes, by appointment

CHÂTEAU PAPE-CLÉMENT

Avenue du Dr. Nancel Penard 216
Pessac
Tel: 0033.5.57263838
www.pape-clement.com

Founded: Mid-fourteenth century, the first bottle labeled in 1893
Production region: Pessac
Wines and grape varieties: 8% whites, 92% reds; Sauvignon Blanc, Semillon, Muscadelle, Cabernet Sauvignon, Merlot, Cabernet Franc, Petit Verdot

GREAT WINES

Château Pape-Clément 1998
Made from hand-selected Cabernet Sauvignon and Merlot grapes (50 percent each). Vinified in steel and aged for twenty months in French oak barrels. Garnet-red color with purplish-blue reflections. Full, powerful, straightforward, and persistent bouquet, fruity and spicy with hints of animal. Dry, rich, and elegant taste, with blackberry, rare wood, and chocolate, and a clean finish. Aged at length, the wine complements grilled meat.

Château Pape-Clément 2001 Blanc
Made from hand-harvested Semillon (53 percent), Sauvignon Blanc (42 percent), and Muscadelle (5 percent) grapes. Fermented and aged for ten months in new French oak barrels. Brilliant straw-yellow color. Full and elegant bouquet, with hints of star anise and bread. Dry, balanced, full taste of great refinement. Long finish with hints of elderberry. Should be drunk after two to five years as an aperitif, or with shellfish.

Visits and tastings: yes, by appointment

CHÂTEAU MARGAUX

Châteaux Margaux BP31
Margaux
Tel: 0033.5.57888383
www.chateau-margaux.com

Founded: Mid-eighteenth century
Production region: Margaux
Wines and grape varieties: 8% whites, 92% reds; Cabernet Sauvignon, Cabernet Franc, Merlot, Sauvignon Blanc

GREAT WINES

Château Margaux 1989
Made from Cabernet Sauvignon (78 percent), Merlot (15 percent), and Petit Verdot (7 percent) grapes vinified in large wood barrels for twenty-four months. Intense ruby-red color, tending to garnet. Full, complex, and persistent bouquet with delicate hints of animal and toast, red berry preserves, brandied cherries, plums, coffee, and rare wood. Dry, powerful, velvety feel, with notes of chocolate, coffee, leather, and licorice, and subtle wild fruit. Extremely long and refined finish. One of the great wines of France, it can be aged at length, and complements truffles.

Pavillon Blanc 2002
Pure Sauvignon Blanc, in production since 1920. Entirely vinified in barrels of French oak. Delicate straw-yellow color. Full, complex, voluptuous bouquet, with floral notes and hints of apricot and exotic fruit. Full, oily, but elegant taste. Clean, persistent finish, with notes of bread crust. Should be drunk immediately, or aged five to six years and drunk as an aperitif.

Visits and tastings: yes, by appointment

CHÂTEAU PICHON-LONGUEVILLE

Route des Château
Pauillac
Tel: 0033.5.56731717
www.chateaupichonlongueville.com

Founded: mid-eighteenth century
Production region: Pauillac
Wines and grape varieties: 100% reds; Cabernet Sauvignon, Cabernet Franc, Merlot

GREAT WINES

Pichon-Longueville Baron 2000
70 percent Cabernet Sauvignon, 25 percent Merlot, and 5 percent Cabernet Franc grapes from old vines. Fermented in steel, aged separately in French oak barrels for fifteen months. Intense ruby-red color, with purplish-blue reflections. Complex bouquet; hints of animal, ripe fruit, leather, and wood. Dry and spicy, with great complexity and balance. Long finish, with licorice and herbs. Should be aged at length, and complements game.

Les Tourelles de Longueville 1995
55 percent Cabernet Sauvignon, 35 percent Merlot, and 10 percent Cabernet Franc grapes, fermented in steel and aged separately for ten months in French oak barrels. Garnet-red color. Fine, complex bouquet of red berries, aged wood, and brandied cherries. Dry, powerful, with a young acidity. Long, clean finish with herbs and licorice. Age from ten to twenty years, pair with poultry and fish.

Visits and tastings: yes

CHÂTEAU LYNCH-BAGES

Route des Château
Pauillac
Tel: 0033.5.56592642
www.lynchbages.com

Founded: 1933
Production region: Pauillac
Wines and grape varieties: 95% reds, 5% whites; Cabernet Sauvignon, Cabernet Franc, Merlot, Petit Verdot, Sauvignon Blanc, Semillon, Muscadelle

GREAT WINES

Blanc de Lynch-Bages 2001
Made from 40 percent Sauvignon Blanc, 40 percent Semillon, and 20 percent Muscadelle. Fermented in steel and aged for ten months in barrels of French oak. Brilliant straw-yellow color. Full, fruity bouquet with hints of white peach and vanilla. Dry, balanced, and elegant taste. Long and clean aftertaste. Should be aged five years, and complements shellfish and salted fish.

Château Lynch-Bages 2000
Made from 80 percent Cabernet Sauvignon, 10 percent Merlot, 8 percent Cabernet Franc, and 20 percent Petit Verdot grapes, from old vines. Fermented in steel and aged for twelve months in barrels of French oak. Complex, persistent, and elegant to the nose, with hints of animal, wild fruit, blackberry preserves, spices, and leather. Dry, powerful taste of great structure and body, and notes of coffee, chocolate, and licorice. A wine of great personality, it should be aged at least twenty years, and complements large roasts and game.

Visits and tastings: yes

CHÂTEAU MOUTON ROTHSCHILD

Pauillac
Tel: 0033.5.56732129
www.moutonrothschild.com

Founded: 1933
Production region: Pauillac
Wines and grape varieties: 100% reds; Cabernet Sauvignon, Cabernet Franc, Merlot, Petit Verdot

GREAT WINES

Mouton Rothschild 1982
Made from four grape varieties and vinified entirely in wood, aged for two years in barrels of French oak. Garnet-red color with brick reflections. Fine, full, complex, and persistent bouquet, with rather restrained hints of animal, cassis, blackberry, blueberry, and rare wood. Dry, full, harmonious taste, with notes of chocolate and licorice. Should be aged at length, and complements game and roasts.

BURGUNDY

WINE TRAIL *Itinerary*

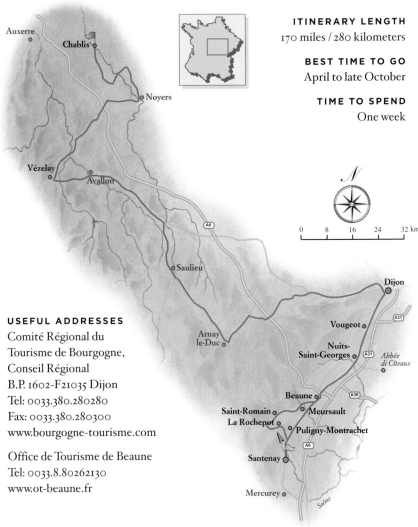

ITINERARY LENGTH
170 miles / 280 kilometers

BEST TIME TO GO
April to late October

TIME TO SPEND
One week

USEFUL ADDRESSES
Comité Régional du
Tourisme de Bourgogne,
Conseil Régional
B.P. 1602-F21035 Dijon
Tel: 0033.380.280280
Fax: 0033.380.280300
www.bourgogne-tourisme.com

Office de Tourisme de Beaune
Tel: 0033.8.80262130
www.ot-beaune.fr

BURGUNDY, THE RURAL heart of France: billowing expanses of precious vineyards and artistic masterpieces; Dijon and Beaune; monasteries and Romanesque churches, solitary castles, canals, and villages untouched by time. For centuries the economy of this inimitable and slender region, which rises northward from the gates of Lyon to Auxerre, has been based on those who tend the countryside and graze their prize herds, working with love and pride. The people's faces tell the story, with lines etched by the wind and terse smiles. Animals are traded when the planting begins at village fairs, and the *fermiers* sell their delicious cheeses in the markets. History confirms it: According to many, traces of local viticulture precede the Roman conquest. Untouched by change, without industrial complexes or useless cement slabs, this land of great wines and tasty delicacies resembles an enormous musical score, with its straight, precise, organized rows. With rare exceptions, two varieties of grapes are grown here with magisterial results: pure Chardonnay and Pinot Noir. The intensity, the refine-

OPPOSITE PAGE, FROM TOP: the Tonnellerie François Fréres, a coop, in Saint-Romain; a road sign on the "Route des Grands Crus"; a corner of the Caves de la Reine Pèdauque in Beaune; the pressing of the grapes in a bas-relief in Dijon.

RIGHT: a view of Auxerre, with the cathedral of St. Étienne.

ment, the perfume, and the complexity of the grand cru is unequalled. "Drink it always and you will never die," wrote François Rabelais, and Erasmus of Rotterdam responded: "Oh happy Burgundy, worthy of being called mother of humanity, since from its breast there gushes forth such exquisite milk."

THE WINE ROUTE

ROW BY ROW, WINE BY WINE

Burgundy's initial visual impact is of a complex mosaic, where the tiles are the endless vineyards, divided by low stone walls and strips of clay earth. These "tiles" encircle the farms, rocks, and castles, and rise up to cover the slopes along the right bank of the Sâone. Then they disappear for brief stretches, only to resume again, as far as the horizon. In the summer Burgundy is cheerful and green, but in winter, when the vines are bare, it reveals its most intimate secrets. This is when one sees the bare earth, the microcomposition of the terrain, the soil that varies from one plot of land to the next. In just a few feet one can see gritty, white limestone and earth veined with pink and clay. Everything is minimal but significant, including the variations—a distance of only a few yards between two plots, and the wine that results is different.

Interior of the Moutarderie Fallot, a mustard mill, in Dijon.

PROTAGONISTS
Domaine of Romanée-Conti

This small vineyard of five acres (two hectares) between Dijon and Beaune on the Côtes de Nuits forms a narrow strip of vines less than 31 miles (50 kilometers) long. It produces perfect grapes, collected during a half-day of harvest, yielding 6,000 bottles a year. This is the home of Romanée-Conti, a fabulous ruby-red Burgundy, the most famous and elegant in the world. The name alone evokes grandeur and uniqueness, and it is difficult, nearly impossible, to find these bottles. Louis François de Bourbon, prince of Conti, created the legend. In 1760 he purchased the Romanée vineyard for a price ten times greater than that of the best vineyards in France at the time. He then withdrew the wine from the market, using it only for his own banquets. Taken over as a national property during the Revolution, the prized parcel of land had various owners before passing into the hands of the De Villaine and Leroy families. The extraordinary quality of the wines from this prestigious house lies in its incredible aromatic complexity rather than in its potency. It is rich, opulent, and exceptionally refined. It can be aged for up to 30 to 40 years. The two most famous bottles of the *domaine* are the Romanée-Conti and the Tâche, and they are joined by four *Grands Cru* reds (Richebourg, Romanée-St-Vivant, Grand-Echézeaux, and Echézaux) and one *Grand Cru* white (Montrachet). Maniacal attention to production on a property of this stature is almost to be expected, as is the careful care given to the preservation of the vineyard's irreplaceable natural conditions. This is one of the reasons why organic cultivation was introduced many years ago.

OPPOSITE PAGE: Gothic turns in the staircase of one of the many maisons particulières that can be visited in Dijon.

RIGHT: the Hôtel-Dieu in Beaune, a jewel of Flemish architecture, established in 1443 by Nicolas Rolin, chancellor to the Duke of Burgundy.

ABOVE: work in the vine-yard outside Vougeot.

OPPOSITE: Work in the cellar (Pierre Naigeon) in the vicinity of Beaune. Ancient wine cellars in the Abbey of the Annunziata, in the Annunziata hamlet.

Stone walls divide the tracts of Chardonnay and Pinot Noir into small and circumscribed properties, carefully tended by their winegrowers. Every individual producer is personally involved with the making of the wine, every small landowner is a "creative" winemaker. There is no standardization of methods, but much inventiveness. The Burgundian wine businesses lack hierarchical structure, and there is no one oenological figure who dominates, decides, and creates the wine. On visits to the cellars (only some are open to the public), it is possible to speak with those who truly make the wine, those who follow it from the ground to the bottle. In this region where waste is frowned upon, it is difficult to find a wine producer willing to uncork a bottle for tasting, but the most "open" among them will pour out wine directly from the barrels—without wasting any.

The great noble and ecclesiastic estates were expropriated and resold during the French Revolution, which is why vineyards in Burgundy are so divided up among various landowners. Napoleonic law, whereby equal portions were assigned to all sons upon the death of a landowner, further increased the fragmentation of the vineyards.

Unlike Bordeaux, where classification of the vintage is assigned to a *domaine*, in Burgundy it is tied to the vineyard (a property unit), which rarely belongs to a single landowner. The Clôs de Vougeot, a vineyard covering 124 acres, is subdivided among some seventy different landowners, some of whom possess only a few rows of vines from which they produce only a few bottles; but they can lay claim to the prestigious title grand cru.

FROM THE CÔTE CHALONNAISE TO THE CÔTE DE BEAUNE

The Côte Chalonnaise is the natural, if less valued, extension of the Côte de Beaune. At the Maison Antonin Rodet in Mercurey, visitors can taste his fantastic Pinot Noir and Chardonnay, which come from various properties. The official "Route des Grands Crus," arriving from the south, begins in **SANTENAY** and traverses the entire Côte d'Or as far as Dijon. The road rises immediately amid the rows of vines cutting through the ridge of the Burgundian hills, dotted with small vineyards. Approximately 4,900 *domaines* compete for just under 100,000 acres, which account for only 3 percent of French wines, and the prices are sky-high.

One should stop to admire the windmill that dominates the countryside just outside of Santenay, and a few miles farther lies the first of Burgundy's mythic names: **PULIGNY-MONTRACHET**, land of sublime whites. Their power comes from the exposure of the vineyards, which receive better sun than those in any other part of the region. Following along a side valley, the road climbs up to the village of **LA ROCHEPOT**, where the austere silhouette of a castle rises up, exuberant and harmonious. Built in the twelfth century, it is considered one of the most beautiful in Burgundy and boasts massive, elegant towers. Looking out from the parapet walk, one can see the entire landscape changing color along with the seasons. The castle

rooms, dining room, and the twelfth-century chapel are also magnificent.

At the top of the hills the woods, faithful sentinels, provide shelter from the winds and maintain the humidity; the best-known vineyards are located halfway up the hillside, and in the plain rows of less-prized grapes alternate with tilled fields. Follow the contour of the slopes as far as **SAINT-ROMAIN**, where for three generations the Tonnellerie François Frères has produced chestnut barrels for aging high-quality wines. Semidarkness, muffled noises, wood, and the magic of fire, the eternal play of creating and destroying—this is how the François Frères barrels come into being, in Burgundy as in Hungary, Australia, and the United States, where other barrel-making facilities have been opened.

The road turns toward the plain and leads to **MEURSAULT**, a cradle of superb wine-producing enterprises and mythic names: Maison Jean-François Coche-Dury, Domaine des Comtes Lafon, and Château de Meursault.

CAPITALS OF BURGUNDY

Beyond the vineyards and the villages of Volnay and Pommard, with their stone houses with slate roofs, lies **BEAUNE**, a wine-producing capital with a wealth of art and charm. The Hôtel-Dieu hospital, a fifteenth-century jewel with its pinnacles and colorfully painted tiles, is the stone symbol of the power of the Burgundian dukes, who in their time also wielded

TAKE A BREAK

LODGING

Beaune: **HÔTEL LE CEP**
Rue Maufoux 27
Tel: 0033.3.80223548
This former residence has been transformed into a charming and elegant hotel.

Nitry: **HÔTEL DE LA BEURSAUDIÈRE**
Chemin de la Ronde
Tel: 0033.3.86336970
www.beursaudiere.com
An actual farm has been converted into a quaint hotel, with great attention to detail. Regional dishes are served.

DINING

Nuits-Saint-Georges: **LE CHEF COQ**
Vallée de la Serrée 13
Tel: 0033.3.80611206
www.lagentilhommiere.fr
Traditional dishes revisited, served in an elegant atmosphere, and an excellent wine list.

The suites have decorative themes such as Zen, Oriental, Pop Art, and colonial.

Chorey Les Beaune: **LE BAREUZAI**
Route Nationale 74
Tel: 0033.3.80249322
An occasion to experience an original wine-maker's table, where excellent wines pair with grilled meat that guests cook themselves.

BELOW: The Moutarderie Fallot in Dijon; the Hotel le Cep in Beaune.

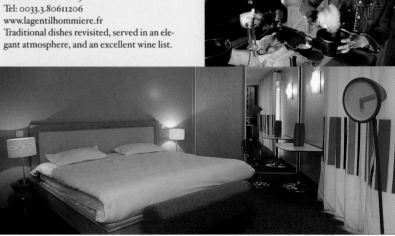

authority in Flanders and the Low Countries. With an act of munificent piety, Nicolas Rolin and his wife Guigone de Salins founded the hospital in 1443 to help the sick and indigent. This was during the Middle Ages, and the poor were treated with respect, as representatives of Christ's suffering. The sumptuous Salle des Pauvres is surprising: beds line the walls, separated by red curtains, and all face toward the flamboyant Gothic chapel. The building's shining gem is Rogier van der Weyden's *Last Judgment*, painted during the same period as the hospital's construction.

The hospital functioned uninterruptedly until 1971, when the health services where moved to more modern facilities. Thanks to generous bequests and donations over the centuries, the Hôtel-Dieu acquired a significant *domaine viticole* of more than 150 acres, which is essential to the most thrilling auction in the world. On the third Sunday in November, the connoisseur elite gather here. The *vente a la bougie* proceeds according to ancient ritual. Two candles are lit, and that year's production is auctioned off until the flames are spent. Then it begins again—more candles, more lots. The proceeds go to the hospital. Now it is also possible to participate in the auction via the Internet.

Leave time to glance at the Museé du Vin de Bourgogne (Museum of Burgundy Wine), leaf through some books on wine at the Athenaeum of vineyards and wine (over 16,000 square feet dedicated to the prized beverage, with publications in all languages, objects, crystal, and a solid selection of wines for sale),

enjoy a tasting at the Caves de la Reine Pédauque, and take a quick stop at the centuries-old Moutarderie Fallot mustard mill to sample the various tastes.

NUITS-SAINT-GEORGES marks the beginning of the Côte de Nuits, home of the most famous wines *domaines* such as Faiveley and Romanée-Conti, the latter being one of the world's most legendary names in oenology, thanks to the production of very few bottles of unequaled quality (and cost).

Wine sanctuaries in Burgundy: above, the Athenaeum de la Vigne bookstore and wine shop in Beaune and, below, the cellar of Domaine des Comtes Lafon in Meursault.

Wine sanctuaries in
Burgundy: the barrel room
at the Domaine Faiveley.

From **VOSNE-ROMANÉE**—the site of the
Domaine Confuron-Cotetidot, another brilliant
example of wines that reflect the region—the itinerary proceeds to the Abbey of **CÎTEAUX**, enveloped
in the pungent odor of the strongest and most boldly
perfumed cheese in Burgundy, Epoisse. *Ora et labora*,
pray and work: The monks follow the rule of Saint
Benedict and live raising livestock and producing
cheese. **VOUGEOT** is home to the Château Clos de
Vougeot, ancient property of the monks of Citeaux
(twelfth to sixteenth century), where they studied and
improved the cultivation of vines. The Cistercian
vaults of the monument house the Confrérie des
Chevaliers du Tastevin, established in the 1930s to
relaunch and improve Burgundian wines. It was a
time of economic crisis: "Given that no one wants our
wines," Camille Rodier and Georges Faiveley said,

"let's invite friends to drink with us." Thus was born
one of the most flourishing and elegant marketing
operations in the world of wine. On November 16,
1934, the confraternity gathered together friends in a
ritual and an atmosphere that would later be repeated
over time, and the worship of Burgundian wines was
reborn, with results that are still evident today.

CHAMBOLLE-MUSIGNY, **GEVREY-
CHAMBERTIN**, **MARSANNAY-LA-CÔTE**: A string
of stone and slate jewels are framed by the world's most
prized vineyards. Then there is **DIJON**, historic capital of Burgundy and splendid city of the fifteenth-
century dukes, who experienced new glories in the
seventeenth and eighteenth centuries under the
Condè princes. It is a city of sumptuous palaces, superb
maisons particuliéres, rich museums, Renaissance monuments, churches, monasteries, and gardens.

TOWARD CHABLIS

Historically, Burgundy was also a crossroads for pilgrims on their way to San Juan de Compostela.
VÉZELAY, the *colline éternelle*, an evocative medieval village north of Morvan, is one of the region's cardinal points. It is a magical and mystical place, the point from which Richard the Lionheart departed in 1190 for the third Crusade. Over time it was forgotten, but in 1840, thanks to architect Viollet-le-Duc, it was rediscovered and restored. Today the pink and ocher mass of the Romanesque basilica of Sainte Madeleine dominates the hill. The monastery's architectural purity has inspired such artists as Marcel Proust, Pablo Picasso, and Le Corbusier. It sits surrounded by the seductive green of the regional natural parkland of Morvan. The enchanted atmosphere continues as far as **NOYERS**, one of the loveliest villages in France—a tiny hamlet with half-timbered houses, piazzas, and paved streets, a castle in ruins, and ancient twelfth-century walls and towers. The waters of the Serein linger at the altitude of the village, captivated by the charm of the setting. **CHABLIS** emerges next from amid the vineyards. A few light stone houses built around the central square form a backdrop for the rows of vines of the world's most famous Chardonnay grapes. Opposite the town, on the right bank of the Serein, are the most highly regarded vineyards, featuring the large white Grand Crus of Chablis, which come exclusively from seven delimited plots. Only the Maison Albert Pic & Fils, belonging to Baron Patrick de Ladoucette, boasts the complete production of the seven grand crus. Extremely aromatic, this wine, with its excellent duration and intense aftertaste, concludes the Burgundian tour with a golden touch.

DOMAINE ROMANÉE-CONTI

Rue Derière de Four, Vosne-Romanée,
Tel: 0033.3.80624880

Founded: 1241
Production region: Vosne-Romanée,
Flagey-Echèzeaux, Montrachet
Wines and grape varieties: 96% reds,
4% whites; Pinot Noir, Chardonnay

GREAT WINES

Romanée-Conti 1996
This is the masterpiece of Burgundy,
which shines in its delicacy, complexity,
and balance. Deep ruby-red color, with
hints of violet as well as raspberry, plum,
cinnamon, licorice, and tobacco. Velvety,
full taste, exceptionally complex and elegant. Should be aged a minimum of ten
years (but also thirty or forty) and should
be drunk by itself.

La Tache Grand Cru 1996
Deep ruby-red color, almost opaque.
Extremely complex and lingering to the
nose, with hints that range from raspberry to plum, from licorice to wild
plants. It is velvety, elegant, and highly
refined to the taste. It should be aged at
length even thirty to forty years, and
should be drunk by itself.

Visits and tastings: no

DOMAINE FAIVELEY

Nuit-Saint-Georges,
Tel: 0033.3.80610455

Founded: 1825
Production region: All of Burgundy
Wines and grape varieties: 25% whites,
75% reds; Pinot Noir, Chardonnay

GREAT WINES

Clos de Vougeot Grand Cru 1996
Fruit of a manual harvest and a narrow
selection of grapes, it has a deep ruby
color with purplish-blue reflections that
tend toward garnet with aging. Full, complex, and rather persistent bouquet with
hints of woods and plum preserves.
Powerful taste, with great structure, concentration, and elegance. Long aftertaste
of ripe fruit with menthol and licorice
notes. Capable of considerable aging, it
should be tasted after the first fifteen
years, and goes well with venison in wild
berry sauce.

DOMAINE CONFURON-COTETIDOT

Rue de la Fontaine 10, Vosne-Romanée
Tel: 0033.3.80610339

Founded: 1964
Production region: Vosne-Romanée, Nuits-
Saint-Georges, Gevrey-Chambertin,
Chambolle-Musigny
Wines and grape varieties: 99% reds,1%
whites; Pinot Noir and Chardonnay

GREAT WINES

1er Cru Vosne Romanée
Les Suchots 1999
Harvested by hand from a strict selection
of grapes. Deep ruby-red color with evident purplish-blue reflections.
Concentrated and complex bouquet, with
clear hints of wild fruit and plum. Dry,
potent taste, structured and balanced.
Complements braised meat, game, and
mushrooms. Needs a decade in order to
fully develop and reveal the fineness of its
texture.

Clos de Vougeot Grand Cru 1996
Harvested by hand from a strict selection
of grapes. Deep ruby-red color, with purplish-blue reflections tending to garnet
with aging. Full, complex, and rather persistent bouquet, with hints of woods and
plum preserves. Powerful taste with great
structure, concentration, and elegance.
Long finish with ripe fruit, mint, and
notes of licorice. Can be aged at length
and should be tasted after the first fifteen
years. Complements venison in wild fruit
sauce.

Visits and tastings: yes, by appointment

MAISON JEAN-FRANÇOIS COCHE-DURY

Rue Charles Giraud 9, Mersault,
Tel: 0033.3.80212412

Founded: 1946
Production region: Meursault, Puligny
Wines and grape varieties: 60% whites,
40% reds; Pinot Noir, Chardonnay

GREAT WINES

Meursault-Perrières 1996
Fruit of a limitied selection of grapes from
vines averaging forty-five years of age
within the Perrières vineyard, on the
boundary between Meursault and Puligny.
An intense straw-yellow color with delicate gilded reflections. Full, complex, and
surprisingly persistent bouquet, with
notes of orange, honey, citrus, tropical
fruit, and rare wood. Powerful, voluptuous taste with great structure and concentration, with an extremely long
aftertaste. Can be aged for some ten years,
and goes well with shellfish.

Visits and tastings: yes, by appointment

MAISON RÉGNARD

Pouilly sur Loire,
Tel: 0033.3.86421045

Founded: 1860
Production region: All of Burgundy
Wines and grape varieties: 40% whites,
60% reds; Pinot Noir, Chardonnay

GREAT WINES

Chevalier Montrachet Grand Cru 2000
This is a wine with an extraordinary concentration of aromas and perfumes,
heightened by its controlled period of
time in the cask. Straw-yellow color with
slightly greenish reflections. Full, complex, and very persistent bouquet, with
mineral hints of flint, grapefruit, citrus,
vanilla, and sandalwood. Powerful to the
taste, rich, opulent, with great structure
and complexity, and an extremely prolonged aftertaste of star anise. Should be
aged at least ten years, and goes well with
medium-aged cheeses.

Visits and tastings: no

DOMAINE DES COMTES LAFON

Clos de la Barre, Meursault,
Tel: 0033.3.80212217
www.comtes-lafon.fr

Founded: 1875
Production region: Meursault, Volnay,
Monthélie
Wines and grape varieties: 65% whites,
35% reds; Pinot Noir, Chardonnay

GREAT WINES

Montrachet Grand Cru 2000
Made from grapes selected and harvested
by hand, fermented in vats of new chestnut and aged two years in barrels of
French oak. Brilliant straw-yellow color
with golden reflections, it has an intense
and very persistent perfume, with hints
of tropical fruit, ripe banana, citrus, acacia honey, and vanilla. Full and opulent
taste of enormous concentration and
complexity. Incredibly long and clean
aftertaste. Excellent for aging, and goes
well with truffles or lobster. A wine for
grand occasions.

Visits and tastings: yes, by appointment

ALBERT PIC & FILS

Boulevard Tacussel 28, Chablis,
Tel: 0033.3.86421045

Founded: 1755
Production region: Chablis
Wines and grape varieties: 100% white;
Chardonnay

GREAT WINES

1er Pic 1990
Made from the selection of grapes from
various grand crus and from vines at least
thirty years old. Intense straw-yellow
color, with antique gold reflections.
Elegant, full, complex, and lingering bouquet, with hints of grapefruit, vanilla,
caramel, and ripe banana. Dry, sumptuous
taste, agreeable and mineral, almost thick,
of great refinement. Long, clean aftertaste. Should be aged at least fifteen years
and drunk by itself.

Chablis Grand Régnard 2001
Brilliant straw-yellow color with slightly
greenish reflections, veering toward gold.
Dry to the nose, clean, very elegant, with
hints of ripe fruit, tropical fruit, and acacia honey. Dry, decisive taste, fresh and
elegant, with good concentration. Should
be aged at least five to six years, and goes
well with fish in sauce or with white meat.

Visits and tastings: yes, by appointment

CAVES JEAN & SÉBASTIAN DAUVISSAT

Rue de Chichée 3, Chablis,
Tel: 0033.3.86421462

Founded: 1899
Production region: Chablis
Wine and grape varieties: 100% white;
Chardonnay

GREAT WINES

Chablis Grand Cru Les Preuses
Made from grapes from forty-five- to
fifty-year-old vines, half is fermented in
steel, the rest in wood. Straw-yellow color
with greenish reflections, tending toward
gold with aging. Full and complex bouquet with notes of vanilla and vestiges of
cedar, lychee, and grapefruit. Elegant and
lingering in the mouth, great balance and
refinement, with a lovely presence of
exotic fruit while the wood remains in the
background, but unmistakable. Should be
aged for about ten years, and goes well
with shellfish.

Chablis 1er Cru Vaillons Vielle Vignes 2000
Made from grapes coming from eighty-
year-old vines, for a production of only
2,500 bottles. Intense straw-yellow color,
it has a complex and persistent bouquet
with notes of vanilla; rich in the mouth,
refined, and very balanced. Should be
aged at least five years, and goes well with
grilled salmon or white meat.

Visits and tastings: yes

CHAMPAGNE

ITINERARY LENGTH
190 miles / 310 kilometers

BEST TIME TO GO
April to late October

TIME TO SPEND
One week

USEFUL ADDRESSES
Centro Informazione
Champagne
Via Savona 19a
Milano
Tel: 02.89423642
Toll-free: 800.846940
www.champagne.fr

Comité Interprofessionnel
du Vin de Champagne
Rue Henri-Martin 5
Epernay
Tel: 0033.3.26511930
www.champagne.fr

WINE TRAIL *Itinerary*

GENTLE HORIZONS, OPEN SPACES, lovely streets, vineyards as far as the eye can see, and an endless supply of bubbly: This is the Champagne region, an hour and a half northeast by car from Paris, in the northernmost wine region in France. It is the land of the mythic "devil's wine," as Champagne was known in the time of Louis XIV, the Sun King. Almost 86,500 acres (some 35,000 hectares) produce three hundred million bottles every year, sold throughout the world. The secret of this wine's success lies in the region's geography. The climate is continental, capricious, and unstable, marked by the Atlantic winds that arrive from Normandy, and so the true fortune lies in the chalky terrain where the vines are rooted. A singular geological cocktail was created 70 million years ago (in prehistoric times the region was covered by the sea), enabling the land to preserve a constant level of humidity, mitigating the effects of dryness and storage and gradually restoring the heat of the sun during the night.

OPPOSITE PAGE, FROM TOP: one of the signs along the Champagne trail; a view of the cellars of Maison Veuve Clicquot Ponsardin in Reims; a view of Bar-sur-Aube; Champagne corks at Maison Krug in Reims.
RIGHT: on the road in Champagne: in the background, the castle of Montmort. The region, located to the southwest of the Ardennes and the Argonnes forest, opens up toward the Île de France and corresponds more or less to the administrative districts of Aube and Marne.

ABOVE: landscape of vineyards in the Aube in the early morning light.

OPPOSITE: expanses of vines around Épernay on the left bank of the Marne, in the heart of the Champagne wine region.

Between the seventeenth and eighteenth century, Dom Pérignon, cellar master (and steward) of the Benedictine abbey of Hautevillers, adopted the cuvée method—blending wines from grape varieties from different farms on the same estate, or from different vineyards in the same wine-producing region and carefully choosing the best grapes to be pressed together. This bubbly sparkling wine, or rather *pétillant*, was received with astounding and unprecedented enthusiasm.

Kings and emperors, aristocrats and the bourgeoisie—in short, anyone who could obtain the wine—agreed that Champagne was a festive beverage, perfect for celebrating grand occasions. Increasing

care and attention was given to the vineyards, and improvements were made to the bottles through the use of thick, dark glass resistant to the internal pressure from the second fermentation. Another decisive advance was the use of cork stoppers instead of the original wooden peg wrapped in oil-soaked hemp. In the nineteenth century, production techniques were further refined to current levels. Champagne is now synonymous with the art of good living.

THE WINE ROUTE
EXPLORING THE AUBE

Leaving the Aube, the southeastern part of the region and its least-known area, the road leads to Marne, home to the best-known labels in the world. The route is varied and engaging, little traveled and enticing. There are intoxicating panoramas of this generous land, dotted with picturesque wine-producing towns scattered over the countryside. Rows of vines follow, one after another, in an area 75 miles (120 kilometers) long, where the hilltops never exceed an altitude of about 1,000 feet (300 meters). Fine Champagne is produced in the Aube, but the names

FLAVORS   *A luxury weekend at Château Les Crayères*

Gerard Boyer, one of the most esteemed chefs in the world, welcomes his guests to a splendid villa, surrounded by a 17-acre (7-hectare) park filled with immense, centuries-old trees and once the residence of Madame Pommery. "The secret to my success," Boyer explains, "lies in a cuisine based on simple ingredients harmonized with unusual flavors." The chateau's Art Nouveau entrance leads to the sumptuous and richly decorated rooms, where an unmistakable French taste for limitless luxury prevails. Service is impeccable, but it is the exclusive atmosphere that leaves a lasting impression. The hushed murmur of diners is interrupted by discreet questions from the waiters, whose black jackets swirl around every table. The choice of wines is so extensive that the list is presented in books of embarrassing dimensions. After dinner guests retire to the extremely elegant rooms, nineteen in all. The windows look out on the cathedral of Reims. Elyane Boyer is in charge, and along with interior designer Pierre-Yves Rochon, she has skillfully maintained the château's aristocratic air.

CHÂTEAU LES CRAYÈRES
64, Boulevard Henry Vasnier
Reims
Tel: 0033.3.26828080
www.gerardboyer.com

OPPOSITE PAGE: the bottles and ambience of the cellar of the Maison Veuve Clicquot Ponsardin in Reims.

BELOW: a collage of images from the Château Les Crayères: details of two dishes, the façade, an interior view.

are not very famous, and they are available for excellent prices for the quality.

The first stop is in Côte des Bar, in **COLOMBÉ-LE-SEC**, for the tasting of Bernard Breuzon Champagne, a small merchant-producer whose wine has a pleasant elegance, thanks in part to the considerable investments he has made in his cellar. The next stop, a few miles away, is **BAR-SUR-AUBE**, with its half-timber houses, and then **BAYEL**, site of Cristalleries Royales de Champagne, the royal glassworks founded at the behest of King Louis XIV in 1666 and purveyors to the court until 1727. Here, gestures learned from master glassworkers in Murano have been repeated for centuries. The entire region

offers spectacular routes, and neither a detailed map nor a compass is required; it is enough to follow the signs for the Champagne trail. The beauty of the trip lies in the pleasure of exploring the region, in meeting wine producers who speak of their craft with passion, in tasting their Champagne to discover which you like best—a difficult task considering the embarrassment of choices, with over 12,000 producers!

The small village of **URVILLE** conceals one of the pleasant surprises of the Aube: the Champagne of the Domaine Drappier, winemakers since 1604 who are now enjoying a period of tremendous fame. The prestigious company offices, in buildings once inhabited by the Cistercian monks of Clairvaux, include

ABOVE: the ancient cellars of Domaine Drappier, a prestigious wine-producer in Urville, in the Aube.

OPPOSITE, RIGHT: Colombé-le-Sec, Maison Bernard Breuzon: the gesture of *remuage*, or riddling, the slight periodic rotation of the bottles, which also gradually changes their tilt to a neck-down position.

WINE *Making sense of the labels*

Every Champagne label must include initials and an identification and control number, which indicate the type and name of the producer. Here is a guide to the principal initials:

CM, *cooperative de manipulation*, a cooperative that receives grapes from its members, and which oversees the processing and marketing of the wines.

ND, *négociant-distributeur*, a merchant who acquires, labels, and markets bottles that are processed by the producer.

NM, *négociant-manipulant*, a producer who buys grapes, must, or wines, usually also cultivating their own vineyards and producing champagne on their own property, such as a *maison*.

RC, *récoltant-coopérateur*, a producer who cultivates their own vines and gives the grapes to a cooperative, which processes and markets them.

RM, *récoltant-manipulant*, a producer who cultivates their own vines, harvests the grapes and produces their own wines. This category is composed mostly by small to average producers, who account for about one-third of the total production.

SR, *société de récoltants*, vinedressers from the same family who join together to share their grapes, process them, and market the wine.

Bottles (and labels) lined up at the Maison Salvatori in Épernay.

splendid vaulted cellars from the twelfth century (the cellars they own in Reims are also spectacular).

The beauty of the landscapes that follow along as far as **ESSOYES** explains why this village was chosen by Auguste Renoir for his retirement. It is a lovely village that hovers amid the silence of deserted streets and the poetry of the surroundings. In the vicinity of the studio where Renoir created some of his greatest works, it is possible to retrace the walks taken by the master as he sought inspiration.

Moving through a dense wooded area that runs along the boundary of the Aube as far as **MUSSY-SUR-SEINE**, the road continues to **LES RICEYS**, home of the rosé wine favored by Louis XIV. This is really three fortified villages in one, and also the only municipality in France with three different guarantees of origin for its wines. In Ricey Haut at Morize Père et Fils, fourth-generation wine producers, it is possible to taste an excellent Champagne, preferably after a visit to the vaulted twelfth-century cellars.

TROYES is surrounded by nearly 15,000 acres (6,000 hectares) of vineyards interspersed with valleys, ridges, forests, and streams. A city of medieval art treasures, its plan must be seen to be believed: It is in the shape of a Champagne cork. The downtown area of the ancient capital of the region abounds with narrow paved alleyways, lovely thatched houses, private Renaissance mansions, ancient churches with superb stained-glass windows, and important museums. In the summer the principal town squares host concerts featuring jazz, classical, and ethnic music.

IN THE SANCTUARIES OF CHAMPAGNE

From **TROYES** the road heads toward **ÉPERNAY**, passing through the prestigious Côtes des Blancs, the limestone cliffs that are home to excellent Chardonnay wines. The eastern slope is completely covered with vines that yield fine and elegant white wines, utilized in the most prestigious blends and in the *blanc de blancs*. Along the way is the spectacular seventeenth-century Château d'Etoges, and in Moulin d'Argensole, outside **VERTUS**, at the foot of the Côtes des Blancs, travelers can taste the 100 percent Chardonnay Champagne of Doyard-Mahé.

ÉPERNAY, on the left bank of the Marne River, marks the entrance to the heart of three great wine-producing regions: the Côtes des Blancs, the Marne valley, and the Reims Mountains. It is said that drinking Champagne in Épernay is a bit like listening to the melodies of Mozart in Salzburg. Walking along the Avenue des Champagne in the center of town, one understands why—nineteenth-century buildings housing the headquarters of the most famous names in Champagne, from Moët et Chandon to Mercier, follow one after another. The frenetic activity on the surface contrasts with the quiet in the cellars below, which hold millions of bottles. Indeed the buildings in Épernay stand over miles of tunnels carved into the chalky soil, where the temperature remains constant and that historically have been used for preserving Champagne. The underground walk, in short, is an experience not to

be missed, and one of the most impressive visits is to the Moët et Chandon cellars, where 90 million bottles line over 17 miles (27 kilometers) of tunnels.

The countryside around Épernay is crisscrossed by wonderful routes that touch upon lovely hilltop villages such as **HAUTVILLERS**, famous for the ancient Benedictine abbey where Dom Pérignon lived, its belvedere, and its display of wrought-iron signs in the small downtown area.

OPPOSITE: the studio of Auguste Renoir in Essoyes.

ABOVE, FROM THE TOP: supervision of the aging of the wine at Maison Tarlant in Oeuilly, between Épernay and Reims; the statue of Dom Pérignon in Épernay.

Throughout the Marne valley, a region particularly suited to the cultivation of Pinot Meunier, a species of grape that gives this magnificent wine its fruity bouquet, vineyards crowned by forests run as far as the eye can see, dotted with villages, castles, and churches. In **OEUILLY**, perched on a hill in a panoramic setting overlooking the infinite expanse of vines, is the Tarlant family winery, founded in 1687. Tarlant works the three heralded grape varieties that form the basis for Champagne—Chardonnay, Pinot Noir, and Pinot Meunier—in different locations, depending on the characteristics of the soil and to bring out the various properties of the grapes.

The journey from Épernay to **REIMS** traverses the Reims Mountains, a small wooded region with lovely historic villages and vineyards that produce the best Champagne grapes. **VERZENAY** is truly unusual: a rural village hidden at the bottom of a valley dominated by a windmill and a lighthouse from 1919, which now houses a wine museum. Early in the morning, when the sun's rays begin to slowly heat the ground and the mist rises, there are beautiful plays of light, and looking up from the street, the silhouette of the windmill rises up like something in a fairy tale.

The Gothic spires of the majestic cathedral of Notre Dame announce the presence of **REIMS**. The

OPPOSITE: the windmill in Verzenay.
RIGHT: Delicacies at the Restaurant Valentino in Troyes; to the right, Champagne bubbles.

TAKE A BREAK

LODGING

Troyes: **LE CHAMP DES OISEAUX**
20, rue Linard Gonthier
Tel: 0033.3.25805850
www.champdesoiseaux.com
Two half-timber houses from the fifteenth and seventeenth centuries in the heart of the city, behind the cathedral, have been transformed into a charming hotel. The suites, on the attic level, are especially desirable.

Vinay-Épernay: **L'HOSTELLERIE LA BRIQUETERIE**
4, Route de Sézanne
Tel: 0033.3.26599999
Surrounded by vineyards and tilled fields, La Briqueterie offers tranquil and well-appointed rooms, in addition to the cooking of Christophe.

DINING

Troyes: **RESTAURANT VALENTINO**
35, rue Paillot de Montabert
Tel: 0033.3.25731414
In an alleyway in the downtown area where cars are banned, this restaurant features traditional dishes with a creative twist, accompanied by an impressive wine list.

church, much loved by Marcel Proust, is besieged by tourists from around the world who travel here, drawn by the Champagne and by the chance to visit the *crayères*—hundreds of miles of tunnels carved during Gallic-Roman times into the chalky rock.

The most famous wine producers are grouped together in the Champ-de-Mars neighborhood and on the slopes of the Saint-Nicaise. These include Louis Roederer Krug, Pommery, Taittinger, Piper-Heidsieck, and Mumm. Maison Veuve Clicquot Ponsardin, one of the oldest houses, boasts a network of 13 miles (20 kilometers) of tunnels carved into the rock at a depth of 80 feet (25 meters), where the temperature remains a constant 10/11°C (50–52°F). Each of the *crayères*, rooms excavated long ago, bears the name of an employee who worked for at least forty years for the maison. The very inviting shop has an infinite variety of gadgets in the unmistakable orange livery of Veuve Clicquot. The Maison Ruinart, the oldest Champagne house, also has spectacular cellars. A staircase descends nearly 100 feet (30 meters) below ground to reach the ancient tunnels excavated by the Romans, the only ones protected as a historic monument of France.

The precious Champagne of Maison Krug in Reims, aging in barrels.

DRAPPIER

Grande Rue, Urville
Tel: 0033.3.25274015
www.champagne-drappier.com

Founded: 1808
Production region: Urville
Wines and grape varieties: 97% whites, 3% rosé; Pinot Noir, Pinot Meunier, Chardonnay

GREAT WINES

Cuvée Grand Sendrée 1996
Made from 55 percent Chardonnay and 45 percent Pinot Noir grapes from the Grande Sandrée vineyard and vinified only in great years. Golden-yellow color with honey reflections, a fine and rather persistent pearliness. Full, fine, and complex to the nose, with hints of peach, apricot, wild fruit, and spiced bread. Dry, decisive taste, clean, excellent structure and balance. Fresh and long aftertaste, with notes of tangerine and licorice. Table wine, excellent for aging.

Cuvée 1152–2002
This blend was created to celebrate the 850th anniversary of the construction of the cellars. Made from a strict selection of 65 percent Pinot Noir, 30 percent Chardonnay, and 5 percent Pinot Meunier grapes from the best vines on the property during the 1999 harvest. Straw-yellow color with pearl reflections. Full, fine, and elegant bouquet, with hints of orange preserves. Dry and refined taste, good structure and balance, with notes of fruit and bread crust. Great prospects for development and aging. Should be drunk as an aperitif or with steamed fish.

Visits and tastings: yes, by appointment

CHAMPAGNE MORIZE PÈRE & FILS

122, rue Général de Grulle
Les Riceys
Tel: 0033.3.25293002
www.champagnemorize.com

Founded: 1830
Production region: Les Riceys
Wines and grape varieties: 88% whites, 12% rosé; Pinot Noir, Chardonnay

GREAT WINES

Brut Prestige
Made from 85 percent Pinot Noir and 15 percent Chardonnay grapes selected and harvested from their own vineyards. Aged seven years in the bottle in the twelfth-century cellars. Intense straw-yellow color with golden reflections, fine and persistent pearliness. Fine and balanced to the nose, with a good palate with floral and fruity hints. Dry, decisive, and clean taste, with impressions of bread crust and yeast. Ready to drink, can be further aged, a table wine.

Brut Rosé
Made from pure Pinot Noir grapes, vinified in red, with brief maceration to reduce to a minimum the contact between pulp and skin. Intense salmon color, fine and persistent pearliness. Full and elegant bouquet, with fruity hints of strawberry and raspberry. Dry, full, delicate taste, excellent structure and complexity. Ready to drink, goes well with smoked salmon and fish antipastos.

Visits and tastings: yes, by appointment

DOYARD-MAHÉ

Moulin d'Argensole
Vertus
Tel: 0033.3.26522385
www.champagne.doyard.mahe.fr

Founded: 1889
Production region: Côtes des Blancs
Wines and grape varieties: 85% whites, 15% rosé; Pinot Noir, Pinot Meunier, Chardonnay

GREAT WINES

Doyard-Mahé Millésime 1998 Brut
Made from pure Chardonnay grapes, exclusively from the Côtes des Blancs and produced only in excellent years. Vivid straw-yellow color with golden reflections and a fine and persistent pearliness. Elegant bouquet, with floral hints and hints of citrus and brioche. Dry, clean taste, good structure, long and refreshing aftertaste. Ready to drink, excellent as an aperitif or with white meat.

Visits and tastings: yes, by appointment

CHAMPAGNE TARLANT

Oeuilly
Tel: 0033.3.26583060
www.tarlant.com

Founded: 1687
Production region: Oeuilly, Boursault, St-Agnan, Celles-les-Condé
Wines and grape varieties: 95% whites, 5% rosé; Pinot Noir, Pinot Meunier, Chardonnay

GREAT WINES

Cuvée Louis Brut
Created in honor of one of the founding fathers of the wine company, this blend is made of Pinot Noir and Chardonnay grapes in equal parts, coming from the most sought-after vineyards in the les Crayères region, where a chalky soil prevails. Vinified in chestnut vats, it has an intense straw-yellow color with amber reflections and a fine and brilliant pearliness. Full and generous bouquet, with toasted notes of undergrowth, dry fruit, and vanilla. Dry, powerful taste, full and structured, with notes of citrus honey. Excellent for aging, and once mature can be a wine for meditation.

Visits and tastings: yes, by appointment

VEUVE CLICQUOT PONSARDIN

1, Place des Droits de l'Homme
Reims
Tel: 0033.3.26895390
www.veuve-clicquot.fr

Founded: 1772
Production region: Reims Mountains,
Marne valley, Côtes des Blancs, Sézannais,
Aube
Wines and grape varieties: 98% whites,
2% rosé; Pinot Noir, Pinot Meunier,
Chardonnay

GREAT WINES

La Grande Dame Rosé 1990
This is a rare blend, the result of an exceptional year. Made from 61 percent Pinot Noir and 39 percent Chardonnay grapes. Salmon-red color with ruby reflections and a fine pearliness. Full, intense bouquet, with hints of dry figs, dates, and vanilla. Dry, concentrated, aromatic, and elegant taste. Long finish with notes of cherry and strawberry. Can be aged at length, and ideal after a meal.

Vintage Reserve 1995
Made from 58 percent Pinot Noir, 9 percent Pinot Meunier, and 33 percent Chardonnay grapes. Brilliant straw-yellow color with reflections tending toward green and a fine, persistent pearliness. Floral hints and notes of almond, fresh hazelnut, apricot, and peach. Dry, decisive, clean, and elegant, with mineral notes, pear, and white peach. Ready to drink, this wine is ideal as an aperitif or an accompaniment to shellfish.

Visits and tastings: yes

RUINART

4, rue des Crayères
Reims
Tel: 0033.3.26775151
www.ruinart.com

Founded: 1729
Production region: Reims Mountains,
Côtes des Blancs
Wines and grape varieties: 92% whites,
8% rosé; Pinot Noir, Pinot Meunier,
Chardonnay

GREAT WINES

Dom Ruinart 1993
A combination of 35 percent Chardonnay from the Reims Mountains and 65 percent Côte des Blancs. Golden-yellow color and a fine and very persistent pearliness. Full, complex bouquet of notable refinement, with hints of almond, toasted bread, citrus, and dried fruit. Dry, powerful, balanced taste, with mango and passion fruit. Long, clean finish with impressions of coffee. Should be aged for long periods, goes well with caviar, foie gras, or apple tart.

Dom Ruinart Rosé 1988
Made from a combination of 85 percent Chardonnay grapes vinified in 15 percent red grapes, from the best vintages on the property. Orange color tending toward Cognac, with fine and very persistent pearliness. Full, complex bouquet with mineral hints of smoke, bread crust, and red berries. Dry, decisive, concentrated, and quite elegant taste. Notes of stewed fruit, spices, and leather to the palate. Long finish, with caramelized nuances. Ready to drink and goes well with smoked salmon or truffles.

Visits and tastings: yes, by appointment

KRUG

5, rue Coquebert
Reims
Tel: 0033.3.26844420
www.krug.com

Founded: 1843
Production region: Reims Mountains
Marne Valley, Côte des Blancs
Wines and grape varieties: Pinot Noir,
Pinot Meunier, Chardonnay

GREAT WINES

Krug Cos du Mesnil 1988
Made from pure Chardonnay grapes from one of the most sought-after pieces of land in the entire region. Intense straw-yellow color with golden reflections, it has a fine and persistent pearliness. Full, complex, and seductive to the nose, with hints of ripe fruit, bread crust, and vanilla. Dry, clear, concentrated taste with great structure and elegance. Long and clean aftertaste with mineral notes. Excellent for aging, and an ideal accompaniment to dishes based on fish or dessert with dry fruit.

Krug 1988
Fermented in small wooden casks and aged in the bottle for ten years before being sold, this vintage perfectly summarizes the Krug style. Brilliant golden yellow color, with a fine and very persistent pearliness, full of personality, rich in hints of fruit, yeast, and bread crust. Dry, explosive taste, clean and elegant with notes of orange flower, quince, and sweet spices. Ready to drink but can be aged at length, goes well with fish in sauce or with white meat.

Visits and tastings: yes, by appointment

CHAMPAGNE LOUIS ROEDERER

21, Boulevard Lundy
Reims
Tel: 0033.3.26404211
www.champagne-roederer.com

Founded: 1776
Production region: Reims Mountains,
Marne valley, Côtes des Blancs
Wines and grape varieties: 98% whites,
2% rosé; Pinot Noir, Pinot Meunier,
Chardonnay

GREAT WINES

Louis Roederer Cristal Rosé Millésime 1996
Made from 30 percent Chardonnay and 70 percent overripe Pinot Noir grapes. Topaz color with coppery reflections, bouquet of tremendous refinement, elegance, and balance with delicate aromas of red fruit, notes of vanilla and bread crust. Dry taste, simultaneously powerful and delicate, of great structure and complexity. Can be aged at length, and goes well with smoked salmon or caviar, or as an aperitif.

Louis Roederer Brut Premiere
At least four great vintages from previous years are added to the wine of the latest harvest for the Brut Premiere blend. Intense straw-yellow color with golden reflections, fine and persistent pearliness. Intense and elegant bouquet, with hints of sagebrush, incense, bay leaf, and linden. Dry, straightforward taste, particularly tasty, harmonious, and pleasant, with an elegant base of toasted almond and ripe rennet apple. Can be aged at length, and goes well with large shellfish, fine fish, and white meat.

Visits and tastings: yes, by appointment

ALSACE

WINE TRAIL *Itinerary*

ITINERARY LENGTH
280 miles /150 kilometers

BEST TIME TO GO
April to October

TIME TO SPEND
Four to five days

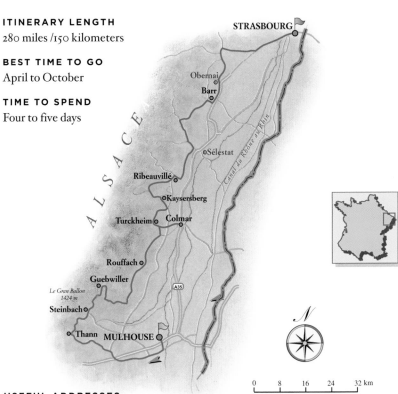

USEFUL ADDRESSES
Comité Régional du Tourisme d'Alsace, Colmar
Tel: 33.3.89247350
www.tourisme-alsace.com
Conseil Interprofessionnel des Vins d'Alsace, Colmar
Tel: 33.3.89201620
www.vinalsace.com

For nearly 2,000 years, the aroma of must has hovered amid the half-timber houses, spired bell towers, medieval villages, cellars, and castles of Alsace. This is the heart of Europe, a land which since the first century BC has been subjected to many different influences—Celtic, Germanic, Gallo-Roman, and Frankish. But the convulsive events that have occurred over the centuries never interrupted the development of wine cultivation, which has continued since Roman times.

During the reign of the Merovingians and the Carolingians, regional wine was considered a "tonic and something that makes you happy," and was consumed in great quantities. Throughout the Middle Ages, this region produced one of the most highly regarded and costly wines in Europe. Then, with the Thirty Years' War and for two centuries thereafter, a series of devastations, epidemics, and plundering decimated the population. The revival of Alsatian wine only began after World War I, when the *vignerons* returned to work the land that had changed hands four times in less than one century, back and forth between France and Germany. Today the many different faces of this smallest French region coexist serenely with the sweetness of the views, made up of endless vineyards that produce 150 million bottles of prized wine annually.

OPPOSITE PAGE, FROM TOP: a view of Strasbourg; smiles and fine bottles at Domaine Sipp Mack in Hunawihr; the cellar of Domaine Paul Blanck, in Kientzheim; Alsace by hot-air balloon.

ABOVE: the landscape in Turckheim.

THE CLIMATE AND THE LAND

The secret to the success of Alsatian wines lies both in the excellent climatic conditions, with scant rainfall (one of the lowest in France) and abundant sun, and in the richness of the soil, which ranges from siliceous to calcareous, sloping down to the alluvial plains. The rows of vines follow the sun-drenched hills, and the Vosges mountains shelter them from the humid ocean winds. The first cultivated variety seems to have been Pinot Noir, introduced by the Romans. Around the twelfth century, white grape varieties gained the upper hand, and by the fifteenth century, Riesling, Moscato, and Gewurztraminer vines were already being grown (the French write it *Gewurztraminer,* without the umlaut), while Pinot Blanc and Pinot Grigio were introduced later.

Unlike other French varieties, in Alsace the wines do not take their name from the region but from the vine variety, of which there are seven. Riesling is certainly the best known and the most eclectic, and it can age for more than ten to fifteen years. The Tokay Pinot Gris—which, now that Hungary has claimed the Tokay name, is called only Pinot Gris—is potent, full-bodied, and persistent. The Gewurztraminer, with its rich aromas of fruit and flowers, is powerful and seductive. The Pinot Blanc, delicate and fresh, goes well with everything. The Sylvaner is fresh, light, and very perfumed. Finally there are the fruity Muscat d'Alsace and the Pinot Noir, the latter being the region's only red wine, which evokes the taste of cherry and violet. In Alsace, as in the Loire valley, it is served cold.

ABOVE: pitched roofs and dense vineyards in Hunawihr.

OPPOSITE: One "piece" from the Musée National de l'Automobile.

FOLLOWING PAGES: Alsace from above, in the twilight mist. Christian Dior said: "A glass of wine from Alsace is like a light dress, a springtime flower, the ray of sunlight that brightens life…"

THE *GRAND CRU* WINES

To have the right to an Alsace Grand Cru Appellation d'Origine Contrôlée (AOC), wines must come from grapes harvested in fifty strictly defined zones of Alsatian vineyards. There are only four authorized varieties: Riesling, Gewurztraminer, Pinot Gris, and Muscat d'Alsace. The minimum alcoholic content must be 10 percent for Riesling and Muscat and 12 percent for Gewurztraminer and Pinot Gris, with a maximum authorized yield of 70 hectoliters per hectare. *Grand cru* labels must indicate not only the authorized name of origin, but also the grape variety and vintage. The *grand cru* panorama is completed by the wines made from late-harvest grapes picked by hand, grape by grape, in separate collection stages, and only when the ideal stage of botrytization (*Botrytis cinerea*) has been reached.

THE JOURNEY
THE ALSATIAN WINE TRAIL

Traveling through this region is a pleasure. The sprawling vineyards descend from the Vosges mountains as far as the Rhine, houses cluster at the foot of the mountains, and innumerable cellars provide an endless feast for the gourmand in the southern part of the region. The journey zigzags across the plain, and the hills graze scores of small villages linked by rows of vines. Everything is graceful, orderly, full of flowers and history.

The itinerary follows the road from **MULHOUSE**, the European capital of technology

CITIES   *Mulhouse, between past and present*

Ancient spinning mills and large-scale industry: At the dawn of the nineteenth century, Mulhouse was considered the "Manchester of France." The city still has a historic downtown, with beautiful homes built by industrialists in the early nineteenth century and a workers' district that served as a model for other cities.

Today it is one of Europe's most important centers for technology museums. The most popular is the Musée National de l'Automobile –Collection Schlumpf. Almost five hundred vehicles are on display, presenting a complete overview of the history of the car industry from 1878 to the present: Rolls Royce, Porsche, Ferrari, Panhard-Levassor, Alfa Romeo, Hispano Suiza, De Dion Bouton, Mercedes, and 120 Bugatti, including the *coupé Napoléon*, Ettore Bugatti's personal vehicle (Avenue de Colmar 192, tel. 0033.3.89332323, fax 0033.3.89320809; www.collection-schlumpf.com). Other museums include: Electropolis (Musée EDF Electropolis), dedicated to electricity; Musée de l'Impression sur Etoffes, the museum of textile printing, which is visited by fashion luminaries, from Christian Dior to Paloma Picasso, who are looking for new ideas from ancient textiles; the Musée Français du Chemin de Fer, a railroad museum that includes the "blue train" that inspired Agatha Christie; and the Musée du Papier Peint, a collection of over 700 wallpapers, including one used in the White House.

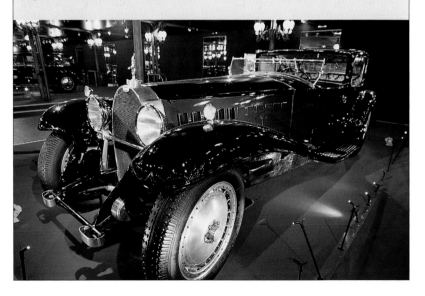

FLAVORS *Arbiters of taste*

If cheese is a passion for many, for Bernard Antony (*below, left*) it is a reason for living. It is with good cause that he says he has worked "in the service of taste for thirty-four years." His customers have included cooks and famous restaurants such as Alain Ducasse, royal palates such as that of Prince Rainier of Monaco, aristocrats such as Baron Elie de Rothschild, and famous figures such as former president Valéry Giscard d'Estaing. Antony gives them the same service that he bestows on those who just happen to stop by his simple shop in Vieux Ferrette, a few miles from Mulhouse. The real reason for entering his Alsatian *Käs Kaller*, in addition to the possibility of making purchases, is to participate in the *"cérémonie du fromage,"* as he calls the tasting of his products (42 euros per person, by reservation only).

At Maison Liesel in Ribeauvillé, your mouth begins to water just looking in the windows. Marco and Marianna Willmann, artisan-refiners, prepare goose and duck foie gras in the workshop-atelier next to their shop. Those who want to take home some products are advised to purchase the *foie gras mi cuit*, cooked like old-style conserves in glass jars, without pasteurization or preservatives, and which last up to six months in a cool place. In Italy people often speak erroneously of *pâté de foie gras* when they are referring to a compound (literally a *pasticcio*, or jumble) made with a minimum percentage of liver and the rest from various other meats, which has nothing in common with true foie gras.

In Niedermorschwihr, the aromas of the region's great white wines are enhanced by the perfume of the jams of Christine Ferber (*below, right*), who was dubbed the "best pastry chef in France" in 1988. Some of her most whimsical confections are made with Veuve Cliquot Champagne, wild strawberries, rose petals, wild black cherry, and mint.

museums, to arrive in **THANN**, the starting point for the 100-mile-long (150 kilometers) wine trail. After a little over 4 miles, in **STEINBACH**, turn down the Route des Crêtes (Route of the Mountain Crests), a treat for the eyes. This spectacular mountain road meanders through the Uffholz forest, climbing the Vosges peaks, from which the view extends over the entire winegrowing region, as far as Germany. Then, in **GUEBWILLER**, the dense vegetation slopes down gently to the plane of vineyards. This itinerary is beautiful for the continuous mix of mountain and forest, vineyards and hamlets.

The ancient village of **ROUFFACH** is dominated by Isenbourg castle, a refined five-star hotel that overlooks the vineyards at the bottom of the valley. This is the loveliest part, where one finds the best vinedressers, in the heart of the wine-producing region. An introduction to the most classic Alsatian wines—Riesling, Pinot Gris, and Gewurztraminer—can be had with a tasting at Zind Humbrecht, a modern wine cellar in **TURCKHEIM**, where the vineyards have been passed down from father to son since 1620. In 1999 they were one of the first to convert to biodynamic viticulture. There is an excellent selection of Pinot Gris *Grains Nobles*, which yield a sweet, struc-

Bernard Antony, left, and pastry chef Christine Ferber, right.

Half-timber houses and open-air tables on the riverbank (Hotel Le Maréchal) in Colmar.

Fantasy of Alsatian vines at the La Sommelière cellar in Colmar.

Strolling in the pedestrian zone, one of the largest in Europe, one can admire a rich artistic heritage that ranges from the medieval to the twentieth century. The Maison de Têtes from the early seventeenth century owes its name to the 111 heads that adorn its façade; the Maison Pfister proves a lovely Renaissance dwelling as does the Dominican church. The collegial church of Saint-Martin stands in pure Gothic style, and the Unterlinden Museum is a thirteenth-century monastery that houses the sixteenth-century Isenheim altarpiece. The Bartholdi Museum is located in the house that was the birthplace of Frederic Auguste Bartholdi, the artist who sculpted the Statue of Liberty in New York. The picturesque Quai de la Poissonerie, the quarter where the fish market once stood, is now known as Little Venice.

tured, and harmonious wine that recalls the character of certain Sauternes.

LITTLE VENICE

Next on the route is **COLMAR**, a mosaic of old buildings, ornate façades, interesting museums, canals, and lanes. The Reformation, the Thirty Years' War, the disturbances of the French Revolution, the Prussian annexation of 1871, and the Nazi occupation of 1940—all seem to have left no trace on the tranquil historic center.

THE HEART OF ALSACE

On the road again, the tranquility of the Vosges mountains leads to **KAYSERSBERG**, a medieval fortified village on the Weiss River, with an extremely beautiful historic center where the shops are embellished with wrought-iron signs. The essence of Alsace can be seen in the storks' nest on the bell tower—home to one of the 354 pairs of these wading birds that have returned to build their nests on the region's chimney tops in recent years. If there is time, stop in **KIENTZHEIM** at Domaine Paul Blanck, owned by a family of winegrowers since 1610. In addition to visit-

TAKE A BREAK

LODGING

Rouffach: **CHÂTEAU D'ISENBOURG**
Tel: 0033.3.89785850 / 0033.3.89785370
www.grandesetapes.com
E-mail: isenbourg@grandesetapes.fr
Accommodation in a scenic castle amid the vineyards, halfway between the Vosges mountains and the Alsatian plain. A stupendous indoor swimming pool is surrounded by rows of vines outside.

Colmar: **ROMANTIC HOTEL LE MARÉCHAL**
Place des Six-Montagnes-Noires 4-6, Colmar
Tel: 0033.3.89416032
www.hotel-le-marechal.com
E-mail: marechal@calixo.net
Lovely frame houses connected to one another, with rooms in the styles of Louis XV, Louis XVI, and Louis Philippe.

DINING

Kaysersberg: **HOTEL-RESTAURANT LE CHAMBARD**

Rue du Général de Gaulle 9/13,
Tel: 0033.3.89471017
E-mail: hotelrestaurantchambard@wanadoo.fr
In every dish by Olivier Nasti, a prize-winning chef of Italian origin, one discovers imagination and creativity in the Alsatian style. His finest creations include two versions of foie gras: sautéed in a pan and served with a Madeira sauce, or flavored with herbs and accompanied by a compote of figs and mango. There is also an excellent wine list.

Riedisheim: **RESTAURANT LA POSTE**
Rue du Général de Gaulle 7 (across from the town hall)
Tel. 0033.3.89440771
The dishes of young chef Jean-Marc Kieny satisfy both eye and palate, and they perpetuate the culinary traditions of the region, with original pairings such as orange and rosemary, or lobster and asparagus. The excellent desserts include champagne, peach, apricot, and cinnamon mousse. The cellar boasts over four hundred Alsatian and French labels. The restaurant is about a ten-minute car ride from Mulhouse.

ing the cellar, excellent wines are available for tasting, which Chantal Blanck describes with passion.

RIBEAUVILLÉ is an important stop on the itinerary—a medieval village on the mountain slopes towered over by the ruins of three ancient castles. Visit Maison Liesel, temple of foie gras, and the Jean Paul Mettè cellar, where over eighty distillates can be sampled. The oddest ones are made from garlic, basil, asparagus, and pepper.

The trip continues in the direction of **BARR**, where one of the last coopers in the region is still at work; then through a landscape structured by the vineyards, turning toward the plane before reaching **STRASBOURG**, with its canals, half-timbered houses, and the headquarters of the European Parliament.

A dish at La Poste in Riedisheim, and an interior of the Hotel-Restaurant Le Chambard in Kaysersberg.

DOMAINE ZIND HUMBRECHT

Route de Colmar 4, Turckheim
Tel: 0033.3.89270205
E-mail: o.humbrecht@wanadoo.fr

Founded: 1959 (the earliest traces date back to 1720)
Production region: Kayserberg, Turckheim, Hunawihr, Gueberschwihr, Thann
Wines and grape varieties: 99% whites, 1% reds; Riesling, Muscat, Pinot Gris, Gewurztraminer, Sylvaner, Pinot d'Alsace, Pinot Noir

GREAT WINES

Riesling Brand 2001
Fermented for over twelve months with little sugary residue, this Riesling is dense and concentrated. Full-bodied in the mouth, but with a clear, dry aftertaste. Fruity hints with floral notes and mineral accents. Ideally should be aged five to twenty years. Perfect complement to fish.

Pinot Gris Rangen de Thann Clos-Saint-Urbain 2001
A wine of great structure that combines mineral aromas of flint and peat with hints of exotic fruit. Complex and balanced, with an aftertaste of spices and smoke. Should be aged at least ten years, and complements dry pastries.

Visits and tastings: yes, by appointment

MARC TEMPÉ

Rue du Schlossberg 16, Zellenberg
Tel: 0033.3.89478522 (or call La Sommelière, tel: 0033.3.89412038)
E-mail: contact@lasommeliere.fr

Founded: 1993
Production region: Zellenberg, Sigolsheim, St. Hippolyte
Wines and grape varieties: 98% whites, 2% reds; Riesling, Pinot Gris, Gewurztraminer, Sylvaner, Pinot d'Alsace, Pinot Noir

GREAT WINES

Gewurztraminer Mambourg 2000
Fermented over twelve months in large wood barrels. Straw-yellow color with greenish reflections. Complex and balanced bouquet with obvious spicy notes. Complements spicy Asian dishes, or cheeses such as Muenster.

Gewurztraminer Mambourg 1998 Sélection de Grains Nobles
A selection of particularly ripe and botrytized grapes, resulting in an opulent, sumptuous wine, where spices combine with honey and ripe fruit. Complements fruit tart or chocolate cake.

Visits and tastings: yes, by appointment

BECKER

Route d'Ostheim 2, Zellenberg
Tel: 0033.3.89478756
E-mail: vinsbecker@aol.com

Founded: 1610
Production region: Zellenberg, Riquewihr, Ribeauvillé, Hunawihr
Wines and grape varieties: 92% whites, 8% reds; Riesling, Pinot Gris, Gewurztraminer, Sylvaner, Pinot Blanc, Pinot Noir, Muscat

GREAT WINES

Gewurztraminer Schoenenbourg Vendanges Tardives 2000
A Gewurztraminer that is very concentrated, rich, and full-bodied, with notes of spices and tobacco. Balanced in the mouth, with a certain acidity that makes it less oily. Should be drunk only after dessert.

Tokay Pinot Gris Grand Cru Froehn 1998
From the most prized vineyard on the property, this *grand cru* reveals regional characteristics: fullness and a very elegant, fruity bouquet. Should be aged at least ten years. Complements chocolate cake.

Visits and tastings: yes, by appointment

DOMAINE WEINBACH

Clos des Capucins, Route du Vin 25, Kaysersberg
Tel: 0033.3.89471321
www.domaineweinbach.com

Founded: 1898
Production region: Kaysersberg, Kientzheim
Wines and grape varieties: 99% whites, 1% reds; Riesling, Muscat, Tokay Pinot Gris, Gewurztraminer, Sylvaner, Pinot Blanc, Pinot Noir

GREAT WINES

2000 Riesling Grand Cru Schlossberg Cuvée Sainte Catherine "L'Inédit!"
From the most prized parcel of the oldest vineyard on the property, this wine is vinified only in exceptional years. It is a dense and full-bodied wine with great balance and a minimum sugary residue. Should be drunk by itself, or with lobster or fish dishes with sauce.

1998 Gewurztraminer Grand Cru Furstentum Sélection de Grains Nobles
This wine is an exceptional combination of power and refinement, with spicy notes. Floral hints and tropical fruit, with an aftertaste of candied grapefruit. Should be aged at length. Complements ripe, green-veined cheeses.

Visits and tastings: yes, by appointment

DOMAINE SIPP MACK

1, rue des Vosges, 68150 Hunawihr
Tel: 0033.3.89736188
www.sippmack.com
E-mail: contact@sippmack.com

Founded: 1698
Production region: Hunawihr, Ribeauvillé,
Riquewihr, Bergheim
Wines and grape varieties: 90% whites,
10% reds; Riesling, Muscat, Tokay Pinot
Gris, Gewurztraminer, Sylvaner, Pinot
Blanc, Pinot Noir

GREAT WINES

Riesling Grand Cru Osterberg 2000
Harvested by hand in mid-October, vinified in steel and then aged four months in
large wooden barrels, this is a Riesling
that needs to be aged. Golden yellow in
color with scents of grapefruit and med-
lar, it is sensuous to the taste, correctly
full and rich. Complements shellfish.

*Gewurztraminer Sélection de
Grains Nobles 1997*
A production of only 1,600 17-ounce
bottles, this is a Gewurztraminer of great
depth. Straw-yellow in color with an unmistakable scent of citrus preserves, it reveals great complexity and richness in the
mouth. Complements foie gras, apple
tart, or fruit pie.

Visits and tastings: yes, by appointment

DOMAINE PAUL BLANCK

32, Grand Rue, 68240 Kientzheim
Tel: 0033.3.89782356
www.blanck.com
E-mail: info@blanck.com

Founded: 1610
Production region: Kientzheim,
Kaysersberg, Sigolsheim, Datzenthal
Wines and grape varieties: 92% whites,
8% reds; Riesling, Muscat, Tokay Pinot
Gris, Gewurztraminer, Sylvaner, Pinot
Blanc, Pinot Noir

GREAT WINES

Gewurztraminer Furstentum 1999
Golden-yellow color with bronze reflections. Full and lingering bouquet with
marked spicy notes. Rich and balanced to
the taste, with a finale of mature fruit. A
wine for contemplation, which can age at
least fifteen years.

Riesling Schlossberg Grand Cru 2000
A strawlike yellow with brilliant reflections and a refined bouquet with floral
scents. Elegant to the taste, sumptuous
without being heavy, rich and lingering.
Can be aged up to twenty years, and complements white fish.

Visits and tastings: yes, by appointment

DOMAINE BOTT FRÈRES

13, avenue du Général de Gaulle,
68150 Ribeauvillé
Tel: 0033.3.89732250
www.bott-freres.fr
E-mail: vins@bott-freres.fr

Founded: 1835
Production region: Ribeauvillé
Wines and grape varieties: Whites 85%, reds
15%; Riesling, Muscat d'Alsace, Tokay
Pinot Gris, Gewurztraminer, Sylvaner,
Pinot Blanc, Pinot Noir

GREAT WINES

Riesling Réserve Personnelle 2000
Dry and elegant, with a fruity scent. A
balanced wine, with a pleasant and mineral acidity. Aged for one year in large, centuries-old wooden barrels. Complements
cold hors-d'oeuvres and fish.

Gewurztraminer Réserve Personnelle 2000
Rich and full-bodied. With aging it develops golden reflections, an unmistakable
scent of rose, and a sumptuous palate. Before being bottled, it matures for one year
in large, centuries-old barrels. Can be
served alone, as an aperitif, or with foie
gras and toast.

Visits and tastings: yes

DOMAINE JEAN SIPP

160, rue de la Fraternité,
68150 Ribeauvillé,
Tel: 0033.3.89736002
www.jean-sipp.com
E-mail: domaine@jean-sipp.com

Founded: 1654 (family archives mention a
certain Jean Guillaume Sipp, but true
commercial development began in the
early 1950s)
Production region: Ribeauvillé, Bergheim,
St. Hippolyte
Wines and grape varieties: 95% whites,
5% reds; Riesling, Muscat, Tokay Pinot
Gris, Gewurztraminer, Sylvaner, Pinot
Blanc, Pinot Noir

GREAT WINES

Riesling Kirchberg 1999
Brilliant yellow color, slightly golden.
Exhibits a particularly rich bouquet with
fruity aromas, specifically of apricot and
citrus preserves. Intense and lingering
taste, it is powerful and rich, with muted
acidity. Splendid alone or with seasoned
fish.

Tokay Pinot Gris Trottacker 1998
Brilliant straw-yellow color, this Tokay
comes from calcareous clay soil. Opulent,
rich, and lingering in both fragrance and
taste, with scents of preserves and spices.
Vinified entirely in the barrel, it complements foie gras.

Visits and tastings: yes, by appointment

MEDITERRANEAN FRANCE

WINE TRAIL *Itinerary*

ITINERARY LENGTH
300 miles / 500 kilometers

BEST TIME TO GO
April to November

TIME TO SPEND
One week

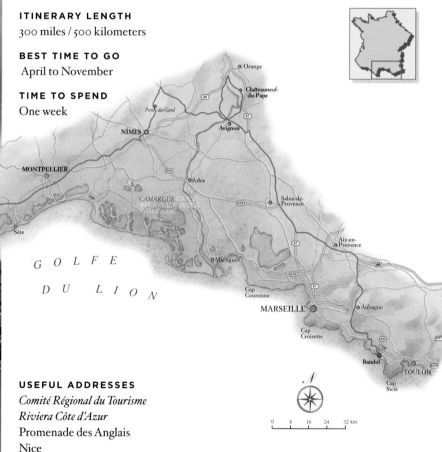

USEFUL ADDRESSES
Comité Régional du Tourisme
Riviera Côte d'Azur
Promenade des Anglais
Nice
Tel: 0033.4.93377878
www.guideriviera.fr

SEA, WIND, MOUNTAINS, rocks, flowers, and vineyards highlight the winding journey through the wildest parts of the Catalan region, providing a surprising combination of the Pyrenees and the Mediterranean in this itinerary through France. Dramatic bluffs dive into the restless blue sea, along which run abandoned terraces, fishing villages, bays, and inlets that unexpectedly open up onto breathtaking views, while the countryside lies behind the other side. The narrow and twisting road follows the coast, offering views of blue sea and monumental rocks.

THE JOURNEY
THE CÔTE VERMEILLE

The vertiginous spectacle continues as far as **BANYULS-SUR-MER**, birthplace of a wine that is the perfect accompaniment to chocolate and the start of the itinerary. A few miles from the border with Spain, the landscape changes and becomes orderly, tended, and geometric, with vines cultivated in terraces. Everything is done by hand, with passion. Like

OPPOSITE PAGE, FROM TOP: still life with labels for the Château-Fortia; an interior of the Hôtel La Mirande in Avignon; the Roman amphitheater in Nîmes; the vineyards and castle of Château des Fines Roches, in the vicinity of Châteauneuf du Pape.
RIGHT: The curving road cuts through coastal vineyards that descend to the sea, near Banyuls-sur-Mer; the Côte Vermeille, with the Catalan coast behind.

LEFT: the spectacular Pont-du-Gard, with its three rows of superimposed arches, spans the Gardon River not far from Nîmes. It was built as an aqueduct in the first century BC.

the sailboats that rule the breakers stirred up by the incessant mistral, the human hand governs this steep, dry land, with vines planted as far as the edge of the beach. This is the Côte Vermeille, which takes its name from the vermilion color that the schistose rocks assume in the half-light at dawn and dusk. Banyuls overlooks the Mediterranean at the foot of the Albères massif, surrounded by vineyards that slope down to the sea. Climbing up steep hillside alleys amid green rows of vines and fragrant brush, one can enjoy unexpected flashes of blue and admire the sea; after dining on fish, when it is time for dessert—based on chocolate—open a splendid bottle of Banyuls Cuvée Parcé Frères from the Domaine de la Rectorie. This curious wine cellar just a few yards from the sea formerly was an underground tunnel excavated by the Germans during wartime to store munitions in expectation of a landing which never took place. Now it is home to prized bottles that lie there, aging.

Further on in **COLLIOURE**, sitting in front of the fortification with feet dangling in the water, one can sip a Rouge Collioure Puig Orio, from the Domaine la Tour Vieille. In the early twentieth century, the radiant, explosive luminosity of this harbor was discovered by artists of rare talent, titans in the history of art. Fauvism, the painting movement whose leading figure was Henri Matisse, was born here, and it was here that André Derain and Pablo Picasso came to steal the colors, moods, and atmos-

FLAVORS *Chef René Bérard*

A temple of gastronomy is hidden in Cadière-d'Azur, a medieval village perched amid the rocks, a short distance from Bandol. This is the realm of René Bérard, born here in 1942 and a renowned Maître Cuisinier de France. Chef Bérard divides his time between his cooking school and restaurant, the Hostellerie Bérard, a small *relais de charme* within the walls of a restored eleventh-century monastery. A serious connoisseur of traditional Provençal flavors, Bérard insists on the quality and purity of basic ingredients. To understand his philosophy, one needs to follow him early in the morning when he goes to the market and then to the wharf to wait for the fishing boats before deciding on the menu for the day. In the garden of Bastide des Saveurs, the splendid country house around which he has created his "garden of tastes," he grows the spices, vegetables, and herbs that enrich his dishes. His ideas are encapsulated by and realized in the food he serves. Surrounded by an explosion of colors and perfumes, wooden cutting boards and copper pans, Bérard communicates his ideas, style, and art with passion, patience, and enthusiasm. It is a full immersion in the truth about food, capable of transforming the most irresponsible hamburger lover into a gastronome.

Hostellerie Bérard
83740
La Cadière-d'Azur
Tel: 0033.494.901143

OPPOSITE: a wing of the ancient buildings of the Château des Fines Roches, in the vicinity of Châteauneuf du Pape, opening up to the plain.

LEFT: René Bérard, and a view of the Hostellerie Bérard.

phere from the earth and sea. With the Fauves, colors—dense, full, and violent—exploded on the canvas in a way never seen before. The Fauves, or "wild beasts" as critic Louis Vauxcelles called them, painted without rules. They wanted to seem rough, but in fact they were cultivated and superior geniuses.

The light of Collioure makes everything seem magical. This stunning seaside abode was home to the kings of Majorca in the thirteenth to fourteenth centuries, became a fortress in the fifteenth century, and then served as a citadel for the kings of Aragon.

FROM THE RHONE VALLEY TO THE CÔTE D'AZUR

The high, rocky Côte Vermeille fades into the sandy coast of the Côte Radieuse, and the journey veers toward the interior. The summits of the Pyrenees rise, blue and distant; moving through the narrow streets and shady piazzas of the Catalan city of **PERPIGNAN**, we reach **RIVESALTES**, city of Muscat wine. Vineyards of Grenache and Macabeu and occasional rows of Malvasia and Muscat line the banks of the Agly River. This is the flat Roussillon plain. The Domaine Cazes in Rivesaltes has been tended by four generations of winemakers, true masters of this type of sweet vinification.

Further on, amid the green of the countryside and the blue of the sea lies **NÎMES**, a city that provides an intelligent example of the benefits of preserving artistic patrimony. Nîmes is both ancient and

LEFT: Nîmes, a view (with a rainbow) of the splendid Jardin de la Fontaine.

OPPOSITE: In Bandol, Château de Pibarnon reds and rosés age in their barrels.

Banyuls-sur-Mer, in the cellar of Domaine de la Rectoire; precious wines in a tunnel excavated during wartime.

contemporary, French and Occitan, conservative and bold. Under the rule of Augustus it was one of the most important cities in the Gallo-Roman empire, precious vestiges of which still remain: Les Arènes, the amphitheater built in the late first century A.D.; the ruins of the temple of Diana; and the Maison Carrée, an Augustan temple in perfect condition that is audaciously mirrored in the mass of glass and steel that comprises the Carré d'Art contemporary art museum, designed by Norman Foster. It is a city of a thousand faces, cooled by the air of the Cévennes mountains and the sea of the Petite Camargue, twin sister to the Camargue area of Provence but less trav-

eled and clichéd. Nîmes is passionate and vital, with the Jardin de la Fontaine, the fabulous park designed in 1745 by architect Gabriel Dardailhon, which includes water in geometric basins on different levels surrounded by balustrades and tall trees.

A short distance outside this "little Rome of France" is the spectacular Pont-du-Gard, spanning the Gardon River. A unique example of a Roman aqueduct, it has three rows of superimposed arches; both impressive and light, it has been celebrated by Stendhal and Jean Jacques Rousseau and beloved by thousands of tourists. A wonder of hydraulic engineering and architecture that shines along the road to

AVIGNON, it transported water to Nîmes from a source in Uzès.

A few miles away Avignon, the "City of Popes" is announced by its mighty bastions. The pedestrian area around the Place de l'Horloge is dotted with tables and painters selling their canvases, with the suggestive architectural backdrop of the Palace of the Popes, which houses a wine cellar inside. This is the most suitable place for an extensive and comprehensive tasting to help the traveler grasp the complex and fascinating oenological range of this Mediterranean corner of France. The Palace of the Popes covers 161,500 square feet (15,000 square meters) and has ten

towers and enormous arches. It is one of the greatest examples of a Gothic palace built in the fourteenth century. Impressive and elegant, the austere pontifical residence dominates the beautiful piazza that in the summer provides the setting for a famous theater festival. There is also the impressive Pont Saint-Bénézet bridge, dating from the twelfth century; destroyed in 1226, it was rebuilt in 1250, and only four of its twenty-two original arches remain.

The subtle and sensual charm of Avignon is revealed at night, when lights expertly illuminate the buildings and little streets. This is the point of departure for a tour of the fabulous vineyard of

The Palace of the Popes in Avignon, which took over thirty years to build in the fourteenth century.

155

CHÂTEAUNEUF DU PAPE, which produces a generous red of great structure that exudes the characteristics of the stony soil in which the vines grow. Little country roads vanish among the rows of vines; they climb the hills, pulling the gaze off into the distance along bends in the Rhone River as far as the mists that herald the Mediterranean, overlooking châteaus and *domaines*. Whether the manor houses are resplendent or in disrepair, this is a land of great wines, the most shining examples of which include Château Fortia and Domaine de la Janasse. Here the harvest is still done by hand, according to traditional rules. The wineries are usually run by families, and the wines reflect not only the land but also the character of the winemaker. The patrimony of this region departs from the usual international varieties to favor indigenous ones, and the resulting flavors are unique. It is a pleasure to taste not only the great reds, but also the fine, elegant, and fresh whites, such as Viognier.

A short trip down the highway that bypasses Marseille soon leads to the heart of a world that is utterly different in both landscape and wines. **BANDOL** was made famous by the Romans and since then has maintained its reputation for its rows of

OPPOSITE: the Gallo-Roman classicism of the Maison-Carré, in Nîmes.
RIGHT: Cadière-d'Azur provides historic atmosphere and gastronomic delights near Bandol.

The nighttime profile of the famous Pont Saint-Bénézet, which long ago linked Avignon to Villeneuve-lès-Avignon, spanning the Rhone.

vines, along with its perfumes, colors, and beaches. Warmed by the hot sun of the Mediterranean, this enclave offers excellent reds, perfumed and tannic, based on the Mourvédre grape, which expresses its best characteristics in these wines; its rosés are superb in elegance and structure. Bandol reds are off-spring of the sea, sun, and rocks—it is a combination that reflects the territory and its geography with its golden beaches and unexpected cliffs. The uniqueness of the wines of Bandol require exceptional care with the food they accompany; reds of enormous body and structure are a perfect complement to fish (not to be missed is the combination of a young Bandol with fried mullet). It is a pleasure for the palate. The many wine producers that stand out in this distinctive

region include Château Pradeaux, with reds capable of extraordinary aging, and Château de Pibarnon, which, along with reds of considerable elegance, offers a rosé of fabulous structure.

The curving profile of the coast outlines spectac-ular views and presents an occasion to make an excur-sion to the Côte d'Azur. Here, the tiny Bellet *appellation* boasts Château de Bellet, which for four centuries has been perpetuating a family winemaking tradition. The winery's top offerings include the Cuvée Baron G. The grapes come from a handful of "urban" vineyards of Folle Noire, Braquet, and Rolle, which perch on the hills above Nice between the coast and the southern Alps. Kissed by the sun, these grapes yield a wine that is fruity and mineral in taste,

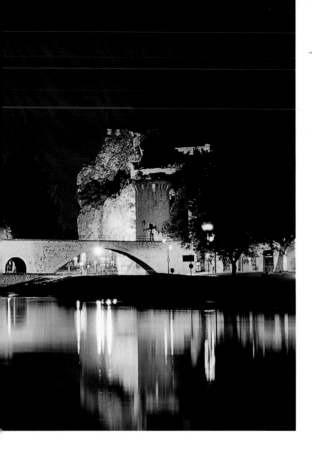

TAKE A BREAK

LODGING

Avignon: **LA MIRANDE**
4, Place de la Mirande
Tel: 0033.4.90859393
www.la-mirande.fr
This exclusive and charming hotel from the eighteenth century near the Palace of the Popes elegantly embodies the sumptuousness and atmosphere of a family residence.

Bandol: **HOTEL ÎLE ROUSSE**
25, Boulevard Louis Lumière
Tel: 0033.4.94293300
This lovely hotel with elegant, light-filled rooms overlooking the sea also has a thalassotherapy

(seawater therapy) center. The excellent gourmet restaurant, Les Oliviers, specializes in fish dishes that go best with the local wines.

DINING

Avignon: **CHRISTIAN ETIENNE**
10, rue de Mons
Tel: 0033.4.90861650
Creative genius Christian Etienne's single-themed menus celebrate the many facets of one ingredient—tomatoes, mushrooms, truffles, artichokes—from hors d'oeuvres to dessert. The terrace has a lovely view of the Place du Palais. The wine list is also excellent.

recalling the fragrances of thyme, wild rose, tropical fruits, and gunpowder. It is a palette of unique perfumes and tastes, emphasizing once again the incredible variety of wines, settings, traditions, and figures linked to this surprising coastal itinerary.

RIGHT: Christian Etienne: a dessert, and a view of the interior.

DOMAINE LA TOUR VIELLE

3, Avenue de Mirador
Collioure
Tel: 0033.4.68823842

Founded: 1981
Production region: Collioure, Banyuls
Wines and grape varieties: 20% whites, 20% rosés, 50% reds, 25% sweet wines; Grenache, Carignan, Syrah, Mourvedre, Grenache Gris, Roussanne, Vermentino

GREAT WINES

Rouge Collioure Puig Oriol 2002
Made from 70 percent Grenache and 30 percent Syrah grapes from vines between eighteen and forty years old, grown exclusively in schistose soil. Deep ruby-red color, deep bouquet, with notes of blackberry and wild fruit preserves. Dry, winy, mineral taste, with hints of ripe blackberry. Should be aged three to five years, and complements all red meat and rabbit.

Banyuls Millesime 1994
Aged in 600-liter oak barrels for eight years. The barrels are not completely filled in order to obtain a certain degree of oxidation. Deep garnet-red color, with brick reflections. Full and deep bouquet, very persistent, with hints of ripe fruit, cherries in brandy, fig, cinnamon, and chocolate. Sweet, velvety taste, complex and structured, with a presence of dates, dry figs, and licorice. Complements green-veined cheeses and chocolate-based desserts.

Visits and tastings: yes, by appointment

DOMAINE DE LA RECTORIE

Banyuls-sur-Mer
Tel: 0033.4.68881345
www.rectorie.com

Founded: 1988
Production region: Banyuls, Cospron
Wines and grape varieties: 25% whites, 10% rosés, 45% reds, 20% sweet wines; Grenache, Carignan, Syrah, Mourvedre, Grenache Gris

GREAT WINES

Banyuls Cuvée Parcé Frères 2001
Made from Grenache Noir and Carignan grapes, gathered in an early harvest and bottled after a brief maturation, fermented exclusively in steel to maintain the fruity notes. Deep ruby-red color with purplish-blue reflections. Full and persistent bouquet, with notes of wild fruit preserves, blackberry, and black raspberry. Sweet and sumptuous in the mouth, with a strong flavor of wild fruit, violet, and cocoa. Complements natural gorgonzola or sweets based on bitter chocolate.

Visits and tastings: yes, by appointment

DOMAINE CAZES

4, rue Francisco Ferrer
Rivesaltes
Tel: 0033.4.68640826

Founded: 1927
Production region: Rivesaltes
Wines and grape varieties: 10% whites, 10% rosés, 50% reds, 30% sweet wines; Muscat, Macabeu, Vermentino, Chardonnay, Syrah, Grenache, Merlot, Cabernet Sauvignon, Mourvedre

GREAT WINES

Trilogy 2000
Made from 70 percent Syrah, 20 percent Mourvedre, and 10 percent Grenache Noir grapes, aged twelve months in French oak barrels. Deep ruby-red color with violet reflections. Intense and persistent bouquet, with hints of red berry, spices, and black pepper. Full, powerful taste, with elegant tannins and hints of vanilla. After aging at least five years, complements grilled lamb or stewed red meat.

Muscat de Rivesaltes 2001
Made from 50 percent Muscat of Alexandria and 50 percent Muscat Petit Grains grapes, from vines that are at least thirty years old. Fermentation in steel is interrupted with the addition of alcohol up to 15 percent and then bottled. Pale straw-yellow color. Sweet, perfumed, and persistent taste. Complements blue cheeses.

Visits and tastings: yes, by appointment

DOMAINE DE LA JANASSE

27, Chemin du Moulin
Courthezon
www.lajanasse.com

Founded: 1963
Production region: Courthezon, Châteauneuf du Pape
Wines and grape varieties: 10% whites, 2% rosés, 88% reds; Roussanne, Cinsault, Viognier, Carignan, Syrah, Grenache, Merlot, Cabernet Sauvignon, Mourvedre

GREAT WINES

Domaine de la Janasse Les Garrigues Côte du Rhône 2001
Made from pure Grenache Noir grapes from vines that are sixty to eighty years old. Aged twelve months in large oak barrels, with 20 percent in casks for the same period. Intense ruby-red color. Full, complex, and persistent bouquet, with hints of wild fruit and cherry. A wine of great structure and notable concentration, rich in fine tannins and acidity, with a soft and elegant result. Should be aged seven to ten years, and complements game and roasts.

Domaine de la Janasse Châteauneuf-du-Pape Vieilles Vignes 2001
Made from 85 percent Grenache Noir and 15 percent Syrah and Mourvedre grapes, from vines over eighty years old. Aged twelve months in large oak barrels (70 percent) and casks (30 percent). Bouquet of notable complexity, with mineral and hints of blackberry, wild fruit preserves, and leather. Full, velvety, elegant taste, with notes of cherries in brandy, toasted bread, chocolate, and licorice. Should be aged ten to twenty years, and complements game and medium-aged cheeses.

Visits and tastings: yes, by appointment

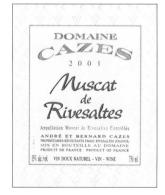

CHÂTEAU FORTIA

Châteauneuf du Pape
Tel: 0033.4.90837225
www.chateau-fortia.com

Founded: 1790
Production region: Châteauneuf du Pape
Wines and grape varieties: 10% whites and 90% reds; Grenache Blanc, Roussanne, Clairette, Bourboulenc, Counoise, Grenache Noir, Syrah, Mourvedre

GREAT WINES

Château Fortia Châteauneuf-du-Pape 2000 (white)
Made from 50 percent Roussanne, 32 percent Clairette, and 18 percent Grenache Blanc grapes, vinified separately. The Roussanne grapes ferment in barrels for six months on their own leavens, while the other grapes ferment in steel for the same period. Intense straw-yellow color, with golden reflections. Full and persistent bouquet, with floral and mineral hints and notes of honey and vanilla. Long and clean aftertaste. Should be drunk within four years, and complements white meat and aged goat cheese.

Château Fortia Châteauneuf-du-Pape 2000 (red)
Made from 30 percent Syrah, 15 percent Mourvedre, and 55 percent Grenache Noir grapes from vines that have an average age of thirty to forty years. Aged for eighteen months in large oak barrels. Full and complex bouquet, with hints of strawberry, morello cherry, and spices. Dry, powerful, and velvety taste, with notes of cherries in brandy. Should be aged ten to fifteen years.

Visits and tastings: yes, by appointment

CHÂTEAU PRADEAUX

676, Chemin des Pradeaux
Saint-Cyr-sur-Mer
Tel: 0033.4.94321021

Founded: 1752
Production region: Saint-Cyr-sur-Mer
Wines and grape varieties: 20% rosés, 80% reds; Mourvedre, Cinsault, Grenache Noir

GREAT WINES

Château Pradeaux Rosé 2002
Made from Mourvedre and Cinsault grapes in equal percentages, harvested by hand. Delicate rosy color with bronze reflections. Fine bouquet, with hints of wild rose, strawberry, and spices. Dry, structured, elegant, and aromatic taste, with mentholated notes. Should be drunk young, is an ideal complement to vegetables, dishes based on eggplant or zucchini, or fish in sauce.

Château Pradeaux Rouge 1999
A classic Bandol red, made from 95 percent Mourvedre and 5 percent Grenache Noir grapes. Intense ruby-red color with brick reflections. Harmonious and complex bouquet, with hints of violet, blackberry, plum, and leather. Dry, powerful, slightly rough and flavorful taste, with notes of toasted bread, spices, cocoa, and licorice. Should be aged from five to fifteen years; when young complements game, and when aged can accompany lamb, grilled tuna, and bouillabaisse. Aged three years in large oak barrels originally used in Bavaria for beer.

Visits and tastings: yes, by appointment

CHÂTEAU DE PIBARNON

La Cadière d'Azur
Tel: 0033.4.494901273

Founded: 1978
Production region: La Cadière d'Azul
Wines and grape varieties: 10% whites, 25% rosés, 65% reds; Cinsault, Mourvedre, Grenache Noir, Clairette, Bourboulenc, Viognier

GREAT WINES

Bandol Rosé 2003
One of finest rosés on an international level. Made from equal parts Cinsault and Mourvedre grapes, harvested by hand. Salmon color with reflections tending to bronze. Full, fine, and persistent bouquet, with floral hints, red berry and spice. Soft, refined taste of surprising structure, with a long and refreshing aftertaste. Should be aged three to four years, and complements Mediterranean cuisine based on fish or vegetables, or spicy dishes.

Bandol Rouge 1997
Made from Mourvedre grapes with 10 percent Grenache Noir, harvested by hand. Fermented in steel and later aged in large French oak vats for a minimum of twenty months. Intense ruby-red color with violet reflections. Full, complex, and very persistent to the nose, with hints of blackberry, pepper, tobacco, and spices. Robust and balanced taste, great body and structure, with a lovely presence of elegant tannins. Long aftertaste with notes of licorice. Should be drunk now or aged ten to fifteen years, and complements black truffles.

Visits and tastings: yes, by appointment

CHÂTEAU DE BELLET

440, Chemin de Saquier
Saint-Roman-de-Bellet, Nice

Founded: 1800
Production region: Saint Roman de Bellet
Wines and grape varieties: 50% whites, 25% rosés, 25% reds; Rolle (Vermentino), Chardonnay, Braquet, Folle Noire, Grenache

GREAT WINES

Château de Bellet Blanc 2002-Cuvée Baron G.
Made from 95 percent Rolle (Vermentino) and 5 percent Chardonnay grapes, fermented in oak barrels. Intense straw-yellow color. Complex and persistent to the nose, with floral hints and notes of gunpowder. Clear, clean taste, with a presence of tropical fruits that become lightly flavorful with aging, with a note of honey. Can be aged for some ten years, and complements fish.

Visits and tastings: yes, by appointment

ITALY

The cultivation of vines is one of many things that Italy owes to ancient Greece. Around 1000 BC, during the period of colonization, the Greeks brought vine cultivation to the Mediterranean basin. Their first Italian colonies developed in Sicily and Calabria, and the precious plants spread rapidly northward and found ideal terrains and climates throughout the peninsula.

As early as the seventh century BC, the Etruscans devoted themselves to viticulture in the region that is now Tuscany, and their wine was a prized commodity. In the third century BC, Hannibal passed through southern Italy, where vines were growing everywhere, on his way to Rome. During the Roman Empire, viticulture and winemaking became rooted in northern Italy and spread beyond the Alps, to France and Germany. The cultivation of vines, which was tied to society's general prosperity, underwent a period of rapid decline during the barbarian invasions, but then experienced a rebirth during the Renaissance. Some of the historic wine producers in Tuscany, such as Antinori and Frescobaldi, became well-established during this period. During the period of Spanish and Hapsburg domination, viticulture underwent another long period of decline. In the nineteenth century, riding the wave of great political and social changes, there was new impetus for wine production and the first attempts were made at high-level vinification, particularly in Piedmont. This period was brief in duration, cut short first by the phylloxera blight and then by the two world wars. It was only beginning in the 1970s that Italian vinification began its rebirth.

RIGHT: the Erste & Neue cellar in Caldaro, along the wine route in Alto Adige. *OPPOSITE PAGE:* a landscape in Chianti.

ITALIAN WINE TODAY

The last thirty years of the twentieth century saw a veritable revolution in the world of Italian wine, and the beginning of the third millennium seems truly promising.

Today Italy is the foremost wine producer in the world, with an average annual production of approximately 60 million hectoliters. However, this is not necessarily altogether a positive thing: There are still regions where quantity is more important than quality. Generally, however, there is a tendency toward lower yield per acre, which signifies a decrease in production and an increase in average quality. One need only go to the Langhe district, Maremma, Sicily, or even the Alto Adige to see vast vineyard regions cleared and replanted anew; old methods of cultivation, developed to obtain extremely high yields (the pergola method, for example), have been replaced by other methods (such as the Guyot method) that result in richer, more concentrated grapes.

The same is true for grape varieties. In recent years many winegrowers have decided to forego strong grape varieties used for blending (such as Trebbiano) to plant nobler varieties.

As a result, changes can be seen in agriculture in general and in wine production in particular. While during the postwar period the countryside was abandoned for economic reasons and winemaking became an industrialized process, today that trend has reversed. Thanks mainly to the example set by France and, more recently, California, people are seeing that high-quality wine pays off. Producers who were able to hold out during difficult times, who were committed to obtaining ever better wines, began to see the wisdom of their choices. High-quality Italian wine has always been more appreciated abroad, and exports are clearly on the rise. This in turn has brought in more money and increased investment possibilities, which will result in even finer wines. In terms of the domestic market, the profile of the Italian drinker shows a considerable decline in consumption; they are drinking less, but better-quality products.

The map of fine wine is also in constant evolution. Next to the better known regions, such as Piedmont and Tuscany, and those

that are gaining prominence, such as Friuli, there are now important producers who are bringing luster to regions such as Sicily, Campania, Alto Adige, and Sardinia.

The future of Italian wine lies in the proper use of the territory. Thanks to its geographic, morphological, and climatic diversity, Italy boasts the highest number of indigenous grape varieties in the world, even more than France. If Italian winemakers take into account this precious heritage instead of limiting themselves to the few international varieties and badly copying the "California style," the country will see the development of local characteristics, which are fundamental to a wine's greatness.

THE ITINERARIES

The Italian wine regions are numerous and very different. There are historical regions and emerging ones, all with a wonderful variety of landscapes and flavors. Wine is produced in every corner of the country, from the islands to the Alps, and from the south to the northern plains. Thus there are an almost infinite number of itineraries and wine routes, and of these we have included six.

One is in Piedmont, where the search is for some historic Italian wines, Barolo and Barbaresco. Many other wines have brought renown to the Langhe region, which not only offers an oenological heritage, but also has a fascinating history, peasant culture, and regional flavors, above all the endlessly enticing truffle.

Alto Adige is one of the regions where wine quality is increasing in an exciting fashion. And so a splendid wine trail starts at the foot of the Dolomites, amid castles, exceptional restaurants, and first-class cellars. The route takes in the abbey in Novacella, Salorno, home of Gewürztraminer, Sauvignon, and Chardonnay wines, but also great Cabernets and Pinot Noirs.

There are two routes in Tuscany: one is the Chianti route, amid olive groves and fine wines, from Florence to Siena, along roads that

have bewitched hosts of visitors, to the Crete Senesi and Montalcino; the other traverses the hills of Maremma, through the region's largest wine zone, amid wild and storied landscapes. There are the wines of Bolgheri, but also some surprises, such as the Ciliegiolo.

An itinerary through Umbria combines the sweetness of the canvases of Perugino and the vine-covered hills of Lake Trasimeno, with the tradition of Torgiano and the robust notes of a Sagrantino di Montefalco.

The Sicilian itinerary, a circuit that starts in Palermo and continues with a visit off-island to Pantelleria, explores an extremely well-established wine world (Marsala, Muscat, Corvo), but also looks at other, more forward-looking developments that are defining an area in the midst of economic and productive ferment.

Finally there is a small piece in the mosaic of Italian wines — Collio Friulano — covered in the section that is beyond Italy's borders, an enclave within the Slovenian itinerary of Istria, Carso, and Collio.

Crests of vineyard-covered hills in the Langhe regions near Grinzane Cavour.

LANGHE

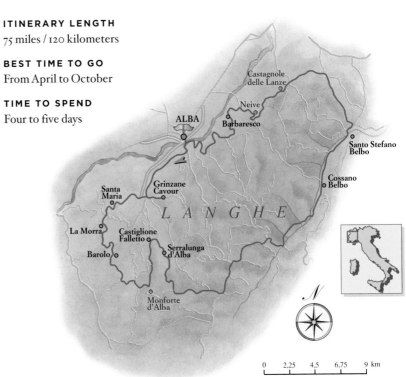

WINE TRAIL *Itinerary*

ITINERARY LENGTH
75 miles / 120 kilometers

BEST TIME TO GO
From April to October

TIME TO SPEND
Four to five days

USEFUL ADDRESSES

Ente Turismo Alba Bra Langhe e Roero
Palazzo Mostre e Congressi, piazza
Medford 3
Alba
Tel: 0173.358333
Fax: 0173.635251

Enoteca Regionale del Barbaresco
Piazza Falletti 1
Barolo
Tel: 0173.56277

THE AUTUMN, WHEN the leaves in the vine-yards are tinged with red and orange, is the best time to visit the Langhe, a strip of land filled with vivid tastes, history, and culture, which extends southwest of Monferrato until it comes up against the Ligurian Alps. This is the season for great oenological and gas-tronomical delights, with truffles and wines of world renown. Barolo and Barbaresco are made from grapes that find their ideal habitat in this fertile and lovely undulating land between Bormida and Tanaro. By summer's end "outsiders" can already be seen in La

Morra, trying to outbid one another for lots by the best producers of Barolo, on the occasion of the only auction in the world dedicated to this king of wines. In October, the race commences for the first white truffles. If one wishes to act decisively without being an expert, the precious *Tuber magnatum* can be pur-chased in specialty shops, which also often sell bottles of important vintages.

Some of the most renowned sellers are located right in the downtown area of **ALBA**, a compact medieval city full of tower houses. The old Via

OPPOSITE, FROM THE TOP: surveying the Langhe from an air balloon; a road that cuts through the vineyards; harvest time in Barolo; an interior of the Relais Santo Stefano in San Maurizio Belbo.

ABOVE: the hypermodern expansion of the Ceretto wine-producing facility, in Castiglione Falletto.

ABOVE: the majestic castle of Grinzane Cavour, which belonged to the family of Camillo Benso, who stayed there for a long period.

OPPOSITE PAGE: gastronomic riches of the Langhe on display at the I Piaceri del Gusto wine cellars in Alba.

Maestra, now the Via Vittorio Emanuele, is like an artery for regional gastronomic shopping, and important addresses can be found, zigzagging from one side of the street to another. The visitor should not leave Alba without stopping in one of the historic locales that re-create the ambience of "old Piedmont," especially the ancient Cantine Pio Cesare, founded in 1881, where high-quality wine has been produced for four generations.

THE WINE ROUTE
TRAVELING THROUGH THE LANGHE

Leaving Alba, the cultural and economic epicenter of the Langhe, one can head toward **GRINZANE CAVOUR**, which is heralded by the massive bulk of the castle where Camillo Benso, count of Cavour, was sent as a young man to oversee the family lands and vineyards and to cool his liberal instincts. This, too, should be included among the significant names in the history of Barolo, as it is generally understood today. From here the tilled fields, walnut trees, and

birch groves gradually disappear, replaced by vast vineyards, following the uneven terrain toward **LA MORRA**, which has a concentration of the most renowned wine masters. At dusk, looking at the crest of the hill, it is possible to witness a spectacle of nature: The setting sun illuminates the severe profile of the Monviso mountain, which stands out black against the fiery colors of the sky.

From Grinzane Cavour toward **SANTA MARIA**, the journey becomes panoramic and brightly colored. The abundant and orderly vineyards of Nebbiolo, Barbera, and Dolcetto are easily recog-

nizable in autumn: Before falling the leaves of Nebbiolo turn yellow, while the Barbera vegetation turns more reddish, and the Dolcetto vines tend toward pink. Arriving in **BORGATA TETTI**, near the church is a grand, late-nineteenth-century farmhouse, the general headquarters for the estates and cellars of Fratelli Oddero, one of the greatest dynasties in the Barolo region. After a series of hairpin turns around a row of hills, the road arrives at the upper piazza of La Morra, where an enchanting vista opens up and it is possible to appreciate the harmony that ties the people to the earth in this region.

THE LANDS OF BAROLO

Halfway up the hill, in the direction of Barolo, is Elio Altare's wine business, one of the first to follow Angelo Gaja's revolutionary idea to place wine in barrels; his wines convey the meticulous research he has carried out for years. Near the Abbey of the Annunziata is another historic wine business: Renato Ratti, where in addition to tasting a great Barolo Marcenasco, it is possible to visit the Alba wine museum created within the walls of the centuries-old

LEFT: the painted Barolo Chapel, not far from Alba, symbolizes today's Langhe region.
FOLLOWING PAGES: the colors and geometries of the vineyards around Grinzane Cavour.

abbey. There are old bottles, equipment, and documents that tell the story of winemaking in the Langhe.

Not to be missed is a visit to the brightly colored Barolo chapel, on the Ceretto property in **BRUNATE**, which has leant its name to one of the most important and famous Barolo wines. The explosion of color on the old building, built by a well-off farmer in 1914 but never consecrated, was brought about a few years ago by two artists—David Tremlett, from Britain, and American minimalist Sol LeWitt— who turned it into a symbolic image of the Langhe.

Descending to the amphitheater, passing through a surprisingly geometric vineyard landscape, one arrives at the thousand-year-old castle of **BAROLO**, birthplace of the prestigious wine of the same name, whose history is interwoven with the Risorgimento and the unification of Italy. The manor, in the Falletti family as far back as the fourteenth century, emerges from amid the red rooftops of the houses located strategically in a hollow exposed to the sun and protected from the wind. It was the Marchesa Giulia Colbert de Maulévrier (1786–1864), wife of Carlo Tancredi Falletti, who was the force behind the creation of the modern Barolo, working with Louis Oudart, a French enologist. With its intense taste and aromatic bouquet, it was said to be appreciated even by King Carlo Alberto. Until that time the wine had been known by the name of the grape variety, Nebbiolo, but the marchesa renamed it

PERSONALITIES *Elio Altare*

"Once there was Langa, a very poor land . . . " Reticent Elio Altare, speaking about himself and his wine, always starts with the region and with those who came before and made the land great. He explains: "It is a moral obligation to recognize that if Barolo reached the top of the international rankings and is sought after throughout the world, I do not take credit for this. I can say I was quick to follow the great Angelo Gaja's propensity for revitalization, to take inspiration from the winegrowers of Burgundy, and to learn a great deal from [Paul] Pontallier, the oenologist of Château Margaux. But I don't forget that until the seventies I was cultivating my vineyard with oxen, and it was only then that I began to use machinery and to honestly compare myself with those who were doing better, competing on equal terms with other producers. We need to remember the historic winegrowers, those who maintained Barolo's high reputation during dark times. To mention a few: Paolo Cordero (thirty years ago in the United States, he was Barolo), Aldo and Giovanni Conterno, Alfredo Prunotto, Pio Cesare, Giuseppe and Bartolo Mascarello. We,

the new generation, began to be involved with producing higher-quality wine, and success began coming step by step with the slowing down of the exodus of young people to industrial centers. It was a team effort, and there were about fifteen of us. When we began the revolution we were all hungry. . . and so we tried so many different things, experiments, comparisons with samples. We also asked customers for their opinions about wines at blind tastings, and the owner of the sample that received the best results explained to the others what he had done in the cellar and in the vineyard. In this way we achieved our early results and my first pupils, including Renato Corino, who was following in his father's footsteps. I am convinced that wine is an interpretation that cannot be codified. It is a continuous evolution: First wine was a staple, now it is a pleasure. However, my great accomplishment is to have created a dream, and it is a success that pleases me." Today the company's production stands at about 50,000 bottles a year. Altare is considered a master, and his Barolo Vigneto Arborina is a masterpiece of the region.

RIGHT: harvest time: vats brimming with clusters of Nebbiolo grapes that, in time, will be turned into prestigious Barolo wines.

OPPOSITE PAGE, FROM TOP: the ancient Relais San Maurizio in Santo Stefano Belbo; a phantasmagoric "tunnel" of bottles at the Le Torri di Alba wine center.

after the region, Barolo. The castle cellars house the Enoteca Regionale, the regional wine center; the piano nobile is occupied by Marchesa Falletti's quarters, the rooms of the librarian Silvio Pellico, the *sala rossa*—the seventeenth-century hall with the family coat of arms—and the gallery.

The yellow house that faces—one might say almost challenges—the Falletti castle and austerely dominates the town is the historic headquarters of the Tenuta Opera Pia Barolo, later the cellars of the Marchesi of Barolo. They are the producers of Barolo Cannubi, an elegant and intensely perfumed wine, garnet in color with ruby reflections, and Barolo Sarmassa, a wine with excellent body.

Leaving this special hill, the wine trail continues toward **MONFORTE D'ALBA**, skirting a placid sea of vineyards, a terrain in transition between two different geographic systems tied to different grapes. The landscape here opens up, sweeping as far as the castle of Serralunga. Monforte is home to the Azienda Agricola Elio Grasso, overlooking the Langhe. Surrounded by rows of vines, the road continues toward **CASTIGLIONE FALLETTO**, dominated by the imposing quadrangular fortress, contested over the centuries by important patrician families.

At the summit of the Bricco Rocche, the geographic center of the Barolo region, is another modern and highly technological work of art, on the property owned by Ceretto winegrowers. Created in 1999 on the occasion of the expansion of the existing

cellar and production facilities, the large glass cube, supported with steel cables and featuring sharp edges and a solid base, easily evokes the initial sharpness of the wine, as well as its robust structure and great staying power over time.

ALONG THE BELBO VALLEY

From here the road descends to the crossroads for **SERRALUNGA** with its long, narrow castle, which originally was a lookout tower, then on toward **RODDINO**. The landscape becomes more severe and is divided between the extemporaneous nature of the woods and the orderly vines that spread out as the journey continues into the Belbo valley. Highway 592 leads to **COSSANO BELBO**, where one finds the Mulino Marino, a mill that still uses an old-style millstone, and where it is possible to buy white flour (needed for making tagliatelle and ravioli) made from organic wheat.

Farther along is **SANTO STEFANO BELBO**, home of author Cesare Pavese (1980–1950) and the setting for a twentieth-century literary masterpiece, *The Moon and the Bonfire*. The Centro Studi Cesare Pavese is located in a lovely house in the center of town and has a wealth of information about the writer, his life, and the local places mentioned in his works; the museum archive also contains some unpublished works and original books, which can be consulted, as well as a photographic exhibition of Pavese-related sites.

FOLLOWING PAGES: **Alba, the wood and stones of the ancient Pio Cesare cellars.**

175

TASTES *Truffles and* trifulau

Every weekend in the fall until mid-November, the finest palates from Europe gather in the Maddalena courtyard in Alba, among the stands of the town's white truffle market, to stock up on the precious mushroom sold by merchants and *trifulau*, as the hunters are called. The strong, composite odor of this mushroom (mushroom, mind you, not tuber) can sometimes be confusing. It must be harmonious, and the fragrances of garlic, honey, hay, or spices should be detectable. To learn more about them, particularly to get tips before buying them, take one of the tasting courses organized by the Centro Nazionale Studi Tartufo (tel. 0173.35833 for reservations) every Saturday and Sunday from 9 am to noon, until November 26, in Grinzane Cavour, where the Enoteca Regionale Piemonte Cavour has its offices.

Alba, two dishes (with truffles) at the Osteria Vento di Langa.

TAKE A BREAK

LODGING

Alba: **PALAZZO FINATI**
8, via Vernazza
Tel: 0173.366684
www.palazzofinati.com
In the shadow of the duomo in Alba, an
early-nineteenth-century palace has been
transformed into a charming hotel.

Santo Stefano Belbo: **RELAIS SAN MAURIZIO**
Località San Maurizio 39
Tel: 0141.841900
www.relaissanmaurizio.it
A seventeenth-century monastery has
been returned to its early splendor (with
modern touches) in the heart of the
Langhe, with an acclaimed wine-therapy
center.

DINING

Alba: **OSTERIA VENTO DI LANGHA**
20, via Elvio Pertinace
Tel: 0173.293282
This up-and-coming restaurant offers
classic dishes with a creative touch made
by Elena, the young chef who enjoys
readapting old Piedmontese recipes.

Barolo: **LOCANDA NEL BORGO ANTICO**
2, Piazza Municipio
Tel: 0173.56355
Chef Massimo Camia is in a class by
himself but puts on no airs. He creates
and invents dishes based on typical
recipes, tied to regional flavors but also
taking risks with bold juxtapositions.
The pastry is a delight to behold, and
the wine list is excellent.

Monforte d'Alba: **IL GIARDINO DI FELICIN**
18, via Vallada
Tel: 0173-78225
Traditional, but not too much so, would
be an apt description of the style of this
restaurant in Monforte, where for three
generations they have been serving typical regional dishes with a personal touch.
Classic *tajarin* (egg noodles) and ravioli
without meat are served with a salad of
ovuli mushrooms and paté, all with truffles. They make their own bread and use
only extra-virgin olive oil. The cellar has
over 12,000 bottles, from 1956 to recent
years. The upper floor has thirteen quiet
rooms furnished with antiques.

THIS PAGE, FROM THE LEFT: a Barbaresco of the Marchesi Grésy; making pasta at the Felicin restaurant; grinding wheat at the Mulino Marino in Cassano Belbo.

OPPOSITE PAGE: Castiglione Falletto, Bricco Rocche: steel vats at the Ceretto wine.

The brand-new Relais San Maurizio hotel is hidden on a hillside, overlooking a superb panorama of vineyards and castles, in a centuries-old park. In the seventeenth century it was the site of a monastery, built by the Franciscan friars as a place where they could follow a life of rigid sobriety, far from the world's temptations. The monks spent their days not only in prayer, but also cultivating the vines that were essential for the economy of the region. The new wellness center, which overlooks the vineyards of San Maurizio, is carved into the tufa stone of the garden, where they grow the ingredients used for wine-based cures in the "Thermarium."

Descending, the landscape one again becomes gentle and rounded. The vines become thicker further toward **BARBARESCO**, once again in the vicinity of Alba, where, some twenty years later than Barolo, a local wine was born that now has an international reputation as one of the finest expressions of Italian oenology.

The journey through this beautiful region continues after a tasting at Tenuta Cisa Adinari, owned by the Marchesi of Grésy. Positioned amid the area's most prized vineyards are the little village and a regional wine center in a tiny deconsecrated Baroque church; tastings of all the great Barbaresco wines take place beneath the frescoed walls.

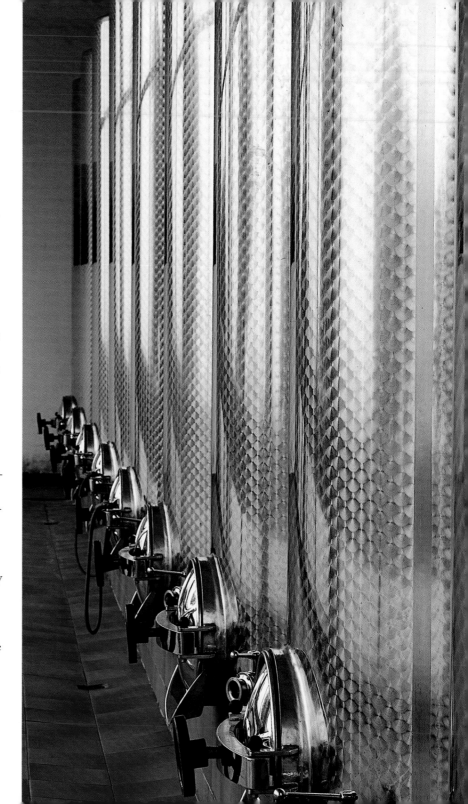

LABELS TO LOOK FOR

GAJA

36, via Torino
Barbaresco
Tel: 0173.635158

Founded: 1859
Production region: Barbaresco, Treiso, Alba,
Serralunga, La Morra
Wine and grape varieties: 8% whites,
92% reds; Chardonnay, Nebbiolo,
Barbera, Cabernet Sauvignon

GREAT WINES

Gaia Rey 1994
Pure Chardonnay from a vineyard planted
in 1973. Intense straw-yellow with golden
reflections. Full, powerful, complex, and
persistent bouquet, with hints of ripe fruit,
acacia honey, vanilla, and elderberry. Dry,
full, opulent, and balanced taste. Notes of
tobacco, sandalwood, and spices. Can be
aged for ten to fifteen years. Complements
first courses, white meat and baked fish.

SPERSS '97
Made from 94 percent Nebbiolo and 6
percent Barbera grapes from Serralunga.
Intense ruby-red color. Full, complex, harmonious, and lingering bouquet, with
hints of minerals, sour cherry, ripe fruit,
and rare wood. Dry, powerful taste of
notable refinement and complexity, with
notes of cherry, tar, and licorice. Exciting,
extremely long aftertaste with mentholated hints. Should be drunk after twelve
to fifteen years, and up to fifty to sixty
years. A wonderful complement to grilled
meats, chops, stewed rabbit, lamb, and
not excessively aged cheeses.

Visits and tastings: no

MARCHESI DI BAROLO

12, via Alba
Barolo
Tel: 0173.564400
www.marchesibarolo.com

Founded: 1861
Production region: Municipality of Barolo
Wines and grape varieties: 85% reds,
15% whites; Nebbiolo, Barbera, Dolcetto,
Cabernet Sauvignon, Moscato d'Asti

GREAT WINES

Barolo Cannubi 1998
Made from pure Nebbiolo grapes from
the Cannubi vineyard. Garnet-red color
with ruby reflections. Very intense, full,
and lingering perfume, with hints of rose,
vanilla, walnut, licorice, and spices. Full-
bodied to the palate, austere and powerful, with great elegance and balance.
Should be aged at length, and an ideal
complement to stews and game.

Barolo Sarmassa 1997
Made from pure Nebbiolo grapes from
the Samassa vineyard. Intense ruby-red
color, bouquet of red berries, particularly
currant, vanilla, licorice, and mentholated
hints. Dry, powerful, honest, and complex
taste, with considerable balance between
body and acidity. Can be aged at length,
and is a perfect complement to game and
stewed meats.

Visits and tastings: yes

ELIO ALTARE

Cascina Nuova, frazione Annunziata 51
La Morra
Tel: 0173.50835
www.elioaltare.com

Founded: 1948
Production region: Dogliani, La Morra,
Castiglione Falletto, Serralunga
Wines and grape varieties: 100% reds;
Nebbiolo, Barbera, Dolcetto, Cabernet
Sauvignon, Syrah

GREAT WINES

Barolo Vigneto Arborina 1999
Made from pure Nebbiolo grapes from
the Arborina vineyard. Ruby-red color
tending toward garnet. Full, complex bouquet of great refinement and persistence,
with mentholated hints and notes of wild
fruit, cherry, and vanilla. Balanced, elegant, refined, and velvety to the mouth.
Extremely long aftertaste with notes of
elderberry and licorice. Should be drunk
young or can be aged for twenty years. Use
as a table wine.

Langhe Larigi 2001
Made from pure Barbera grapes. Intense
ruby-red color with purplish-blue reflections. Full, fine, and lingering bouquet,
with notes of red berry, undergrowth, and
cherries in brandy, against a slightly mineral base of graphite. Dry, powerful, elegant, and balanced taste. Should be aged
for ten to fifteen years, and goes with
corned tongue, *bollito misto*, and *bagna
cauda*.

Visits and tastings: yes

FRATELLI ODDERO

La Morra
Tel: 0173.50618
www.odderofratelli.it

Founded: 1878
Production region: La Morra, Monforte
d'Alba, Serralunga d'Alba, Castiglione
Falletto
Wines and grape varieties: 95% reds, 5%
whites; Chardonnay, Nebbiolo, Barbera,
Dolcetto, Cabernet Sauvignon, Freisa

GREAT WINES

Barolo Vigna Rionda 1998
Made from pure Nebbiolo grapes from
the Vigna Rionda vineyard in the municipality of Serralunga d'Alba. Traditional
vinification in red fermenters and subsequent aging in wood for two years.
Brilliant garnet-red color, intense, complex, and lingering perfume, with hints of
fruit, undergrowth, and hay. Powerful,
masculine in the mouth, rich with
extracts, very fruity, with notes of licorice.
Quite long-lasting, will improve with
aging. Complements stewed meats.

Barolo Mondoca di Bussia Soprana 1998
Made from pure Nebbiolo grapes from
the homonymous vineyard in the municipality of Monforte. Traditional vinification in red fermenters and subsequent
aging in wood for two years. Brilliant
garnet-red color, lingering, delicate bouquet of great refinement. Dry, decisive,
austere, and harmonious taste. Long and
clean aftertaste. Ages well, an ideal complement for large roasts.

Visits and tastings: yes, by appointment

RENATO RATTI

Antiche cantine dell'abbazia
dell'Annunziata, frazione Annunziata
La Morra
Tel: 0173.50185
www.renatoratti.com

Founded: 1965
Production region: Municipality of
La Morra, Novello, Mango d'Alba,
and Costigliole d'Asti
Wines and grape varieties: 100% red;
Dolcetto, Barbera, Nebbiolo de Barolo,
Cabernet Sauvignon, Merlot

GREAT WINES

Barolo Marcenasco Rocche 1999
Made from Nebbiolo grapes harvested by
hand in the Rocche dell'Annunziata vineyard. Intense garnet-red color, characterized by a rather persistent bouquet of wild
fruits, cherries in brandy, vanilla, tobacco,
and spices. Dry, powerful, and austere but
elegant to the palate. Long and clean
aftertaste with memories of licorice.
Should be kept in a cellar for at least ten
years, and goes well with dishes based on
meat in sauce.

Barolo Marcerasco Conca 1999
Made from Nebbiolo grapes harvested in
the Conca vineyard in La Morra.
Produced only in great years. Full and persistent bouquet with fruity hints, particularly of morello cherry and raspberry,
wood, and vanilla. Dry, powerful taste,
still a bit rough but quite promising, with
a long and clean aftertaste, rich in mentholated hints. A robust wine, complements strong dishes based on game and
aged cheeses.

Visits and tastings: yes, by appointment

ELIO GRASSO

40, Località Ginestra
Monforte d'Alba
Tel: 0173-50185
elio.grasso@isiline.it

Founded: 1928
Production region: Monforte d'Alba
Wines and grape varieties: 5% whites;
95% reds; Nebbiolo, Barbera, Dolcetto,
Chardonnay

GREAT WINES

Barolo Gavarini Vigna Chiniera 1998
Made from Nebbiolo grapes from the
Chiniera vineyard in Monforte d'Alba.
Intense garnet-red color. Full perfume,
complex and persistent, with blackberry
and spices. Dry, powerful, seductive taste,
with considerable presence of sweet tannins. Will need ten to twenty years to find
its maximum expression. Goes well with
cheeses and braised meats.

Barolo Runcot 1997
Made from Nebbiolo grapes from the
Runcot vineyard in Monforte d'Alba.
After vinification in steel, it ages for
thirty months in new barrels of French
oak. Intense garnet-red color, with a full
and persistent bouquet, with hints of wild
rose, wild fruits, tobacco, and licorice.
Dry, powerful, and elegant taste.
Excellent for aging, and goes well with
braised meats and hard, aged cheeses.

Visits and tastings: yes, by appointment

CERETTO

34, Località San Cassiano
Alba
Tel: 0173.282582
www.ceretto.com

Founded: 1937
Production region: La Morra, Serralunga,
Castiglione Falletto
Wines and grape varieties: 50% reds,
50% whites; Arneis, Nebbiolo, Barbera,
Dolcetto, Cabernet Sauvignon, Pinot
Noir, Merlot, Riesling, Moscato d'Asti

GREAT WINES

Barolo Bricco Rocche 1998
Made from pure Nebbiolo grapes from
the Castiglione Falletto vineyard.
Impenetrable ruby-red color, with a full,
complex, and very persistent bouquet,
with hints of rose, violet, and spices. Dry,
powerful, sumptuous, and velvety taste,
with great balance between tannins and
acidity. Can be drunk young but improves
in fifteen to twenty years after bottling.
Goes well with roasts and stewed meats.

Barolo Asili Barbaresco Bernadot 1999
Made from pure Nebbiolo grapes from
the Bernadot vineyard in the municipality
of Treiso. Garnet-red color, with a full and
persistent perfume and hints of violet, red
berry fruits, and tobacco. Powerful, complex, elegant, and quite balanced to the
palate. Can be aged for long periods and
enjoyed with game.

Visits and tastings: yes, by appointment

PIO CESARE

6, via Cesare Balbo
Alba
Tel: 0173.440386

Founded: 1881
Production region: Serralunga d'Alba,
Grinzane Cavour, La Morra, Treiso,
Novello, Sinio d'Alba, and Diano d'Alba
Wines and grape varieties: 20% whites,
80% reds; Nebbiolo, Barbera, Dolcetto,
Freisa, Grignolino, Cortese, Chardonnay,
Arneis, Moscato d'Alba

GREAT WINES

Ornato 1998
Made from select Nebbiolo grapes from
certain "special" rows on the Cascina
Ornato property in Serralunga d'Alba.
Intense ruby color with garnet reflections, a full and persistent bouquet with
hints of red berry, plum, cocoa, and
licorice. Richly structured in the mouth,
concentrated and powerful, with a long
and elegant aftertaste. Can be quite long-
lasting, goes well with stews and with
meats in red wine–based sauces.

Barbaresco Il Bricco 1998
Made from selected Nebbiolo grapes from
specific rows in the vineyards of Cascina
Bricco, in the municipality of Treiso.
Intense garnet-red color and full and persistent perfume, with hints of ripe fruit
and spices. Dry, powerful taste, rich in
extracts and tannins. Long aftertaste with
notes of wild fruit. Should be aged for at
least a decade, and goes well with game.

Visits and tastings: no

ALTO ADIGE
SOUTH TYROL

WINE TRAIL *Itinerary*

ITINERARY LENGTH
75 miles / 120 kilometers

BEST TIME TO GO
May to October

TIME TO SPEND
The distances are short; everything
depends on the duration of the visit
(and the inclination to linger...)

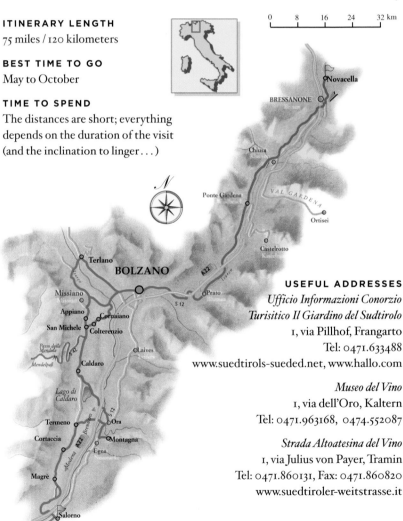

USEFUL ADDRESSES
*Ufficio Informazioni Conorzio
Turisitico Il Giardino del Sudtirolo*
1, via Pillhof, Frangarto
Tel: 0471.633488
www.suedtirols-sueded.net, www.hallo.com

Museo del Vino
1, via dell'Oro, Kaltern
Tel: 0471.963168, 0474.552087

Strada Altoatesina del Vino
1, via Julius von Payer, Tramin
Tel: 0471.860131, Fax: 0471.860820
www.suedtiroler-weitstrasse.it

NEARLY EVERYONE HAS passed through
these valleys: first the Reti, Etruscans, and Romans,
then the Goths, Swabians, Huns, Visigoths, and
Ostrogoths; crowned heads going to Rome, with their
retinues, to receive a papal investiture; pilgrims, merchants, and soldiers. Whether spurred on by noble,
religious, or bellicose intentions, they all passed
through Alto Adige, or South Tyrol, a land characterized by its widely varied landscape that over the centuries has preserved splendid evidence of the region's

colorful past. It is also a land that has always been tied
to the cultivation of grapes and to wine production.

The Alto Adige wine trail is located in the northernmost wine region in Italy. Rows of vines blanket
the hills, almost brushing up against the mountains. It
is a spectacular and bucolic setting, the result of a
laborious commitment by generation after generation
of winegrowers.

In the early Christian era the cultivation of vines
was encouraged by the Roman legionaries. Later in the

OPPOSITE PAGE, FROM TOP:
harvest in Alto Adige;
driving outside Santa
Maddalena/Sankt Magda-
lena; a colt leaping among
the vines; bottles in a
Cornaiano/Girlan cellar.

ABOVE: a view of the
monastery of Sabiona,
slightly north of
Chiusa/Klausen.

OPPOSITE: an expanse of
vines proceeds in an
orderly fashion along the
wine trail.

THIS PAGE: an elderly
woman farmer harvesting
grapes by hand.

Middle Ages, when Alto Adige became a crossroads
between the Germanic and Latin worlds, the first international wine trade began with the Teutonic monasteries. During Charlemagne's empire, many bishops and
fifty convents in southern Germany chose South Tyrol
to provide them with wine, thereby encouraging production far in advance of neighboring regions.

In the early twentieth century winegrowing here
reached its greatest expansion, with a cultivated area
of almost 25,000 acres (over 10,000 hectares) and 60
percent of the total production of light, reasonably
priced red wine, which crossed the border to central
Europe (since at that time South Tyrol was part of
Austria). Today the winegrowing area has been
reduced by half, due to urbanization and a boom in
fruit growing.

The principal production areas are located in the
Adige valley, between Merano/Meran and
Salorno/Salurn, and in the Isarco valley, between
Bressanone/Brixen and Bolzano/Bozen. The varied
landscape, charming with its gentle hills, arbors, and
terraces framed against the backdrop of the rock walls
of the Dolomites, corresponds to a great variety of
grapes due to the favorable climatic conditions and
the vineyards' diverse terrain and exposure. Alto
Adige's indigenous grape varieties are Lagrein,
recently discovered and always used for blending,
Schiava (or Vernatsch), and Traminer Aromatico, from
which is made a spiced white wine known throughout
the world. For over a century, however, grapes with

ABOVE: **The splendid land-scape of vineyards along the Alto Adige wine trail.**

OPPOSITE: **An image of the Ristorante Zur Rose.**

origins in Bordeaux, Burgundy, and the Rhineland have also been cultivated (including Pinot Nero, Merlot, and Cabernet Sauvignon for the reds, and Pinot Blanc, Pinot Grigio, Chardonnay, Riesling, Sauvignon, Sylvaner, Veltliner, Müller-Thurgau, Moscato Rosa, and Moscato Giallo for the whites).

Although the production percentage of reds (66 percent) is considerably greater than that of whites (34 percent), it is really the variety of the latter that embodies the greatness of the region's wine and its potential for the future.

THE WINE ROUTE
THE ABBEY OF NOVACELLA AND THE WINE'S ORIGINS

A wine itinerary in the Alto Adige, along with the region's history, begins in the vineyards and cellars of the Abbazia dell'Ordine dei Canonici Regolari di Sant'Agostino di Novacella—or more briefly, the abbey of Novacella, just north of Bressanone/Brixen. This imposing architectural gem comprises buildings from different eras and is situated in the Isarco valley. It was founded in 1142 by Bishop (later Saint) Hartmann, with the help of the governor of Sabiona

TAKE A BREAK

LODGING

Appiano: **HOTEL SCHLOSS KORB**
Tel: 0471.636000
www.highlight-hotels.com/korb
This fourteenth-century-style hotel has a large
terrace overlooking the Catinaccio mountains
and their vineyards.

Caldaro: **SCHLOSSHOTEL AERENTAL**
Tel: 0471.962222
www.schlosshotel.it
A luxurious seventeenth-century castle has been
converted to a hotel with a refined atmosphere.

DINING

Appiano: **RISTORANTE ZUR ROSE**
2, via Josef Jnnerhofer
Tel: 0471.662249
Herbert Hintner, the artist-chef, creatively
combines ancient flavors and modern tastes,
while his wife, Margot, the sommelier, oversees
the 650 labels on the wine list.

Caldaro: **RISTORANTE
CASTEL RINGBERG**
1, via San Giussepe al Lago
Tel: 0471.960010
www.castel-ringberg.com
Diners can now enjoy regional dishes with
Mediterranean and Asian influences alongside
a good regional wine list.

Terlano: **RISTORANTE WEINGARTEN**
Tel: 0471.257888
An informal setting for traditional dishes.

Cortaccia: **RISTORANTE ZUR ROSE**
2, via Endergasse
Tel: 0471.880116
Arno Baldo and his wife offer excellent
regional dishes with imaginative touches.

Regimberto and his consort Cristina, and from the
beginning it offered refuge to pilgrims traveling to the
Holy Land or passing through on their way to papal
Rome. There are many reasons, in addition to the
spiritual, to visit this architectural complex. For those
who are ardent about history and literature, an
archive and library abound with rare books, illuminated manuscripts and rococo stuccowork; for those
who love art, there are the paintings and proportions
of the architecture itself; and for wine enthusiasts,
there is the cellar, where wines produced on the property can be sampled.

A view of the sumptuous private cellar of the four-teenth-century Schloss Korb, near Appiano.

Traveling the little country roads that wind up and down the surrounding hills, it is the rows of vines that draw the gaze to the abbey, whose lands also include the Markhof estate near **CORNAIANO/ GIRLAN**, in the heart of the principal production region of Alto Adige, and another vineyard at the small convent of Santa Maria, on the outskirts of **BOLZANO**. The sandy, dry terrain and airy climate of these hills result in excellent red wines, good for aging, which include those made in the abbey's cellars. Leaving Novacella, the itinerary continues in search of Alto Adige's ancient winemaking tradition.

PERFUMES OF WHITES IN THE ISARCO VALLEY AND THE VAL D'ADIGE

Descending toward Bolzano along the Isarco River, the traveler approaches the land of Santa Maddalena, one of the most spectacularly beautiful regions on this journey. Small farmsteads and family businesses here produce excellent wines from Schiava grapes. The road, which rises toward the plateau of Renon/Ritten, traverses an area of steep vineyards that frame the Sciliar and Catinaccio massifs. Take the time to visit the Waldgries winery, where Heinrich Plattner produces Langrein, an excellent Pinot Bianco, Pinot Grigio, and Santa Maddalena, and a Moscato Rosa Passito that is much sought after by German tourists. The itinerary continues on to **BOLZANO/BOZEN**, a city that now encompasses

the old municipality of Gries, autonomous until 1925 and home to the Lagrein grape. The latter is one of the oldest indigenous grape varieties in Italy, already praised by Charles IV as the best wine of Bolzano in a rural ordinance of 1370. Some of the finest wine producers have a presence on the central piazza: Gries Kellerei and Muri-Gries Benedictine Convent, whose members—following the rule of their order to *ora et labora*, or pray and work—supplement their prayer with the production of an excellent wine.

Surrounded by vineyards that ascend and descend the hilly terrain, the road leads to **TERLANO/TERLAN**—home of the famous Terlaner Weissburgunder and also known for the cultivation of white asparagus that in this region often accompanies a young, cool Sauvignon. Val d'Adige, all apple orchards and vineyards, is the birthplace of an important chapter in regional wine cultivation. In 1953, when many were criticizing the perfumed and somewhat "feminine" wines produced in the region, Sebastian Stocker, *kellemeister* of the community cellar, was a confident supporter of the whites from these well-drained terrains, which receive constant exposure to the sun and are oriented to the south. Indeed, he claimed they would become symbolic of the wine cellar's production. Thanks to his intuition and to the gradual transition of the vineyards from the traditional arbor system to a guyot vine-training method, excellent Gewürztraminers and Sauvignons are now produced, along with an unforgettable

PERSONALITIES   *Alois Lageder*

Alois Lageder has a love of wine in his DNA—even as a child, he cheerfully played in his family's vineyards and wine cellar. This is how he describes it in a calm, tranquil tone, and yet he is a decision-maker, convinced that in a few years he has succeeded in transforming his land, worked for 150 years according to the most traditional cultivation methods, into a high-tech operation, one of the most environmentally advanced in the world.

The historic buildings on the Löwengang estate in Magrè were expanded, applying ecologically conscious and environmental building solutions with low energy consumption and natural colors. The photovoltaic power plant installed in 1996 is the high point of these improvements. "Beneath the sun of Alto Adige grapes of excellent quality have always ripened," Lageder explains. "I wanted to use this same

positive energy to build the company."

"The decision to renovate the buildings in the most natural way was also pursued in the cellar, following two fundamental concepts: the force of gravity and the circular form. The vinification tower, 46 feet [14 meters] tall, benefits from the application of these principles. Taking advantage of the difference in height, the grapes, the must, and the wine drop downward without the use of mechanical means, to the great benefit of the wine's quality."

Integrated wine production, biodynamic methods, and self-produced compost with stalks and leaves, coupled with the phases of the moon as a guide for working the land and the music of Bach playing where the wine is aged whenever the wind awakens the turbine located outside: This is the language of Alto Adige's foremost private producer of wine.

Terlaner that is capable of remaining full of life and fresh for decades.

It is useful to know that the community wine cellars of Alto Adige, unlike in other regions of Italy, often represent the qualitative apex of local production.

IN THE VAL D'ADIGE, AMID VINEYARDS AND CASTLES

After crossing the Adige River, the itinerary continues toward the **APPIANO/EPPAN** production region, which boasts one of the greatest concentrations of castles, fortresses, and noble residences in Europe. A winding road of curves and hairpin turns that cut through the vineyards leads to the Hotel Schloss Korb, a romantic fourteenth-century manor house with a large terrace that overlooks the Catinaccio mountains and rows of vines. From here, continuing on foot along the dirt path that enters the woods, one arrives at the ruins of Boymont castle and a spectacular setting opens up that stretches from Bolzano to the Dolomites.

Moving downstream, the road passes the late-Gothic parish church of San Paolo—known as the "country cathedral" for its unusual sixteenth-century bell tower rising 275 feet (85 meters) tall, and its onion dome—before arriving at the lovely village of **CORNAIANO/GIRLAN**. Here, the wine cellars carved out of the clay earth were connected to each other by an effective tunnel system to drain off rainwater into the Adige. Today many of the tunnels and

canals have caved in or been closed because they are no longer usable. Visitors to the Niedermayr winery can sample and purchase wine and visit the small, private museum. Inside, in addition to the many wine-making implements, there is a cart with vats that the family once used to deliver wine to local inns and

ABOVE, FROM TOP: costumes, smiles, and local color.

hotels. The **COLTERENZIO/SCHRECKBICHL** cooperative, also worth a visit, has become famous for the Cornelius line, an expression of the highest quality vintages.

The next stop is **SAN MICHELE/SANKT MICHAEL-EPPAN**, whose community cellar, the pride of the regional wines, produces the mythic Sauvignon of the Sanct Valentin line, as well as a great Chardonnay.

colored palaces face onto the main piazza, along with the old Signoria di Caldaro-Laimburg hospital, which houses a wine museum that contains documents related to the centuries-old history of wine production in the region.

The antique objects on display in the museum include the original costume of the land warden, which in itself is a work of art. This guardian of the vineyards was armed with a large knife and dressed in terrifying fashion; from Assumption Day (August 15) until the third Sunday of October, he was responsible for discouraging grape thieves. An exception was made for the poor and for pregnant women who were permitted to gather a few grapes, but on the condition that they ate them on the spot. The land warden position no longer exists, but there lingers a memory of this personality, who terrorized and deterred would-be thieves for generations.

Caldaro also has the picturesque Erste & Neue wine cellar, completely frescoed in 2000 on the occasion of the centennial of its founding.

Descending toward the Lake Caldaro/Kalterersee, as an alternative to the main road a scenic route climbs up to Monte di Sotto and then descends again in the vicinity of **ORA/AUER**. From here, a detour of a few miles leads to the town of **MONTAGNA/ MONTAN**, home to the Franz Haas winery. The splendid Manna, a Riesling blend from a late harvest of Traminer Aromatico, Sauvignon, and Chardonnay, and the Pinot Nero are worth tasting.

THIS PAGE: vineyards as far as the eye can see along the Weinstrasse.

FROM CELLAR TO CELLAR, FROM CALDARO TO SALORNO

The itinerary continues to **CALDARO/KALTERN**, an extremely charming village set amid the vineyards that slope down to the lake of the same name. Pastel-

193

RIGHT: barrel-making implements.

BELOW: barrels in the community cellar in San Michele.

Ten minutes or so away, the road reaches **TERMENO/TRAMIN**, realm of the mythic Gewürztraminer. Right in the main piazza, in the shadow of the centuries-old bell tower, is a building that combines aesthetics and functionality using typical regional materials such as wood and iron, along with cement and steel. Inside is the Hofstätter wine cellar, which produces a much-admired Pinot Nero: Urban Villa Barthenau. This vineyard also has reduced its production in favor of quality to obtain grapes that are more concentrated and rich in extracts.

A little farther along is the property of Elena Walch, one of the few women in the Alto Adige wine world. Her best vineyards, which are truly spectacular, are those that surround the seventeenth-century Castel Ringberg and the Kastelaz estate.

A few miles separate Termeno from **CORTACCIA/KURTATSCH**. Proceeding up to Castel Turmhof Tiefenbrunner, it is possible to taste the Feldmarschall, made with Müller-Thurgau grapes cultivated at an altitude of over 3,200 feet (1,000 meters). The garden and pond in front of the castle are decorated with curious figures and masks created by Johan Tifentaler, a wine producer and cheerful philosopher who took pleasure in frescoing and decorating his property with allegorical statues and images.

A stop in **MAGRÈ/MARGREID** is unforgettable thanks to the wines of Alois Lageder, who set up production with invaluable advice from Robert Mondavi, the California wine king, and whose wines are now much sought after throughout the world (see inset on page 190).

Then the road suddenly descends toward the plain. Here the arbors and vineyards that embellish the gentle slopes and hills fall away into other type of cultivation, bringing the Alto Adige wine trail to its conclusion in **SALORNO**.

PERSONALITIES   *Elena Walch*   IL PERSONAGGIO

Enchanted by the precious inlay work of the bottles in her family wine cellar in Termeno/Tramin and by the beauty of their two properties—Castel Ringberg, on Lake Caldaro, and the Kastelaz estate, a hill that dominates Termeno—Elena Walch decided to close her architecture office in Milan and devote herself to making wine.

She immediately became one of the most innovative producers, accepting the qualitative challenge that the market requires of Alto Adige labels. Her husband, Werner Walch, descendant of one of the oldest wine dynasties in Alto Adige and owner of the historic Wilhelm Walch winery founded in 1869, had faith in her and entrusted her with the two family jewels: the hillside vineyards of Castel Ringberg and Kastelaz.

She made her debut with two labels: Istrice, made from Cabernet Sauvignon (85 percent) and Cabernet Franc (15 percent), with a robust flavor; and Chardonnay Cardellino, with a pronounced hint of fruit. Working with intuition and passion, Walch has pushed to qualitatively transform her vineyards, replanting them and setting them up to produce low yields per acre with selected clonal grapes, maintaining both indigenous vines and international varieties. Wherever possible she has introduced the most modern guyot methods in place of the traditional Alto Adige pergola system. Her international success was consolidated with the Gewürztraminer Kastelaz, made from rigorously selected grapes, fermented and aged in steel. Her latest creation is "Beyond the Clouds," an evocative and international name for a blend that is linked to the colors and scents of her beloved Alto Adige.

ALOIS LAGEDER, TENUTA LÖWENGANG

Magreid
Tel: 0471.809500
www.lageder.com

Founded: 1855
Production region: Magrè, Cortaccia, Termeno, Caldaro, Bolzano
Wines and grape varieties: 40% whites, 60% reds; Pinot Bianco, Chardonnay, Pinot Grigio, Traminer Aromatico, Sauvignon Blanc, Müller-Thurgau, Riesling, Moscato Giallo, Schiava, Pinot Nero, Merlot, Lagrein, Cabernet Franc, Cabernet Sauvignon, Moscato Rosa

GREAT WINES

Löwengang Chardonnay 1997
A Chardonnay of great fineness and elegance, made from a careful selection of grapes. Brilliant straw-yellow color with greenish reflections, tending toward gold with aging. Elegant, balanced, and fresh body. Long and clean aftertaste with notes of almond. Can be aged for surprising periods, and goes well with fish (including shellfish and mollusks) and white meat.

"Cor Römigberg" Cabernet Sauvignon 1997
Made from Cabernet Sauvignon grapes with the addition of a percentage of Petit Verdot, aged in barrels of French oak. Perfume ranging from violet to cherry to black currant, from tobacco to rare wood. Dry, powerful, and velvety taste, with tannins that are never aggressive and a long finish distinguished by elegant herbs. Should be aged eight to ten years, and goes well with roasts, lamb, and game.

Visits and tastings: yes, by appointment

CANTINA SOCIALE DI TERLANO

7, via Siberleiten
Terlan
Tel: 0471.257135
www.kellerei-terlan.com

Founded: 1893
Production region: Municipality of Terlano
Wines and grape varieties: 60% whites, 40% reds; Pinot Bianco, Chardonnay, Pinot Grigio, Traminer Aromatico, Sauvignon, Müller-Thurgau, Schiava, Pinot Nero, Merlot, Lagrein, Cabernet

GREAT WINES

Lunare Gewürztraminer 2003
Fermented and aged in 500-liter barrels (tonneaux) for over twelve months. Straw-yellow color of exceptional vitality, very complex, sumptuous, and spicy bouquet, with hints of roses and hay. Full, soft, and elegant taste. Very persistent. Should be aged for three to four years, excellent as an aperitif and goes well with spicy Thai dishes.

Porphyr Lagrein 1999
Vinified in steel containers and aged in barrels, this Lagrein fully reveals the character of its native soil—rich in porphyry. Garnet-red color, intense perfume of bitter chocolate and nuances of violet. It has a full, robust taste, with soft, very persistent tannins. Should be aged four to six years, and goes well with roasts, large game, and lamb.

Visits and tastings: yes

AZIENDA VINICOLA NIEDERMAYR

Gerlan
Tel: 0471.662451
www.niedermayr.it

Founded: 1852
Production region: Municipalities of Appiano and Caldaro, Bolzano and Santa Maddalena basin.
Wines and grape varieties: 25% whites, 75% reds; Pinot Grigio, Pinot Bianco, Chardonnay, Traminer Aromatico, Müller-Thurgau, Lagrein, Pinot Nero, Cabernet, Merlot, Schiava

GREAT WINES

Aureus 2000
Raisin wine made from different varieties of white grapes, produced at a high altitude. Full and lingering taste, sweet, aromatic, and velvety. Can be served with foie gras, aged cheeses, gorgonzola, and plain pastries.

Euforius 2000
A blend of Lagrein, Cabernet Sauvignon, and Merlot. Fermented in steel and aged in barrels for twelve months. Intense ruby-red color and marked perfume of sour cherry, currants, wild fruit, and fresh grass. Can be aged for four to six years, and goes well with game dishes and roasts.

Visits and tastings: yes

COOPERATIVA PRODUTTORI COLTERENZIO

8, Strada del Vino, Gerlan
Tel: 0471.664246
www.colterenzio.com

Founded: 1960
Production region: Municipalities of Appiano, Cornaiano, Salorno, Settequerce, Bolzano basin
Wines and grape varieties: 50% whites, 50% reds; Pinot Grigio, Pinot Bianco, Chardonnay, Traminer Aromatico, Müller-Thurgau, Sauvignon, Lagrein, Pinot Nero, Cabernet, Merlot, and Schiava

GREAT WINES

Cornell Chardonnay 1997
Made from grapes cultivated in Cornaiano, fermented and aged in the barrel for eleven months. A wine of particular complexity and fineness. Golden yellow color, bold perfume with delicate notes of vanilla and exotic fruit. Palatable and clean taste, with refined aftertaste of toasted almond and golden apple. Ages well, and may be drunk as an aperitif or as a complement to hot hors d'oeuvres, fish, and white meat.

Cornell Cornelius 1997
The result of a combination of Cabernet Sauvignon (60 percent) and Merlot (40 percent), aged twenty years in the barrel. Great structure. Intense ruby-red color and perfume of cassis, wild fruit, and spices. Should be aged for up to ten years, and goes well with game, grilled red meat, and venison.

Visits and tastings: yes, by appointment

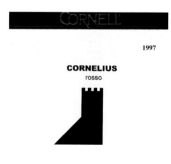

CANTINA PRODUTTORI SANKT MICHAEL-EPPAN

17/19, via Circonvallazione, Eppan
Tel: 0471.664466
www.stmichael.it

Founded: 1907
Production region: San Michele and the entire municipal region of Appiano, Cornaiano, Colterenzio, San Paolo, Missano, Frangarto, and Monticolo, as well as parts of Caldaro, Termeno, Cortaccia, Montagna, Gries, and Santa Maddalena
Wines and grape varieties: 50% whites, 50% reds; Pinot Bianco, Chardonnay, Pinot Grigio, Traminer Aromatico, Sauvignon, Müller-Thurgau, Riesling, Moscato Giallo, Schiava, Pinot Nero, Merlot, Lagrein, and Cabernet

GREAT WINES

Chardonnay Sanct Valentin 1999
Made from a strict selection of the best Chardonnay grapes given to the cooperative, fermented, and then aged in the barrel for eleven months. Golden straw-yellow color and full, complex, and persistent bouquet, with hints of vanilla and exotic fruit. Should be aged for up to five to six years, and drunk as an aperitif or combined with refined dishes and white meat.

Lagrein Dunkel 2000
Made from pure Lagrein grapes, an excellent example of wine from this region. Scarlet-red color, variegated perfume with hint of vanilla and ripe red fruit. Full, forward, and velvety taste with a pleasant finish of licorice. Can be aged for a moderate period, and goes well with roasts.

Visits and tastings: yes, by appointment

AZIENDA AGRICOLA FRANZ HAAS

6, via Villa
Montan
Tel: 0471.812280
www.franz-haas.it

Founded: 1880
Production region: Montagna, Egna Neumarkt, Mazzon Mazon
Wines and grape varieties: 50% whites, 50% reds; Pinot Bianco, Pinot Grigio, Traminer Aromatico, Müller-Thurgau, Moscato Rosa, Pinot Nero, Lagrein

GREAT WINES

Manna 2000
Blend of Riesling, late-harvested Traminer Aromatico, Sauvignon, and Chardonnay. Intense straw-yellow color and full, complex, and aromatic bouquet. Dry, velvety taste with good structure and depth. Should be aged up to five to six years, and goes well with fish dishes and white meat.

Pinot Nero Cru 2001
The result of a selection of the best grapes collected on the property. Delicate ruby-red reflections. Full, aromatic, and lingering bouquet with hints of ripe wild fruit. Dry, soft, and enveloping taste of considerable complexity. Should be drunk within four to six years, and goes well with fine poultry and aged cheeses.

Visits and tastings: yes, by appointment

CANTINA HOFSTÄTTER

5, piazza Municipio, Tremin
Tel: 0471.860161
www.hofstatter.com

Founded: 1907
Production region: Municipalities of Termeno, Cortaccia, and Mazzon
Wines and grape varieties: 40% whites, 60% reds; Pinot Bianco, Chardonnay, Pinot Grigio, Traminer Aromatico, Sauvignon, Riesling, Müller-Thurgau, Pinot Nero, Merlot, Lagrein, and Cabernet

GREAT WINES

Steinraffler 2001
Aged fifteen months in small oak barrels and then another six months after being assembled in large barrels, this Lagrein has a deep garnet-red color with black tones. Dense, concentrated, and pleasantly typical, its perfume brings together earthy mineral and fruity aromas. Both its fruity and its mineral aromatic components are evident again to the palate. Should be aged four to six years, and goes well with strong game dishes, lamb, and roasts.

Barthenau Vigna S. Urbano-Pinot Nero 2000
Its aging in wood includes two distinct phases, each lasting one year: The first phase is in small barrels of French oak; the second involves the assembly of the different elements in a single large oak barrel. Ruby-red with a perfume of sour cherry and raspberry with delicate tones of finely spiced vanilla. Elegant and balanced to the palate with well-integrated tannins and exceptional aromatic concentration. Complements duck and pheasant, game, and aged cheeses.

Visits and tastings: yes, by appointment

ELENA WALCH CASTEL RINGBERG AND KASTELAZ

1, via Andreas Hofer, Tremin
Tel: 0471.860172
www.elenawalch.com

Founded: 1975
Production region: Castel Ringberg, above Lake Caldaro, and Kastelaz, in the municipality of Termeno
Wines and grape varieties: 50% whites, 50% reds; Pinot Bianco, Chardonnay, Pinot Grigio, Traminer Aromatico, Sauvignon, Müller-Thurgau, Riesling, Moscato Rosa, Schiava, Merlot, Lagrein, Cabernet

GREAT WINES

Beyond the Clouds 2002
A blend of the best whites with a prevalence of Chardonnay, made from selected grapes. Intense, brilliant yellow color. Dry to the palate, good structure, elegant and balanced, with notes of vanilla, peach, and a touch of wood. Should be drunk after a couple of years, and goes well with fish dishes and white meat, or as an aperitif.

Gewürztraminer Kastelaz 2003
A truly elegant Gewürztraminer, despite the vintage having yielded wines that are often excessive. Straw-yellow color with golden reflections, full and complex bouquet with hints of rose and spices. Powerful, aromatic, almost sumptuous taste, but harmonious and well-balanced. Can be aged four to five years and is excellent as an aperitif or combined with spicy dishes.

Visits and tastings: yes, by appointment

CHIANTI

WINE TRAIL *Itinerary*

ITINERARY LENGTH
125 miles / 200 kilometers

BEST TIME TO GO
April to late October

TIME TO SPEND
Three to four days

USEFUL ADDRESSES

Agenzia per il Turismo di Firenze
16, via A. Manzoni
Tel: 055.23320, Fax: 055.234628
www.firenzeturismo.it

Agenzia per il Turismo di Siena
56, piazza del Campo
Tel: 0577.280551, Fax: 0577.281041
www.terredisiena.it

THE PART OF Tuscany that the English have familiarly christened "Chiantishire," as if it were a branch of their own island, includes gentle hills covered with vineyards, olive groves, oak and pine woods, castles, and ancient villages. It is a sort of region within a region, whose wine-producing fame—like that of Bordeaux, Burgundy, and Champagne—has been known throughout the world for centuries. Chianti, which for non-Italians is synonymous with Italian wine and for Italians with Tuscan wine, has acted as a driving force for important regional and national labels. Its importance is such that one finds it even in the superb paintings that celebrate the glory of the Medici in the Palazzo Vecchio in Florence.

THE WINE ROUTE
CHIANTI AT THE
PALAZZO VECCHIO

FLORENCE fascinates, excites, astonishes. An abundant and generous cultural center, it delights with its ancient and intense atmosphere of the Renaissance capital. Fillipo Brunelleschi's dome, Giotto's bell tower, the Uffizi Gallery, and Michelangelo's *David* are masterpieces that should be admired—as they

ABOVE: A row of cypress trees rising up to a farm-house, marking the undulation of the hills, between Crete Senesi and Chianti.

have been over the centuries by emperors, kings, and popes. But one should not overlook the subtle pleasures of simply walking through the streets on both sides of the Arno a bit haphazardly, discovering the piazzas, narrow alleyways, and typical corners, and finally arriving in the Piazza della Signoria where the austere Palazzo Vecchio, a political hub and symbol of the city for seven centuries, dominates. It is one of the most visited and yet least-known places in the city: Few people know about the impenetrable network of hidden ceilings, storerooms, closets, and

other rooms that exist within. Few also realize that a journey through Chianti can begin here in the Hall of the Five Hundred, the grand scale of which was conceived by Girolamo Savonarola to house the Assemblea dei Giusti, or the "Gathering of the Righteous." With Giorgio Vasari's renovation, begun in 1555, the ceiling of the hall became the apotheosis of the power of Grand Duke Cosimo I, with various representations of the Florentine victories over Pisa and Siena. At the bottom of this celebration of the power of the Medici dynasty, one can make out the

TASTES *Enoteca Pinchiorri*

The success of this restaurant, numbered among the top ten in the world, is explained by the determination, class, and passion of Giorgio Pinchiorri and Annie Féolde. A sixteenth-century building on Florence's Via Ghibellina, the same street where the Bargello Museum is located, houses Enoteca. Crossing the threshold is significant, as it brings one into a temple of gastronomic culture, prized by all the guides, where a refined atmosphere of gestures, colors, and decor reigns: old rose for the sofas and tablecloths, pastel yellow for the walls, suffused lighting, antique furniture, carpets, paintings, fresh flowers, and silverware and luminous crystal on the dining table. The first room is a lounge where people can consult the menu and wine list, while the main room and mezzanine are intimate and welcoming.

Service is irreproachable. Annie adroitly sees to the kitchen and the crowd of coworkers. Giorgio oversees and takes pleasure in the wine cellar: 140,000 bottles (4,500 labels) resting with great care in their original crates or in those made especially for them. At the table, a leisurely sequence of dishes interwoven with delicate flavors is accompanied by an incredible wine list. It is eloquent, tasty, and creative cuisine with a Tuscany touch. Eating and drinking are harmonized as never before in a careful exercise of style that distinguishes Enoteca Pinchiorri. It is a true gustatory experience, which can be repeated in Tokyo where a second location opened in 1993.

Enoteca Pinchiorri, Via Ghibellina 87, Florence: tel. 055.242757
www.enotecapinchiorri.com

allegory of Chianti to the right and with his back to the audience. "This gentleman, he is Chianti," Vasari wrote, "with the Pesa and the Elsa rivers, its horns of plenty filled with fruit, and at its feet a Bacchus of a more mature age, for the excellent wines of this region; and in the distance Castellina, Radda, and Broglio are portrayed with their insignia; and the arms in the shield held by that young man, who represents Chianti, is a black rooster against a yellow field."

It is only a few steps from the sixteenth-century allegories in the Palazzo Vecchio frescoes to the first

OPPOSITE: the parish church of Castellina in Chianti.

RIGHT: building stones and cobbled streets in Montefioralle, an ancient village in Chianti, near Greve.

tastings. In the shadow of Piazza della Signoria, it is possible to taste the best offerings from the two oldest Florentine families connected to wine: the Antinori and the Frescobaldi. If the former has devoted itself to wine production for more than 600 years, since Giovanni di Piero Antinori began participating in the Arte Fiorentina dei Vinattieri in 1385, the Frescobaldi family, which includes illustrious men of letters, explorers, composers, bankers, and political figures, has produced wine for thirty generations. The Solaia and the Tignanello are best tasted in the warm, welcoming spaces of the small Antinori cellar in the family's aristocratic Florentine palace, in the piazza of the same name, opposite the Baroque church of San Gaetano. The Montesodi and the Mormoreto are served between the sumptuous walls of the Frescobaldi Wine Bar and Restaurant, in Via dei Magazzini.

IN THE COUNTRYSIDE OF CASTLES AND WINES

Leaving Florence—perhaps after a stop at Enoteca Pinchiorri, a true temple of Italian gastronomy, and a visit to its prestigious cellar—one heads for Chianti following, if possible, Vasari's points of reference. This is a land so rich that it seems like a jewel case brimming with treasures, particularly for those who know enough to slow down the frenetic rhythm of today's aggressive and stampeding tourism. The unique landscape, interwoven with reminders of different eras from the

Contrasting wine cellars and atmospheres: *ABOVE,* the cellar of the Ricasoli barons' Brolio castle; *BELOW,* the cellar of Casa Vinicola Querciabella, near Greve, a site of organic wine production.

medieval to the present, still offers the tranquility of its small towns, the silence of its parish churches, the simple mysticism of its tabernacles, the history of its farmhouses, the secrets of its rural culture, its oils, and above all its wine. The latter was appreciated as far back as the time of Leonardo, who wrote: "... and I think, however, that people who are born where good wines are found are extremely happy."

Chianti's fortunes are tied not only to wine and to the countryside, but also to its strategic position between Florence and Siena. Throughout the Middle Ages the two rival cities contested this land, and for this reason many fortified towns and castles punctuate the region. Many towns were established for trade; the porticoed, triangular piazza of **GREVE** in Chianti, for example, reveals its historic function as a marketplace.

From Greve the road climbs slightly to the west to **MONTEFIORALLE**, an ancient and tiny town surrounded by walls, at the summit of a hill that overlooks the Greve valley. The narrow little streets, the beautiful stone houses, and the views of the surrounding countryside make this one of the most evocative places in the region. Verrazzano is one of the castles in Chianti that illustrates the medieval defensive concept of towering over one's enemy. This is also the native land of the family of Giovanni de Verrazzano, the navigator who in 1524 was the first to explore the Atlantic coast of North America, in his ship *Delfina,* and discovered the bay that New York City now overlooks. In the vicinity of Greve is the Querciabella cellar, whose wine is a brilliant example of organic production. In addition to its wonderful red wines, the Batàr is perhaps one of the most important Tuscan white wines.

Highway 222 continues along a splendid route through a landscape that varies from cultivated fields to wooded areas, to **CASTELLINA** in Chianti, in a dominant position on a hill between the valleys of the Arbia, the Elsa, and the Pesa. The town is pleasant, but the main attraction is the succession of wine

Historic barrels at the
Fattoria di Felsina, near
Castelnuovo Berardenga.

shops with barrel-vaulted ceilings along the medieval Via delle Volte.

Descending to **MONTERIGGIONI** by way of **LILLIANO**, preferably in the early morning, one sees a typical Chianti landscape: rows of cypress trees and isolated country houses that emerge from the mist, almost like a mirage. It is a winding road that follows the natural, gentle slope of the hill as it descends and crosses one of the many areas that have preserved the distinctive character of the agrarian landscape—originally based on a sharecropping system—with an unmistakable parceling of the terrain planted with vines and olive trees, embellished with farmhouses and villas that peek out here and there. It is one of the most spectacular drives of the entire trip. Monteriggioni, a small village completely surrounded by thirteenth-century walls, seems untouched by time with its fourteen imposing, fortified towers that emerge like gigantic sentinels.

Rows of vines that alternate with olive groves and woods divide Castellina, where the itinerary returns, from **RADDA** in Chianti, a town protected by medieval walls that marks the watershed between the Pesa and Arbia valleys. The Podestà palace, at the center of town, is a reminder that beginning in the mid-fourteenth century Radda was the seat of the League of Chianti. A few kilometers farther on lies Ama castle, near **GAIOLE** in Chianti, in a region described admiringly by Grand Duke Pietro Leopold of Hapsburg-Lorraine in his 1773 report on the government of Tuscany.

LEFT: an image of Chianti: slopes of olive trees and vineyards, fields and cypresses, outlines of villages among hills traversed by up-and-down roads.

FOLLOWING PAGES: the vineyards of Chianti.

In a region as vast as Chianti, which occupies much of Tuscany spreading out between Arezzo, Florence, Pisa, Pistoia, Prato, and Siena with more than 125 miles (200 kilometers) of roads through the hills, it is normal to taste a wide variety of wines, even if the same Sangiovese grape predominates in all of them. The same wine can stimulate different sensory reactions, depending on the microclimate, the terrain, and the cultivation methods. Chianti is regulated according to two different regulations, one for Chianti Classico between Florence and Siena, and one for Chianti, which is subdivided into seven smaller zones: Colli Aretini, Colli Fiorentini, Colline Pisane, Colli Senesi (south of Siena), Montalbano (the area around Carmignano), Montespertoli, and Rufina (in the area around Pontassieve).

Prized bottles at Castello di Brolio, a historic site in the Chianti region; the baron Ricasoli.

Once again crossing through woods, vineyards, and olive groves, we arrive at Brolio castle, ancestral home to the Ricasoli barons, whose history has been closely linked to this land since the twelfth century. In the mid-nineteenth century Bettino Ricasoli codified modern Chianti. Casabianca wrote that the beauty and grandeur of the complex (which can be toured) and its crenellated towers seemed to audaciously challenge the sky itself, and there are many stories and legends about the site. With its pentagonal form and brick ramparts, it is an architectural exception among Chianti's small fortresses. Baron Francesco Ricasoli, after pursuing other interests, salvaged the company and has begun offering a line of high-level wines.

At a crossroad near **CASTELNUOVO BERARDENGA** continue to the right, for Borgo San Felice, which in 1990 was transformed into a luxurious resort. This medieval village in the heart of Chianti Classico is striking by night, with its wrought-iron lanterns that cast a warm light on the houses and stone doorways, the brick arches, stairways, and little piazzas. But it is equally enchanting by day, when augmented by the color and cheer of the flowers that abound in every corner, the green explosion of ivy that clings to the ancient buildings, and the silent comings and goings of the people who work in the renowned agricultural concern, famous for having launched one of the first Super-Tuscan wines. The vineyards that surround the village provide a spectacular panorama.

ABOVE: Tuscany's culture of eating well: the Osteria del Vecchio Castello, in the countryside of Montalcino.

OPPOSITE: A view of the Hotel Helvetia & Bristol and a dish of stuffed rabbit, a traditional Tuscan fare.

From here the landscape opens up over the spacious hills that overlook Castelnuovo Berardenga, toward the broad basin of Siena. Visitors can inhale the charm along with the elegant wines on the Felsina estate, in the farthest foothills of the Chianti mountains. In business since the early eighties, the estate offers an admirable selection of clonal and small production wines to increase the potential of the individual vineyards. The success of this approach is seen in the Fontalloro, 100 percent Sangiovese, a Super-Tuscan wine that is atypical and highly prized. Giuseppe Mazzocolin, a professor of literature, is the driving force behind the farm. A fervent believer in the power of understatement, with the help of oenol-

ogist Franco Bernabei he has been able to turn himself into one of the most respected wine producers in this part of Italy. In addition to wine, the professor-turned-agriculturalist devotes himself body and soul to the production of a sublime extra-virgin olive oil.

FROM CRETE SENESI TO THE HOME OF BRUNELLO

Passing **SIENA**, the route continues through the region known as Crete Senesi, an expanse of stark clay hills without vineyards or tall trees, marked by deep gullies. It is a fascinating landscape, almost lunar in its austerity. The earth takes on different tones and reflections, depending on the time of day and the season. If the grazing light of winter rekindles the grayness of the clay earth with the yellow tones of dusk, in summer the green of the pastures is interwoven with the orange of the sunflower fields and the brilliant gold of the expanses of wheat. The Benedictine abbey of **MONTE OLIVETO MAGGIORE**, surrounded by a forest of cypress, pine, oak, and olive trees, merits a visit.

Approaching **MONTALCINO**, home of the renowned DOCG Montalcino wine, the woodland turns into vineyards. Medieval villages and ancient farm complexes, parish churches, and fortified strongholds can be glimpsed along the way. The road to Montalcino traverses one of the most fascinating landscapes in Italy, enriched by human works inserted harmoniously into the natural scenery. Here, hidden amid olive trees and rows of vines, is Tenuta il Greppo, birthplace of Brunello di Montalcino, which was first bottled in the late nineteenth century by Ferruccio Biondi Santi, the man who identified a particular clone, the Sangiovese Grosso, and purified it for production. His son Tancredi standardized the Brunello, creating the foundation for future regulation and above all confirming the development of a true individual wine with an exceptionally long shelf life. Today Franco and his successor Jacopo continue the tradition. The sanctum sanctorum of the family contains their most prized wines, veritable oenological gems that are refilled every now and then, in accordance with a ritual ceremony that involves all the owners of vintages for that year.

TAKE A BREAK

LODGING

Florence: **HOTEL HELVETIA & BRISTOL**
Vie dei Pescioni 2
Tel: 055.287814
www.royaldemeure.com
Charm and refinement characterize this luxurious hotel, located across from the Strozzi palace. The warm and welcoming atmosphere is echoed in the parlors and guestrooms.

Castelnuovo Berardenga: **HOTEL RELAIS BORGO SAN FELICE**
Località San Felice
Tel: 0577.3964
www.borgosanfelice.it
The restaurant, Poggio Rosso, is noteworthy. Excellent wines from the vineyard are considered among the best in the region.

DINING

Montalcino: **OSTERIA DEL VECCHIO CASTELLO**
Località Poggio alla Mura - La Pieve
Tel: 0577.816026
In a former thirteenth-century monastery, chef Susanna Fumi creatively reinterprets splendid regional dishes. Service is impeccable, as is the wine list with some 800 labels. Reservations are advised.

Siena: **GRAND HOTEL CONTINENTAL**
Banchi di Sopra 85
Tel: 0577.5601
Interesting tastings are held in the Grand Hotel Continental's ancient cellar, which was discovered during the building's last renovation.

LABELS TO LOOK FOR

MARCHESI DE FRESCOBALDI

Via Santo Spirito 11
Florence
Tel: 055.27141
www.frescobaldi.it

Founded: 1300
Production region: Castello di Nipozzano, Castello di Pomino, Montalcino, Tenuta di Castiglioni
Wines and grape varieties: Reds 90%, whites 10%; Chardonnay, Sangiovese, Cabernet Sauvignon, Cabernet Franc, Merlot

GREAT WINES

Montesodi 2000
Made from pure Sangiovese grapes from vineyards on the Castello di Nipozzano estate. Aged in new casks of French oak for at least twelve months. A dry, elegant taste with cherry, plum, licorice, chocolate, and coffee. Can be aged for long periods, and goes well with grilled red meat and game.

Mormoreto 2000
Made from 65 percent Cabernet Sauvignon grapes, Cabernet Franc and Merlot, from the Castello di Nipozzano estate. Aged twenty months in small barrels. Dry, velvety taste, with robust but elegant tannins, balanced acidity, and a long aftertaste of licorice. Can be aged for a considerable period, and goes well with grilled meats, particularly lamb.

Visits and tastings: yes, by appointment

ANTINORI

Piazza Antinori 3
Florence
www.antinori.it

Founded: 1385
Production region: Chianti Classico
Wines and grape varieties: Reds 95% whites 5%; Trebbiano, Chardonnay, Sangiovese, Cabernet Sauvignon, Cabernet Franc, Syrah

GREAT WINES

Tignanello 2000
Made from a selection of 80 percent Sangiovese grapes and the remaining portion Cabernet Sauvignon. Produced in large wooden vats and subsequently aged in casks of French oak. Intense ruby-red color with purplish-blue highlights. Full, complex, and lingering aroma with hints of cherries in brandy, morello cherries, wild fruit, and fruit preserves. Dry, powerful, elegant taste, with notes of chocolate, coffee, and licorice. Long, clean aftertaste with mentholated traces. Can be aged for even ten to twelve years, and goes well with a classic T-bone steak.

Solaia 2000-13.5°
Made from 75 percent Cabernet Sauvignon grapes, 5 percent Cabernet Franc, and 20 percent Sangiovese, from the homonymous vineyard on the Tignanello estate. Intense ruby-red color. Full, intense, and lingering bouquet, with hints of red berries, rare wood, and spices. Dry, complex taste with strong structure and elegance. A velvety wine, rich in soft tannins with a long, clean aftertaste with hints of licorice. Should be aged at least eight to ten years, and goes well with red grilled meat and game.

Visits and tastings: yes, by appointment

AGRICOLA QUERCIABELLA

Via di Barbiano 17
Creve in Chianti
Tel: 055.853834
www.querciabella.com

Founded: 1972
Production region: Ruffoli
Wines and grapes varieties: 90% reds, 10% whites; Sangiovese, Cabernet, Merlot, Syrah, Chardonnay, Pinot Bianco

GREAT WINES

Batar 2001
Made from 65 percent Chardonnay and 35 percent Pinot Bianco grapes from an extremely select harvest from the proprietary vineyards on the hill of Ruffoli. Fermented and aged in casks of French oak for nine months. Full, lingering, and complex bouquet. Impressive structure supported by considerable acidity. Hints of wood, vanilla, honey, acacia flowers, and anise. After it has aged from four to ten years, it goes well with young Parmigiano Reggiano, ripe goat cheese, and honey-based sweets.

Camartina 2000
Made from 60 percent Sangiovese and 40 percent Cabernet Sauvignon grapes. Vinified in steel and aged for two years in casks of new French oak. Full bouquet with notes of undergrowth, spices, and rare wood. Dry, powerful, and velvety taste with ripe fruit, wood, chocolate, and licorice. Capable of great aging, it goes well with game and even chocolate.

Visits and tastings: no

CASTELLO DI AMA

Gaiole in Chianti
Tel: 0577.746031
www.castellodiama.com

Founded: 1966
Production region: Gaiole in Chianti
Wines and grape varieties: 70% reds, 30% whites and rosés. Sangiovese, Merlot, Cabernet Sauvignon, Colorino, Canaiolo, Black Malvasia

GREAT WINES

Al poggio 2002
A pure Chardonnay made from a select harvest of grapes from the Poggio vineyard. Twenty percent is fermented in steel, while the rest is kept in French oak casks for nine months. Intense straw-yellow color and a full, complex, and almost opulent bouquet, with hints of bread crust, vanilla, and tropical fruit. Dry and balanced taste, with grapefruit, acacia honey, toast. Should be aged three to four years, and goes well with fish-based first courses or with white meat.

Castello di Ama 2001 Chianti Classico
The result of a select harvest made of 80 percent Sangiovese, 8 perent Canaiolo, and 12 percent Black Malvasia and Merlot. Fermentation is done in steel vats with delicate repassings of must over the grape dregs, before aging in casks. An elegant, fine, full wine, with excellent balance and concentration, and soft and well-integrated tannins. Can be aged ten years or so, and goes well with red meat.

Visits and tastings: yes

BARONE RICASOLI

Cantine del Castello di Brolio
Gaiole in Chianti
Tel: 0577.7301
www.risasoli.it

Founded: 1141
Production region: Gaiole in Chianti and
Castelnuovo Berardenga
Wines and grape varieties: 95% reds,
5% whites; Chardonnay; Malvasia,
Sangiovese, Cabernet Sauvignon, Merlot

GREAT WINES

Castello di Brolio 1999
Made from 90 percent Sangiovese and 10
percent Merlot and Cabernet Sauvignon
grapes. Vinified in cement and aged eighteen months in casks of French oak. Intense
ruby-red color with purplish-blue highlights. Full and lingering bouquet with hints
of wild fruit, spices, and rare wood. Dry,
clean, pure, masculine taste with notes of
leather, wood, chocolate, and licorice.
Prolonged and clean aftertaste of anisette.
Should be aged five to ten years and goes
well with grilled red meat and game.

Casalferro 2000
Made from 75 percent Sangiovese and 25
percent Merlot grapes. Vinified in cement
and aged eighteen months in casks of
French oak. Intense ruby-red color with
purplish-blue highlights. Full, complex, and
lingering bouquet. Notes of spices, sandalwood, and anisette. Dry, powerful, muscular
taste of considerable body. Notes of leather,
wood, and licorice. Can be well aged, and
goes well with large roasts and game.

Visits and tastings: yes

AGRICOLA SAN FELICE

Castelnuovo Berardenga
Tel: 0577.3991
www.agricolasanfelice.it

Founded: Early twentieth century
(primi del novecento)
Production region: Castelnuovo Berardenga
Wines and grape varieties: 80% reds,
20% whites; Sangiovese, Merlot,
Cabernet, Colorino

GREAT WINES

Vigorello 2000
One of the precursors of the famous
Super-Tuscans. Made from 45 percent
Sangiovese, 40 percent Cabernet
Sauvignon, and 15 percent Merlot grapes.
Deep ruby-red color with purplish-blue
highlights. Full, complex, and lingering
bouquet with hints of vanilla, cherries in
brandy, and coffee. Dry, powerful, velvety,
and balanced taste, with notes of coffee,
licorice, bitter chocolate, and an aftertaste
of anise. Can be aged for long periods, and
goes well with well-aged hard cheese.

Poggio Rosso Riserva 2000
Chianti Classico made from 90 percent
Sangiovese and 10 percent Colorino
grapes. Vinified in steel and aged in 500-
liter (130-gallon) French oak barrels for
about 18 months. Very intense ruby-red
color with purplish-blue highlights. Full,
complex, and lingering bouquet, with
notes of spices, tobacco, undergrowth,
and fruit preserves. Full, powerful, and
balanced taste. Notes of chocolate, coffee,
and licorice. Extremely long and elegant
aftertaste with memories of cinnamon.
Can be aged for up to twenty years, and
goes well with grilled red meat and game.

Visits and tastings: yes

FATTORIA DI FELSINA

Strada Chiantigiana SS 484
Castelnuovo Berardenga
Tel: 0577.355117
www.felsina.com

Founded: 1966
Production region: Castelnuovo Berardenga
Wines and grape varieties: 92% reds, 8%
whites; Sangiovese, Cabernet Sauvignon,
Chardonnay

GREAT WINES

Felsina Chianti Classico Riserva Rancia 2000
Made from pure Sangiovese grapes from
the Rancia estate. Vinified in steel and subsequently aged in casks of French oak for
eighteen months. Intense ruby-red color
with purplish-blue highlights. Full and lingering bouquet with notes of red berries
and tobacco. Dry, powerful, elegant, and
full-bodied taste. Long and clean aftertaste
with mentholated hints of chocolate and
licorice. Can be aged from five to ten years,
and goes well with grilled meats.

Fontalloro 2000
Made from pure Sangiovese grapes from
select vines in the proprietary vineyards in
the Chianti Classico and Colli Senesi
regions. Vinified in steel and subsequently
aged in casks of French oak for twenty
months. Deep ruby-red color with purplish-blue highlights. Full, complex, and
lingering bouquet with hints of cherry,
tobacco, and spice. Dry, soft, elegant taste
with mentholated notes of licorice and
chocolate. Long, clean aftertaste.
Can be aged considerably, and goes well
with grilled red meat and game.

Visits and tastings: yes, by appointment

BIONDI-SANTI-TENUTA GREPPO

Montalcino
Tel: 0577.848087
www.biondisanti.it

Founded: 1825
Production region: Tenuta Greppo,
Montalcino
Wines and grape varieties: 100% reds;
Sangiovese Grosso

GREAT WINES

Brunello di Montalcino 1970
Ruby-red color with brick highlights. Full,
complex, and lingering bouquet, with
notes of ripe fruit, rare wood, licorice, and
cherries in brandy. Dry, warm taste of
great fineness and balance. Long aftertaste with mentholated hints. A wine for
meditation, of incredible elegance.

Brunello di Montalcino 1990
Deep ruby-red color with highlights tending toward garnet. Full, lingering bouquet
of great complexity, with hints of red
berries, leather, tobacco, and rare wood.
Dry, velvety taste of great balance, with
notes of undergrowth, sandalwood,
leather, chocolate, and licorice. Extremely
long, clean aftertaste, with mentholated
notes. Can be aged for extremely long
periods. A wine of exceptional elegance
and refinement, that goes well with large
roasts or can be a wine for meditation.

Visits and tastings: yes, by appointment

MAREMMA

WINE TRAIL *Itinerary*

ITINERARY LENGTH
190 miles / 300 kilometers

BEST TIME TO GO
April to November

TIME TO SPEND
Six to seven days

USEFUL ADDRESSES
Consorzio la Strad del Vino
Costa degli Estruschi
Località San Guido 45
Bolgheri
Tel: 0565.749768
Fax: 0565.749705
www.lastradadelvino.com

Consorzio Strada del Vino Monteregio
di Massa Marittima
Via Norma Parenti 22
Massa Marittima
Tel: 0566.940095
www.stradavino.it

Centro Informazioni Consorzio la Strada
del Vino Colli di Maremma
Piazza Garibaldi 51
Pitigliano
Tel / fax: 0564.617111
www.collidimaremma.it

MAREMMA. JUST THE name of this slice of Tuscany, which until a century ago was a swamp and a desolate wasteland, now evokes the intense green and perfume of pinewoods and Mediterranean brush land, distant hills dotted with towers and castles, traces of ancient villages, the secret charm of deserted beaches, immense expanses of prized vineyards, tireless herdsmen, the backdrop of steep mountains, and the pleasures of fine dining. The region's long isolation that lasted until the land reclamation begun by the Lorraine dynasty is one of the reasons for its integrity. One is struck by the sense of balance in a landscape where nature and humankind coexist in harmony. Past and present, environment and culture, merge in a singular whirl of historic settings, landscapes, light, and color. And the Maremma, where vines have been cultivated since Etruscan times, now yields some of the greatest wines in Italy.

THE WINE ROUTE
PEARLS OF THE MAREMMA
PITIGLIANO, a town set on a tufa cliff that austerely dominates the surrounding hills, almost cut off from

OPPOSITE PAGE, FROM THE TOP: herdsmen in the Parco dell'Uccellina; wines, alembics, and goblets at the Fattoria Le Pupille in Grosseto; children on the streets of the ancient Jewish ghetto in Pitigliano; Fattoria La Parrina in Albinia.
RIGHT: in Castagneto Carducci, the Grattamacco estate that yields renowned wines.

the rest of the world, comes into view unexpectedly and in spectacular fashion. The rows of houses lined up one against another, built on the edge of the cliff, jut out from rock that is the same color, breaking the soft lines of the countryside. The effect is impressive, particularly at twilight. The sense of wonder continues with the sixteenth-century arched aqueduct and the grand fortress-palace of the Orsini counts. The visitor can then continue through the stepped medieval streets, terraces, narrow lanes, and twisting alleys, to the ghetto where the important Jewish community of Pitigliano once lived. Beneath the buildings

a second city is hidden—where grottoes, underground tombs, and oddly shaped tunnels have been transformed into wine cellars where wine is made and preserved. There is the Cantina Medievale for example, where it is possible (by reservation) to taste the products of the Cantina Sociale.

The itinerary continues inland, where Maremma is carved by deep valleys, gorges, and ravines—ideal receptacles for primitive human settlements. It is no accident that this is precisely where the Etruscans, a civilization that, while much studied, is still enveloped in an aura of mystery, excavated into the tufa stone to

OPPOSITE: the spaces of the hypogeum, carved out of the tufa stone of the medieval cellar in Pitigliano.

ABOVE: a magical view of Pitigliano, where the houses are the same color as the tufa cliffs upon which they are built.

EXCURSIONS *The Siren's Call*

You board the fishing boat *Sirena* early in the morning, undo the moorings, and if the winds are favorable head toward the open sea. Then, once you arrive at the "right" spot, you bring in the mile or so of nets cast out the night before. The highlight of the day is eating the fish that has just been caught, which is cooked on the grill right on the boat. Paolo Fanciulli learned his trade from his father and from the old men of Talamone, and he thoroughly knows and loves his slice of Maremma—a love shared by all who get to know it. During the outing at sea it is possible to glimpse the sheer rocks where peregrine falcons and ravens nest and the grot- toes along the coast of Collelungo. Sometimes Fanciulli disembarks on the beaches of Maremma Park, perhaps at Cala di Forno where you are likely to see boar and deer that approach a few yards from the sea. It is a form of tourism that allows people to experience the lure of the ancient fisherman's trade, practiced by men who have always lived in close contact with and respected the sea. For information, contact Paolo Fanciulli, tel. 33328461199, e-mail: pescaturismo@tiscali.it.

A fisherman in Orbetello; Paolo Fanciulli intent on bringing in his nets.

create dwellings and monumental necropolises. They also created an exceptional system of hollowed-out passageways—a labyrinth of corridors miles long and about 10 feet (3 meters) wide, with walls as high as 65 feet (20 meters), which from time immemorial has linked three villages: the jewel-like **SORANO**, medieval in appearance; **SOVANA**, an architectural marvel of this land of tufa stone; and Pitigliano.

The wine cellars of the Azienda Sassotondo, halfway between Pitigliano and Sovana, are also carved out of tufa; here it is possible to taste the San Lorenzo, a brilliant example of the regional wine, with a pure cherry taste that is truly unforgettable. Along the road that traverses the Fiora hills, vineyards alternate with olive groves in the deep valleys carved into the tufa; descending toward the coast, castles and small fortified villages dot the summits of the knolls.

FROM ARGENTARIO TO MASSA MARITTIMA

Arriving near the coast, the view changes completely. The woods and forests give way to Mediterranean brushland and the hills fade away into the gulfs, now transformed into "reclaimed" ponds, sandbars, and

OPPOSITE: one of the deep Etruscan "hollow roads" in the vicinity of Sovana.
RIGHT: some of the great wines of the Azienda Agricola Massavecchia, in Massa Marittima.

The duomo in Massa Marittima, captured in the clever, fascinating asymmetry of the lines of the buildings and the piazza.

lagoons, due to the action of the sea and winds as well as ancient deposits from the rivers. The first stop along the coast is at Fattoria la Parrina, where in addition to tasting the Ansonica Bianco, an extremely ancient grape variety that probably originated in the Middle East, and the excellent Parrina Riserva Rosso, it is also possible to sample goat and sheep cheeses produced on site. A few kilometers from **ALBINIA** is **MONTE ARGENTARIO**, a succession of beaches,

creeks, inlets, majestic rocks, verdant flora, and more Ansonica vines. Since ancient times the natural bays of the promontory, sheltered from the winds, have drawn sailing peoples and settlements of great civilizations—Phoenicians, Etruscans, Romans, and Spaniards—traces of which remain visible along the scenic road that runs from **PORTO ERCOLE** to the sailing village of **PORTO SANTO STEFANO**. A visit to **ORBETELLO** is mandatory; it is built at the center of a broad lagoon delimited by the two sand-bars of Giannella and Feniglia, long, sandy strips that link the mountain to the mainland.

Heading back as far as **TALAMONE**, at the southern boundary of Maremma Regional Park, the road turns inland, traversing immense expanses of greenery and solitary pastures. Here and there are farms and picturesque villages, ancient and silent. These include **MAGLIANO**, surrounded by impressive walls that overlook the sea, and **SCANSANO**, a city with medieval origins, home of Morellino wine and site of the Museum of Vines and Wine, housed within the praetorian palace.

On the road to **GROSSETO** is the Fattoria Le Pupille. Elisabetta Geppetti, who runs it, has always devoted herself to the world of wine, first with the help of Giacomo Tachis, and then Riccardo Cotarella. International success came with wines such as the Saffredi, a blend of Cabernet Sauvignon, Merlot, and Alicante, and the Poggio Valente, a pure Morellino di Scansano.

The undulating hills continue as far as the enchanting town of **MASSA MARITTIMA**, which boasts one of the most charming piazzas in Italy. The lovely setting is the result of the location of the duomo, simultaneously irregular and harmonious, and the palaces that surround it: a refined play of symmetry gone mad.

A few steps from the duomo, in the ancient Cantina Moris, it is possible to purchase Moris Farms

PROTAGONISTS   *The herdsmen's realm*

Often it is difficult to spot wild animals in their habitat, but the majestic Maremman cows do not hide. They live in the wild on the prairies, on the edges of cleared land. These ancient beasts came here from the steppes with nomadic barbarians and adapted to the harsh environment of the Maremma.

Maremman horses, the horses of the herdsmen, also run wild, and they, too, have illustrious ancestors. The Etruscans were the first to select a breed suited to this land. They were followed by the Romans, who used Berber horses from Numidia, the Medici, and finally the troops of the Kingdom of Italy, who also used the Maremman horses in wartime.

As early as the sixteenth century, herdsmen were living together with the horses that they tended throughout the year, through rain, snow, or summer heat, challenging malaria and solitude, their worst enemies. It was unforgiving and constant work, handed down from father to son in rugged dynasties accustomed to a life of sacrifice. A difficult profession, but at the same time a noble one, which in recent years has run the risk of disappearing.

Near the Azienda Regionale Agricola Alberese, having made reservations in advance, those who have the requisite skill can follow the herdsmen as they work. It is also possible to work for a few days in close contact with the cowboys who raise wild horses and cows on Equinuus, an organic agricultural complex of about 740 acres. Work with the cowboys as they move their herds, cut out and isolate certain animals, separate colts from their mothers, brand the animals, and break in the colts. It is the Far West in Maremma.
www.alberese.com

PERSONALITIES *Angelo Gaja*

Angelo Gaja speaks about the new wine cellar in Bolgheri and his eyes light up: "Architect Giovanni Bo succeeded in integrating it into the environment, creating large underground spaces held up by thick, recycled metal piers, and concealing two rows of iron and copper pyramids that emerge from the ground with 350 centuries–old olive trees from neighboring properties."

It is not easy to meet Gaja, one of the greatest proponents of the Italian wine world—he is extremely busy. But then, hearing him speak, the success of his wines seems natural. He is open-minded, sharp, and attentive. At work, he is capable of instilling the team of professionals that surround him with profound enthusiasm. Since 1859 his family has been involved with the production of high-quality wines in Barbaresco, in Piedmont. When his moment came, in 1961, the winery was already one of the leaders in the region. "The roots of my success come from my father's and my grandfather's hard work, in the vineyard and in the cellar, based on respect for the characteristics of the region and the indigenous grapes."

Gaja is an optimist, and he explains why: "The future of Italian wine is brilliant and full of great prospects, thanks to two strong points. The first is natural and is connected to the wealth of grape varietals (more than 350), the climate, the microclimates, and the terrain, due to Italy's geography, with vineyards that go from over 3,000 feet (900 meters) above sea level in the Val d'Aosta region to sea level in Sicily. The second factor is human. If the population density is translated into a culture that filters into the region, the great desire and will to work are now recognized throughout the world. Moreover, there is a significant and growing interest on the part of cultured and knowledgeable entrepreneurs who want to create high-level and unique wines, while in other countries, including France, wine has often been seen more than anything as a financial investment."

Gaja concludes, "Italy is only at the beginning. The revolution is arriving now, with great wines that are coming from the most unthinkable corners of the peninsula."

Angelo Gaja, one of the greatest connoisseurs and producers of Italian wine.

wines, including the Avvoltore, a red wine with ruby reflections made from Sangiovese, Cabernet Sauvignon, and Syrah grapes. Until the mid-nineties, it was said that the wine in this area had a salty taste. Moris and the owners of Le Pupille farm—staunch supporters of their region—were the first to know how to offer wines of excellent quality, transforming the "defect" into an asset. The organic wines from the Azienda Agricola Massavecchia are also extraordinary. Fabrizio Niccolaini, a true character, transfers his unique qualities into his wine. The high points are the velvety and enveloping Matto delle Giuncaie, made from Aleatico grapes, and the powerful, unusual La Fonte di Pietrarsa, a wine of tremendous personality, and an expression of the region, although it is made from international varieties such as Cabernet Sauvignon and Merlot.

FROM BOLGHERI, A WINE REVIVAL

Descending from **SUVERETO** toward the flat, sunny spaces more typical of Maremma, the road follows the route of the ancient consular Vecchia Aurelia road, and curves again toward the north as far as **BOLGHERI**. Although signs clearly indicate the turn,

RIGHT, FROM THE TOP: a taste of time at the Cantina Moris di Massa Marittima; Azienda Agricola Massavecchia, the winemaker's pride.

a careful glance will first note the 3-mile-long (5 kilo-meter) avenue of "cypresses, tall and straight, in a double line" described in Giosuè Carducci's poetry. The treetops stand out clearly against the surrounding fields. Upon entering the long road that runs perpendicular to the sea, the first impression is of the small chapel that inspired the poet to write his famous ode, *Davanti a San Guido* (In Front of San Guido). From here the road continues straight on, following the slightly hilly rise of the land. Along the entire boulevard, the site is so awe-inspiring that the visitor is left almost breathless. At the end stands the

centuries-old entrance to the little village enclosed within medieval walls.

The poetry of this place can be discovered in the great wines that in the late sixties signaled the revival of Italian oenology. Sassicaia came into being on a whim of Marchese Mario Incisa della Rocchetta, who was searching for an important wine on the model of the great Bordeaux, based on Cabernet instead of Sangiovese, the ruling grape variety in Chianti. A few years later Marchese Ludovico Antinori, from the historic and ancient family tied to wine, introduced Ornellaia, a blend of Cabernet Sauvignon, Merlot, and Cabernet Franc, which has often been judged to

TAKE A BREAK

LODGING

Albinia:
ANTICA FATTORIA PARRINA
Via Aurelia km 146
Tel: 0564.865586
This perfectly restored old farmhouse provides the pleasant atmosphere of an aristocratic country estate.

Porto Ercole: **IL PELLICANO**
Cala dei Santi
Tel: 0564.858111
www.pellicanohotel.com
This luxurious residence overlooking the sea is a refined beauty farm and spa. It also has an excellent restaurant.

Campiglia Marittima:
CASTELLO DI MAGONA
Tel: 0565-851216
www.castellodimagona.it

Between Suvereto and the coast, the grand duke of Tuscany transformed this house into a veritable castle during the historic land reclamation works in the Maremma. The five suites are furnished with Tuscan and Venetian antiques, valuable carpets, and seventeenth- and eighteenth-century paintings. Every parlor has a large hearth lit in winter.

DINING

Massa Marittima:
RISTORANTE BRACALI
Località Ghirlanda, Via di Perolla 2
Tel: 0566-902318
The elegance of the tables, set with tablecloths from Flanders and silver, is combined with regional cuisine interpreted with creativity by the young chef, Francesco. The wine cellar (which can be visited) holds some 800 labels.

Montemerano:
RISTORANTE DA CAINO
Via Canonica 3, Montemerano
Tel: 0564-602817
In a simple restaurant heated by a lovely hearth, diners can taste dishes prepared by Valeria Piccini based on a knowledgeable and scrupulous search for ingredients—a cornerstone and strong point of this restaurant—which is one of the most popular in Italy. The great quality of the food and the refinement of the flavors are complemented by a truly unique choice of wines. Maurizio Menichetti oversees the two beautiful and well-stocked cellars, one devoted to national wines, the other to international vintages.

be one of the best wines in the world. The road that leaves Bolgheri winds among olive trees, vineyards, tilled fields, and manor houses toward the village of **CASTAGNETO CARDUCCI**, where the reputation of the Tenuta dell'Ornellaia grew even more in the late eighties thanks to the Masseto, a Merlot vinified in purity, which immediately became legendary and has been sold at the most prestigious international auctions. Another mythic red from this region is the Bolgheri Superiore from the Grattamacco estate. Bolgheri's soil is truly fortunate, as is the surrounding territory. It is no accident that the elite of international winemaking, from Robert Mondavi to Angelo Gaja, compete over every tiny plot of this precious corner of Tuscany.

The vines on the Grattamacco estate, one of the temples of great red wines in the Bolgheri region.

AZIENDA SASSOTONDO

Azienda Agricola Carla Benino
Pian di Conati 52
Sovana
Tel: 0564.614218
www.sassotondo.it

Founded: 1990
Production region: Pitigliano, Sovana
Wines and grape varieties: 70% reds,
30% whites; Ciliegiolo, Sangiovese,
Merlot, Alicante, Trebbiano, Sauvignon
Blanc, Greco di Tufo, Sovana

GREAT WINES

San Lorenzo 2000
Made from pure Ciliegiolo grapes. Aged
in new barrels for eighteen months and in
the bottle for another year. Deep ruby-red
color with purplish-blue reflections. Full,
persistent bouquet, with hints of red
berry. Dry, decisive, and clean taste. Good
structure and concentration, long aftertaste with notes of licorice. Ages well.

Numero 6 2001
Made from 50 percent Sovana and Greco
di Tufo grapes, vinified in red and fermented in the barrel for eighteen months;
and 50 percent Sauvignon Blanc grapes,
vinified and fermented in steel. Vivid
golden yellow color, intense and persistent perfume with hints of citrus flowers,
ripe fruit, cedar, and notes of balsam.
Structured, full taste, oily but simultaneously balanced and fresh. Ready to drink
but also can be aged for four to five years,
and goes well with medium-aged cheeses.

Visits and tastings: yes, by appointment

FATTORIA LA PARRINA

Albinia
Tel: 0564.862636
www.parrina.it

Founded: 1830
Production region: La Parrina
Wines and grape varieties: 70% reds,
30% whites; Trebbiano, Ansonica,
Chardonnay, Sauvignon Blanc,
Sangiovese, Cabernet Sauvignon, Merlot

GREAT WINES

Parrina Riserva 1999
A blend of 70 percent selected
Sangiovese, 20 percent Cabernet
Sauvignon, and 10 percent Merlot, from
the most prized vineyards on the estate,
vinified in steel. Intense ruby-red color,
tending to garnet. Complex and persistent bouquet, with hints of red berry, rare
wood, and leather. Full, smooth taste,
good structure and concentration, with
soft tannins. Should be aged five to ten
years and goes well with roasts, stuffed
guinea hen, and game.

Ansonica-Costa dell'Argentario 2003
Made from pure Ansonica grapes that are
vinified in steel vats. Delicate straw-
yellow color, characteristic slightly fruity
perfume, with hints of star anise. Dry, harmonious taste. Clean aftertaste with aromatic notes. Should be drunk young, and
excellent as an aperitif, or as a complement to fish-based first courses.

Visits and tastings: yes

FATTORIA LE PUPILLE

Piagge del Maiano
Grosseto
Tel: 0564.409517
www.elisabettageppetti.com

Founded: 1982
Production region: Magliano, Pereta,
Scansano
Wines and grape varieties: 80% reds, 20%
whites; Traminer, Sauvignon Blanc,
Sangiovese, Cabernet Sauvignon, Merlot,
Alicante, Petit Verdot

GREAT WINES

Saffredi 2001
A blend of select Cabernet Sauvignon,
Merlot, and Alicante grapes from the
Saffredi vineyard, located near Pereta.
Aged in new barrels of French oak for ten
to twelve months. Intense ruby-red color,
full, complex, and persistent bouquet.
Dry, powerful taste with great structure
and concentration, with notes of spices,
fruit preserves, and chocolate. Ages well,
and complements large roasts and grilled
meat.

Poggio Argentato 2002
Made from Traminer and Sauvignon Blanc
grapes from vineyards located in the
municipality of Scansano. Vinified in
steel, brilliant straw-yellow color. Fine,
intense, and persistent bouquet, aromatic
and elegant. Dry, harmonious, seductive,
and slightly spicy taste. Excellent aperitif
wine, can accompany white meat and
medium-aged cheeses.

Visits and tastings: yes, by appointment

MASSAVECCHIA

Podere Fornace 11, Zona Rocche
Massa Marittima
Tel: 0566.904144

Founded: 1985
Production region: Massa Marittima, Massa
Vecchia area
Wines and grape varieties: 70% reds, 30%
whites; Ansonica, Trebbiano, Malvasia di
Candia, Vermentino, Sauvignon Blanc,
Aleatico, Alicante, Cabernet Sauvignon

GREAT WINES

La Fonte di Pietrarsa 1999
Made from 60 percent Cabernet
Sauvignon and 40 percent Merlot grapes.
Aged in oak barrels of varying sizes for
twenty-four months. Deep ruby-red color,
tending to garnet. Explosive and very persistent bouquet with hints of minerals,
flint, smoke, red fruit, and leather.
Powerful, muscular taste, great concentration and complexity. A wine with strong
character that clearly expresses its
regional ties. Can be aged for ten to fifteen years, and goes well with game, particularly ragout of hare.

Ariento 2002
Made from 85 percent Vermentino and 15
percent Malvasia di Candia, Trebbiano,
and Ansonica grapes. Aged in oak barrels
for eighteen months. Intense straw-yellow
color with golden reflections. Intense and
very persistent bouquet with hints of
tropical fruit, ripe banana, mango, and
vanilla. Full, oily, and voluptuous taste. A
white of enormous structure, rich in personality and character. Can be aged for ten
years or so, and can be drunk by itself to
taste its distinctive characteristics, or as a
complement to robust fish-based dishes.

Visits and tastings: yes, by appointment

MORISFARMS

Località Curanova
Massima Marittima
Tel: 0566.919135
www.morisfarms.it

Founded: 1971
Production region: Massa Marittima,
Poggio la Mozza area
Wines and grape varieties: 97% reds,
3% whites; Sangiovese, Cabernet
Sauvignon, Syrah

GREAT WINES

Avvoltore 2000
Made from 75 percent Sangiovese, 20 percent Cabernet Sauvignon, and 5 percent
Syrah grapes. Aged in barrels where it
undergoes malolactic fermentation and
then ages for twelve months. Ruby-red
color with violet reflections, has a complex
and persistent bouquet, with hints of ripe
fruit and vanilla. Dry, powerful but velvety
taste, large body and concentration. Long
and clean aftertaste. Can be aged for considerable periods, and an ideal complement to large grilled meats and boar.

Morellino di Scansano Riserva 1998
Made from 90 percent Sangiovese grapes
and 10 percent other authorized red berry
varieties. Intense ruby-red color, full and
persistent to the nose, with fruity and
spicy hints. Dry, decisive taste, good body,
and harmonious. Should be aged five to
ten years, and goes well with game.

Visits and tastings: yes

TENUTA DELL'ORNELLAIA

Via Bolgherese 191
Bogheri
Tel: 0565.71811
www.ornellaia.it

Founded: 1981
Production region: Bolgheri
Wines and grape varieties: 100% reds;
Merlot, Cabernet Sauvignon, Cabernet
Franc

GREAT WINES

Masseto 1998
Made from pure Merlot grapes exclusively
from the homonymous vineyard and the
Vigna Vecchia vineyard. Deep ruby-red
color with garnet reflections. Full, complex bouquet of great refinement. Dry,
powerful taste with notable structure and
concentration. Quite long-lasting, goes
well with game and large roasts.

Ornellaia 1999
A blend of 30 percent Merlot, 65 percent
Cabernet Sauvignon, and 5 percent
Cabernet Franc grapes, from vines transplanted to Bolgheri in 1982. Deep ruby-red
color, full, complex, and very persistent
bouquet. Ripe red and black fruit on the
palate. Great balance aned velvety tannins
give this a wine excellent body and a very
long finish. Goes well with red meat or,
once aged, can be a wine for meditation.

Visits and tastings: yes, by appointment

CA' MARCANDA

Località Santa Teresa 272
Castagneto Carducci
Tel: 0565.763809

Founded: 1996
Production region: Castagneto Carducci.
Wines and grape varieties: 100% reds;
Merlot, Cabernet Sauvignon, Cabernet
Franc, Syrah, Sangiovese

GREAT WINES

Magari 2001
Made from the separate vinification of 50
percent Merlot, 25 percent Cabernet
Sauvignon, and 25 percent Cabernet Franc
grapes. Intense ruby-red color with purplish-blue reflections. Full, complex, and
very persistent to the nose, with hints of
spices, gunpowder, violet, wild fruit, and
rare wood. Dry, powerful, velvety taste,
rich in cherry, plum, and vulcanized rubber. Long finish with herbal and licorice
notes. Can age well, and complements
roasts or stewed meats.

CAMARCANDA 2000
Made from 50 percent Merlot, 40 percent
Cabernet Sauvignon, and 10 percent
Cabernet Franc grapes. Intense ruby-red
color with purplish-blue reflections.
Intense and persistent perfume with hints
of earth, plum, sour cherry, and wild fruit.
Dry, powerful taste. Long licorice finish.
Can be drunk with grilled red meat, game,
and cheeses, or, once aged, simply accom-
panied by bread.

Visits and tastings: no

SASSICAIA

Tenuta San Guido, località Capanne 27
Bolgheri
Tel: 0565.762003
www.sassicaia.it

Founded: Nineteenth century
Production region: Bolgheri
Wines and grape varieties: 100% reds;
Cabernet Franc, Cabernet Sauvignon

GREAT WINES

Sassicaia 1999
Representative of high-quality Italian wine
throughout the world. A local progenitor of
Bordeaux emulations, it is an exceptional
wine in its refinement, elegance, and
longevity. Made from Cabernet Sauvignon
and Cabernet Franc grapes, it is aged for
twenty-two months in French oak barrels
and then refined for six more months in the
bottle before being sold. Deep ruby-red
color with purplish-blue nuances. Full, complex, and persistent bouquet, with floral
hints and hints of red berry, plum preserves,
and rare wood. Decisive, straightforward,
and balanced in the mouth. With considerable concentration and depth, it shines in
its elegance and cleanness. Long, clean
aftertaste, where notes of licorice and
chocolate can be detected, with mentholated memories. Can be aged for long periods, and should be drunk by itself, as a wine
for meditation, or as a complement to red
meat, game, and roasts.

Visits and tastings: yes, by appointment

UMBRIA

WINE TRAIL *Itinerary*

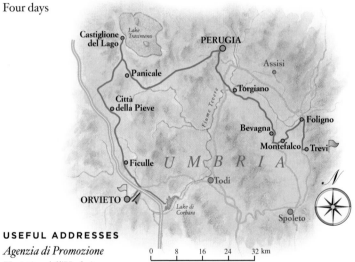

ITINERARY LENGTH
130 miles / 210 kilometers

BEST TIME TO GO
March to November

TIME TO SPEND
Four days

USEFUL ADDRESSES
Agenzia di Promozione
Turistica dell'Umbria
Via Mazzini 21
Perugia
Tel: 075.575951, Fax: 075.5736828
www.umbria2000.it

Associazione Strada del Sagrantino
Piazza del Comune 17
Montefalco
Tel / fax: 074.2378490
www.stradadelsagrantino.it

Associazione Strada del Vino
Colli del Trasimeno
c/o Comunità Montana
Magione
Tel: 075.847411, Fax: 075.8474120
www.montitrasimeno.umbria.it

THE LANDSCAPE STILL resembles those found in the quiet, cerebral canvases of Perugino and the early Raphael, with the same brilliant greens, delicate blues, and gentle, hazy hills. The timeless atmosphere vibrates with the spirituality of Saint Francis of Assisi, Saint Rita of Cascia, and Saint Benedict of Norcia. The flourishing rows of vines that characterize the landscape are receiving significant international recognition. Umbria—a region of hills, picturesque villages, and olive groves in the heart of the Apennines—has joined the wine elite.

Here the art of winemaking has been updated without forsaking the historic relationship between the people and the countryside, viticulture and the culture of wine. The indisputable success of the Torgiano and Montefalco wineries is spurring on other Umbrian products—aside from the already successful Orvieto, one of the few wines in the world that bears the same name as the place where it is produced, like port, Marsala, and madeira—such as denominations like Sagrantino, considered a bit like the new Italian Brunello, and Grechetto, which, along with Chardonnay, is yielding whites of great personality and unquestioned charisma.

A view of the Orvieto grottoes, a labyrinth of differently shaped chambers, tunnels, and passages excavated from the tufa stone for a variety of purposes.

THE WINE ROUTE

IN THE SHADOW OF THE DUOMO

The itinerary begins in spectacular **ORVIETO**, perched on the flat summit of a sheer tufa spur in the Paglia river valley. The city's medieval structure has undergone few changes over the centuries, so it presents a maze of alleys and narrow streets that unexpectedly open up to bucolic panoramas. Walking through Orvieto, one comes across treasures that have attracted generations of travelers before: the grand Palazzo del Popolo, now a conference center; the papal palaces built around the original twelfth-century building; the Palazzo Comunale, rebuilt in the sixteenth century on the remains of a medieval building; the church of Sant'Andrea, flanked by an unusual twelve-sided bell tower; and the duomo, a masterpiece of Italian Gothic architecture embellished with fourteenth-century rose windows by Orcagna.

Underneath the city hides another, subterranean one, carved out of the soft volcanic stone: a maze of intersecting grottoes (only two of which are equipped for visits—a former fifteenth-century furnace and a former columbarium), carved below the urban fabric over the course of 3,000 years. They have been used by various cultures over time, beginning with the Etruscans, and today they are a precious source of historical information about *Urbs Vetus*, as Orvieto was known. The Pozzo della Cava, a recently rediscovered vast well, is interesting to visit, as is the Pozzo di San Patrizio (St. Patrick's Well), an underground burial

---

MUSEUMS   *The history of wine in Torgiano*

Thirty years ago, early supporters of Umbrian wines led by Giorgio Lungarotti and his wife, Maria Grazia conceived of and created the Museum of Wine in Torgiano, a medieval village near Perugia and Assisi, and home to the Lungarotti family winery.

The goal to support and showcase regional wine production has been achieved—each year the museum is visited by over 20,000 people. The collection is installed on the lower levels of the seventeenth-century Palazzo Graziani-Baglioni. There are twenty rooms where visitors can examine historical, archaeological, and artistic documents that illustrate the continuous presence of vines and wine, from the third millennium BC to the present. The curiosities on display include a trick jug, also known as a *bevisepuoi* ("drink if you can"), that was used for a social game spanning various eras and social classes, in which a group of friends would gather around a table to try to discover the mechanism that made it possible to drink from the jug. There is also a monumental seven-

teenth-century winepress, known as "Cato's winepress" because of the description given by the Roman politician (and agronomist) in the second century BC. One of the best-known pieces in the museum is a glazed ceramic plate from 1528, signed by Maestro Giorgio Andreoli; it depicts Bacchus as a child, offering some grapes to the satyr that has raised him.

A more recent arrival is the Olive and Oil Museum, created in an old oil mill. The exhibition offers a historical perspective of the origins and dissemination of olive-growing and the various uses of the oil, from medicine to religion to mythology. The many valuable objects include the alabastron, a red figureware container for ointment (below) from the fifth century BC signed by the so-called "Painter of the Foundry," and which depicts a smith giving the Greek goddess Athena a shield with the owl, symbol of knowledge and wisdom and thus of the goddess herself. There is also an interesting three-holed marble oil lamp from Paros, dating back to Daedalic culture (seventh century BC).

chamber over 200 feet (60 meters) deep; this almost counterbalances the 200-foot (60-meter) height of the Torre del Moro, erected in the late thirteenth century during the city's period of greatest economic power. The two spiral staircases, which never intersect, are the brilliant creation of Antonio Sangallo the Younger and date back to the first half of the sixteenth century.

AMID ORVIETO'S VINEYARDS

Leaving the city's sheer, rocky walls, a view opens up toward the hillsides covered by traditional vineyards of Orvieto Bianco, which in recent years have been increasingly taken over by red berry grapes. Orvieto is a wine of Etruscan origin, about which various legends have been told. However, it is certain that around the year 1500, when Luca Signorelli was called to fresco the chapel of San Brizio in the duomo, his contract included a clause stipulating "that he would be given as much of that Orvieto wine as he wanted."

To taste one of the best, continue on for 10 miles (15 kilometers) toward **LAGO DI CORBARA**, to the Azienda Agricola Decugnano dei Barbi, a property formerly owned by the church, with a splendid view of Orvieto. In the brand-new tasting room—a space that used to be a modest temple—visitors can taste not only Orvieto Classico Superiore DOC, but also a memorable, "traditional method" spumante brut, and a *pourriture noble*, a "noble rot" wine for the record books, one of the foremost Italian sweet wines. With great pride, Claudio Barbi, a second-generation winemaker, harvests his grapes by hand, in small crates, and the grapes are pressed immediately after picking. Once bottled, the wine is kept in the spectacular grottoes carved into the tufa beneath the hill.

AMIDST HILLS AND CASTLES, TOWARD TRASIMENO

The trip continues northward to **FICULLE,** with a visit to the monumental Castello della Sala, built for the Monaldeschi della Vipera and one of the most beautiful medieval fortresses in Italy. Piero Antinori, who is known internationally for his excellent red wines, risked his reputation by starting to produce white wines, such as the elegant Cervaro della Sala and the Conte della Vipera. Years of experimentation,

Città della Pieve, rising above its walls, which are medieval like its fortress and the layout of the town.

under the guidance of Renzo Cotarella—who with his brother was named the best winemaker in 2001 by *Wine Enthusiast*—led to results, and today the whites are of the highest quality. In addition to the aforementioned Cervaro della Sala, considered one of the best in Italy, there is the Muffato, a sweet wine, fine in structure and harmonious, and an excellent complement to desserts and cheeses marbled with green mold.

After leaving the castle, take the Nibbio pass (at an altitude of over 1,900 feet [580 meters]), which

offers a splendid 360-degree panorama of the gentle slopes that yield the grapes for DOC Colli del Trasimeno, one of the best in Italy. A bit farther along is **CITTÀ DELLA PIEVE**, birthplace of the artist Pietro Vannucci, known as Perugino. Descending toward the lake, an expanse of vineyards and the typical Umbrian landscape of woods and olive groves surround **CASTIGLIONE DEL LAGO**. This village on the shore of Trasimeno lake is home to the remains of a medieval castle and, in the church of the Maddalena, the *Madonna and Child with Saints* by a follower of Perugino.

A broad panoramic road along the lake leads to Panicarola, a hamlet of the medieval village of **PANICALE**. Here the strong-willed Patrizia Lamborghini took over the reins of her family's winery, La Fiorita, and completely overhauled its production. Today its wine has a presence on the international market, with two successful reds, the Trescone and the Campoleone, the company's leading wine.

A beautiful road amid the vineyards stretches from Perugia to the illustrious Lungarotti cellars in **TORGIANO**. This is where, twenty years ago, the rediscovery of Umbrian wines—and in a certain sense, a rediscovery of the wines from the entire region—began. The winery is run by two sisters, Teresa Severini, an oenologist, and Chiara Lungarotti, an agronomist. Under their leadership, two new labels with strong personalities have come to the fore—Aurente, a Chardonnay, and Giubilante, a red. And there are two

A view of Panicale, a scenic village on the hills south of Trasimeno.

other reds that are also doing well, the Rubesco Riserva Vigna Monticchio DOCG and the San Giorgio.

It is advisable to visit the cellars and attend a tasting in the company of Angelo Valentini, a great scholar of the history of Italian wine production who came to doubt the primogeniture of the Champagne conceived by Dom Perignon. Valentini's theory is based on a text by Francesco Sacchi where, in 1622, forty-six years prior to the official birth of the French monk's "bubbles," there is a description of a sparkling wine produced by Benedictine monks in Umbria. Because of this, Valentini suggests replacing the phrase "traditional method" with "Benedictine method." In any case, the entire region, which is now brimming with tourists and shops, has benefited from the success of the cellars, as well as the Museum of Wine and the more recent Olive and Oil Museum, both established by the Fondazione Lungarotti.

IN THE LAND OF SAGRANTINO

The journey continues toward **BEVAGNA**, a sort of open-air medieval museum and among the towns with the highest standards of living in Italy, and then **MONTEFALCO**, home of Sagrantino. In recent years the Montefalco Sagrantino DOCG, a full-bodied and elegant red that should be tasted after it has aged, has met with extraordinary success, contributing to the region's popularity. The Passito, which has few rivals in the world, and the Montefalco DOC are also excellent.

TAKE A BREAK

LODGING

Città della Pieve: **LOGGE DEL PERUGINO PARK HOTEL**
Viale Cappuccini 7
Tel: 0578.298927, Fax: 0578.297340
In a Renaissance palace just outside the center of town, this hotel's few rooms offer a view of the hills; there is also a fully equipped spa.

Trevi:
ANTICA DIMORA ALLA ROCCA
This hotel offers an elegant and romantic stopover in a seventeenth-century palace, where care is paid to every detail.

DINING

Orvieto: **IL GIGLIO D'ORO**
Piazza Duomo 8
Tel: 0763.341903
This restaurant right in the Piazza del Duomo, awarded three stars by Michelin, serves country dishes interpreted by chef Enzo Santoni: *invol-tini* of lettuce and ricotta, *lombrichelli* (a type of spaghetti with Umbrian pesto), rack of lamb with thyme served with leek sauce. The wine list is superb. Leave room for dessert—all made to order and presented impeccably.

Castiglione del Lago:
RISTORANTE L'ACQUARIO
Via Vittorio Emanuele 69
Tel: 075-9652432
Ilio Chiuchiulotto presents his creations based on fish from the lake: Trasimeno caviar, or carp eggs served with grilled bread, linguine with smoked tench, and rolls of bass stuffed with lake shrimp. There is an extremely original dessert, only by special order: the *tarzminas*, a bass mousse with "queen carp" eggs caramelized with Cognac. The extensive wine list includes about twenty-five Trasimeno labels.

Typical products of Orvieto; an interior in the Logge del Perugino Park Hotel.

Local success stories include the historic Antonelli San Marco winery, first mentioned as far back as the thirteenth century and which also produces organic oils, and the winery of the great Arnaldo Caprai, in **TORRE**. The latter has been a leading figure in the rebirth of wines in the region. His Sagrantino di Montefalco from 1999, which his son Marco had strongly encouraged since 1993, is warm, soft, and enveloping in the mouth but robust in structure; it is a point of reference and recognized for its quality. The winery's continuous experimentations, which have contributed to the dissemination of dry Sagrantino, are carried out by a team of young graduates in collaboration with the School of Agriculture at the University of Milan.

From Montefalco the road descends to **FOLIGNO**, whose vigorous medieval past is revived every September with the "Giostra della Quintana," a courtly jousting tournament.

The last stop on the journey is **TREVI**, built on a hill of olive groves that dominates the plain of Spoleto. This is the capital of Umbrian olive oil, and tastings and purchases are a must. The numerous possibilities include an excellent extra-virgin Frantoio oil. Visitors to the facility can observe the various phases of processing by walking through a Plexiglas tunnel that traverses the entire length of the establishment.

Beyond the entrance to the cellar of the Azienda Agricola Decugnano dei Barbi, a great Orvieto ages in barrels.

LABELS TO LOOK FOR

AZIENDA AGRICOLA DECUGNANO DEI BARBI

Località Fossatello
Orvieto
Tel: 0763.308255
www.decugnanodeibarbi.com

Founded: 1973
Production region: Orvieto
Wines and grape varieties: 50% whites, 50% reds; Grechetto, Procanico, Verdello, Drupeggio, Chardonnay, Sangiovese, Canaiolo, Merlot, Cabernet Sauvignon

GREAT WINES

"IL" Decugnano dei Barbi Bianco 2000
A blend of Grechetto, Procanico, Verdello, Drupeggio, Chardonnay, and Sauvignon grapes. Refined in the barrel for at least four months. Straw-yellow color and full and intense perfume with hints of ripe fruit and spices. Elegant, flavorful, and balanced. Complements hors d'oeuvres, fish, and shellfish.

"IL" Decugnano dei Barbi Rosso 1998
Made from Sangiovese, Canaiolo, Montepulciano d'Abruzzo, Merlot, and Cabernet Sauvignon grapes. Aged for two years in barrels of French oak. Ruby-red color with purplish-blue reflections. Intense and persistent bouquet of wild fruit, licorice, and juniper. Austere and full-bodied in the mouth, with a long, pungent finish.

Visits and tastings: yes, by appointment

FATTORIA CASTELLO DELLA SALA

Località Sala
Ficulle
Tel: 0763.8605
www.antinori.com

Founded: 1940
Production region: Ficulle
Wines and grape varieties: 90% whites, 10% reds; Grechetto, Procanico, Chardonnay, Sauvignon Blanc, Pinot Noir

GREAT WINES

Cervaro della Sala 1998
A mix of 80 percent Chardonnay and 20 percent Grechetto, vinified separately. Fermentation in new barrels for five months and then aged in bottles for another ten months. Intense straw-yellow color. An intense, fruity perfume with nuances of vanilla. Complex and structured taste with very persistent aftertaste. Should be drunk by itself, as an aperitif, or as a complement to savory fish dishes.

Muffato della Sala 1997
Made from 60 percent Sauvignon and 40 percent Grechetto, Traminer, and Riesling grapes. Grapes are exposed to the *Botrytis cinerea* mold. The golden yellow color intensifies with aging. Intense perfume with hints of peach and honey, and a harmonious and complex taste. Excellent dessert wine, and also goes well with marbled cheeses.

Visits and tastings: yes, by appointment

AZIENDA AGRICOLA LA FIORITA

Località Soderi 1
Panicale
Tel: 075.8350029
www.lamborghinionline.it

Founded: 1971
Production region: Panicale
Wines and grape varieties: 100% reds; Sangiovese, Merlot, Ciliegiolo, Cabernet Sauvignon

GREAT WINES

Campoleone 1998
A blend of 50 percent Sangiovese and 50 percent Merlot, with the two varieties vinified and aged separately. Dark purplish-blue red color, with hints of wild fruit, chocolate, and licorice. Full, oily, and velvety taste. Should be aged five to ten years, and complements red meat and aged cheeses.

Trescone 1998
A blend of Sangiovese (50 percent), Ciliegiolo (30 percent), and Merlot (20 percent), fermented in steel and then refined for four months in oak barrels. Intense ruby-red color, with hints of wild fruit and spices. Soft to the palate, with tannins and good acidity. Benefits from aging for at least five years, and should be served with roasts.

Visits and tastings: yes, by appointment

ARNALDO CAPRAI

Val di Maggio
Località Torre di Montefalco
Tel: 0742.378802
www.arnaldocaprai.it

Founded: 1971
Production region: Montefalco, Colli Martani
Wines and grape varieties: 30% whites, 70% reds; Chardonnay, Grechetto, Ciliegiolo, Sagrantino, Sangiovese, Merlot

GREAT WINES

Sagrantino di Montefalco25
Anni DOCG-1999
Made from pure Sagrantino grapes, this is the Caprai winery's top wine. It is refined for twenty-four months in the barrel and another eight months in the bottle. Ruby-red color with dark garnet reflections. Very intense and persistent on the nose, with hints of ripe fruit, spices, and vanilla. Powerful, soft, and velvety to the palate. Can be aged for long periods, and complements roasts and game.

Montefalco Rosso Riserva DOC 1998
A wine of rare elegance made from Sangiovese (70 percent), Sagrantino (15 percent), and Merlot (15 percent) grapes. Vivid ruby-red color with purplish-blue reflections. Full and intense bouquet, with hints of wild fruit, spices, and vanilla. Full-bodied and persistent taste. Complements roasts and aged cheeses.

Visits and tastings: yes, by appointment

AZIENDA AGRICOLA ANTONELLI SAN MARCO

Località San Marco 59
Montefalco
Tel: 0742.379158
www.antonellisanmarco.it

Founded: 1881
Production region: Montefalco
Wines and grape varieties: 10% whites, 90% reds; Grechetto, Sagrantino, Sangiovese

GREAT WINES

Sagrantino di Montefalco DOCG 1999
Made from pure Sagrantino grapes, refined for six months in 350-liter casks of French oak, then in Slavonian oak barrels for nine months, and then in the bottle for six months to one year. Intense ruby-red color. Intense and persistent to the nose, with hints of blackberry, morello cherry, undergrowth, and violet. Full-bodied with elegant tannins. Complements red meat and game.

Montefalco Rosso Riserva DOC 1999
Made from Sangiovese (70 percent), Sagrantino (15 percent), and Merlot (15 percent) grapes. Intense ruby-red color tending to garnet. Very intense perfume, with hints of currant, cherry, plum, rose, vanilla, licorice, and tobacco. Dry to the taste, warm with great structure. A harmonious and balanced wine that complements savory main courses and well-aged hard cheeses.

Visits and tastings: yes, by appointment

AZIENDA AGRICOLA LUNGAROTTI

Piazza Matteotti 1
Torgiano
Tel: 075.988661
www.lungarotti.it

Founded: 1962
Production region: Torgiano
Wines and grape varieties: 50% whites, 50% reds; Chardonnay, Grechetto, Trebbiano, Pinot Grigio, Cabernet Sauvignon, Cabernet Franc, Canaiolo, Merlot, Sangiovese, Pinot Noir

GREAT WINES

Aurente 2001
A Chardonnay with 10 percent Grechetto. Aged in the barrel for seven months. Golden yellow color, full and complex perfume with hints of ripe banana and vanilla. Harmonious, dry, and full taste, with subtle oak. Complements risotto with truffles, fish in sauce, and white meat.

Rubesco Riserva Vigna Monticchio 1995 DOCG
Made from Sangiovese (70 percent) and Canaiolo (30 percent) grapes aged for long periods. Aged one year in oak barrels and then for eight to ten years in the bottle. Intense ruby-red color and enveloping perfume. Warm, harmonious, and velvety in the mouth. Can be aged for long periods, and complements red meat, game, and braised meats.

Visits and tastings: yes, by appointment

SICILY

WINE TRAIL *Itinerary*

ITINERARY LENGTH
385 miles / 620 kilometers

BEST TIME TO GO
March to December

TIME TO SPEND
Eight to ten days

Map labels

San Vito lo Capo
PALERMO
Bagheria
Casteldaccia
Cefalù
Erice
Segesta
Termini Imerese
Castelbuono
Paceco
ISOLE EGADI
Alcamo
S I C I L Y A
Regaleali
Castellana Sicula
Marsala
Petrosino
Sambuca di Sicilia
Chiusa Sclàfani
Caltanissetta
Mazara del Vallo
Selinunte
Sciacca
MEDITERRANEAN SEA
Pantelleria
I. di Pantelleria
Valle dei Templi
Agrigento

0   8   16   24   32 km

USEFUL ADDRESSES

*Istituto Regionale
della Vite e del Vino*
Via Libertà 66
Palermo
Tel: 091.6278111
www.vitevino.it

Regione Sicilia
www.regione.sicilia.it/
turismo.web

THERE ARE SO many different Sicilies to know and love. At sunset it is a vivid land, tinged with striking reds, turquoises, and gold. Then there is the wind-blown Sicily, with hot African breezes that shape the dunes and golden beaches and dominate the ruins and the fragrant Mediterranean brush. There is the Sicily lapped by a sea that rages against the rocks, echoing the din of historical battles and duels. And for those who don't spurn the sins of gluttony, there is also another Sicily: one of wines and wine cellars, and intense colors and perfumes that delight the eye and the palate.

In recent years Sicily's oenological terrain has experienced a radical transformation, tied to a new generation that has worked to have Sicily's wines appreciated internationally. This success goes beyond historic labels, such as Corvo di Salaparuta and Marsala, and encompasses the entire region.

THE WINE ROUTE
FROM BAGHERIA TO THE WORLD
Our itinerary begins in noble **PALERMO**, where the perfume of jasmine blends with the hum of the mar-

OPPOSITE PAGE, FROM TOP: In Palermo, a courtyard of the Palazzo Ajutamicristo; on the road between Trapani and Erice; Pantelleria, a sign for the Azienda Agricola Valenza; a windmill at the saltworks between Marsala and Trapani.
RIGHT: a forest of supports for young vines, on the Tasca d'Almerita estate in Regaleali.

The Abbazia Santa Anastasia cellar in Castelbuono, on the slopes of the Madonie mountains.

kets, and elegant Baroque silhouettes alternate with modern cement buildings and extraordinary monuments from the Arab and Norman past, in neighborhoods eroded by time.

The first stop is in **CASTELDACCIA**, site of the historic Duca di Salaparuta wine cellar, founded in 1824 by Prince Giuseppe Alliata. Thanks to the illustrious guests who often stayed at his house—the Villa Valguarnera in Bagheria—his wines moved out from the confines of Sicilian drawing rooms and into the world at large. Today, along with traditional products such as Corvo di Salaparuta, which is sold in some

forty countries, there are great wines such as Duca Enrico (pure Nero d'Avola), Bianca di Valguarnera (pure Inzolia), and a new high-quality line that includes Kados (100 percent Grillo), Megara (Frappato and Syrah), and Triskelè (Nero d'Avola, Cabernet Sauvignon, and Merlot).

TOWARD THE INTERIOR

The journey resumes along the coast, passing through **CEFALÙ**, dominated by its famous Norman cathedral, to **CASTELBUONO**, home to the Abbazia Santa Anastasia cellar, appreciated above all for its Litra, a

Cabernet Sauvignon aged in French barrels. It is located in the Madonie mountains, and the road to the hillside winery climbs through immense fields of flowers and vineyards. The Benedictine abbey that has given its name to the property, founded in 1100 by Count Ruggero d'Altavilla, has been restored and transformed into a luxurious hotel overlooking the sea.

Leaving the abbey, the route heads toward the heart of the island, along scenic and twisting roads, through a fascinating landscape of meadows and hills, as far as **REGALEALI**. In 1830, Count Tasca D'Almerita purchased a large property here that ranged from 1,500 to 2,300 feet (460 to 700 meters) above sea level, which he transformed into a modern estate. Innovations have been made since then to 865 acres (350 hectares) of vineyards and the ultramodern wine cellar. The leading wine is Rosso del Conte Nero d'Avola, with a small percentage of Perricone, brilliant ruby in color and with an intense perfume.

SPLENDORS OF CLASSICAL ANTIQUITY

Continue across the island in the direction of **AGRIGENTO**, passing through another long stretch of hilly countryside, to arrive at the Valley of the Temples—stone prayers raised up to the sky in the fifth century BC—the magnificent remains of the Greek colony of Akragas. The ideal time to arrive is twilight, when the evening light mixes with the artificial illumination, lighting up the amber warmth of the

LANDSCAPE   *The Phoenicians and the saltworks*

Leaving Marsala, intoxicated from the scents and soothed by wine tastings that invite conversation, one can take the coastal route toward Trapani, driving past the lagoon, the Stagnone Islands, and the saltworks of Ettore and Infersa. The latter provide a unique spectacle that changes with the light—the best time of day is sunset, when the mounds of salt protected by the *ciaramire*, the sixteenth-century mills, and the saltworks are tinged with red and orange. As the sun sets and the wind dies down, the light is reflected in different tones in each of the many evaporation tanks. Climbing onto the terrace of the great Infersa mill, which recently has been restored, including its wooden gears, one is confronted by a mosaic of fiery colors that as soon as the sun disappears becomes a sheet of silver. Silence reigns.

Among the gullies of the Ettore and Infersa saltworks is the oldest wharf for boats leaving for Mozia, the small island at the center of the Stagnone group. Phoenician in origin, it was destroyed in 397 BC by the Syracusans, and exiles from the island settled on the coast, laying the foundations of what would later become Marsala.

Doric buildings, enveloping in magic the grandeur of this rich legacy from the Greeks.

Leaving Agrigento in the direction of Selinunte, head back toward the interior, toward **SAMBUCA DI SICILIA** to visit the Planeta cellar. For several generations the family has been engaged in agricultural activities, and since 1985 the young descendants—Alessio, Francesca, and Santi—have devoted themselves to wine, in particular working to bring attention to indigenous varieties, to restore the island's oldest and most prized production. They are also planting and adapting certain international grape varieties, initially concentrating their efforts on Sambuca di Sicilia and Menfi. They achieved success with the Chardonnay, which they produce along with a splendid Cometa (100 percent Fiano) and a red Santa Cecilia (100 percent Nero d'Avola).

"Classic" Sicily, the heart of the ancient Greek Mediterranean, is evoked most intensely in the area of **SELINUNTE**, where in the springtime masses of flowers frame the temple ruins. Built in the seventh century BC by the inhabitants of Megara Hyblaea, this Greek settlement near Syracuse enjoyed an extraordinary level of development, as evinced by the splendid monuments that remain. In 409 the Carthaginians destroyed the settlement, which was

Square foundations stones, fallen column drums, and surviving pediments at the Selinunte temples stand out against the yellow of the juniper bushes.

Faces of Pantelleria;
ABOVE: **Marco De Bartoli, in an image that symbolizes his passions, wine and period cars.** *BELOW:* **the low vines of Pantelleria.** *OPPOSITE PAGE, ABOVE:* **Azienda Agricola Valenza.** *BELOW:* **a selection of De Bartoli bottles, and a young vine that is sprouting.**

DAUGHTER OF THE WIND   *Pantelleria*

Black rocks and immense flowering prairies, *dammusi* (the typical cubic stone houses), dry masonry walls, vines, the sirocco and the mistral: This is Pantelleria. The Arabs called it *Bent el-Rhia*, daughter of the wind, and this small volcanic island seems lost in the sea between Sicily and Tunisia. The dry coasts, without beaches, are in contrast with the green interior, with tilled terraces where vines raised from saplings are planted in small hollows to protect them from the wind. These volcanic lands are planted with Zibibbo (from the Arabic *zabib*), also known as Muscat of Alexandria, a type of aromatic, sun-ripened Muscat grape, used to make Passito di Pantelleria and Moscato di Pantelleria. A result of the scant rainfall, high temperatures, and volcanic soil, these two wines celebrate the perfumes and tastes of the island, with a predominant sweetness that is never cloying, in part because of the aromatic quality of the aftertaste.

The finest Passito di Pantelleria is found in three labels: Ben Ryè, from Donnafugata (it can be tasted only at the winery's Marsala location); Bukkuram, from Marco De Bartoli; and Monastè, from Azienda Agricola Valenza (the latter two can be sampled on site).

PERSONALITIES   *Leaders*

Marco De Bartoli and Salvatore Valenza are two wine artists who have sought to produce passito as it has been created for centuries on the island, without succumbing to the market. One only has to talk to these two great winemakers to understand the enthusiasm they bring to their product.

The straightforward and direct manners of De Bartoli, a nonconformist by conviction, have turned him into a true leader in the Sicilian wine world. People either love him or hate him; there is no in-between. He was the first to offer a Marsala wine made only with his own grapes, so that he could constantly check for quality control. For this reason he withdrew for years to the old family property in the district of Fornaia Samperi, just outside Marsala, where wine has been produced for over 200 years. His first mission was to reestablish Marsala, a project he began in the early 1980s, going against everyone's advice. After a few years, it was his turn to shine. "Marsala is often produced as an industrial product," De Bartoli explains, "while we are an artisan winery. We have always worked in search of quality, cultivating a limited quantity of Grillo and Inzolia on each acre, selecting the grapes and perfecting our vinification and aging methods. After struggling to re-create a place for Marsala, my challenge was to launch a Passito di Pantelleria, made in the traditional manner. Now, I can say with satisfaction that the other great houses are following my example." Amid the disorganized charm of Samperi's old barrels and cellars, there are also cars, another great passion of this repeat winner of the Targa Florio auto race.

FROM THE LEFT: an assortment of wines at the Cantina Planeta, in Sambuca di Sicilia; tasting the Nero d'Avola at the Casa Vinicola Firriato, in Paceco.

OPPOSITE: Fish and fava beans in a refined presentation at the Hotel Elimo, and a plate of busiati (long coil-shaped pasta) with Trapani-style pesto.

ily began marketing it as an extremely high-quality product. The first Italian wine to be granted a guarantee of origin, it comes in three categories: fine, superior, and aged. Three cellars should not be missed: the Florio cellars, the historic originators of Marsala; the cellars of Marco De Bartoli; and the Donnafugata winery, created by the Rallo family.

A visit to the Cantine Florio, one of the most beautiful wineries in Italy, is a truly wonderful experience. The cellars were built by architect Giovan Battista Basile—father of Ernesto, who among other things designed the Teatro Massimo in Palermo, in the late nineteenth and early twentieth century. At that time the family had become so wealthy and powerful through the sale of the fortified wine (in the United States they even managed to sell it during Prohibition, adding the phrase "Hospital Size" to the label and a dosage—one spoonful twice a day), that it owned a shipping company, foundry, fishery, bank, sulfur mines, a ceramics factory, boatyards, the Egadi islands, and the villa Igea in Palermo.

A visit to the Donnafugata wine cellars is fascinating, particularly if followed by a tasting of their famous wines, such as the Mille e Una Notte, the Chiarandà del Merlo, or the Ben Ryè (a passito from Pantelleria). These three are all outstanding for their superb elegance.

Alongside the network of roads leading toward **PETROSINO**, immense expanses of vineyards of Grillo, Inzolia, and Catarratto Latino grapes appear—

abandoned and forgotten until its rediscovery in the early nineteenth century.

THE CELLARS OF MARSALA

Twenty-five miles (40 kilometers) beyond Selinunte lies **MARSALA**, a pleasant seaside town on Cape Boeo, and the center of one of the island's most important wine-producing regions. Marsala was appreciated and marketed throughout Europe by the English more than two centuries ago—the first exporter was John Woodhouse—until the Florio fam-

TAKE A BREAK

LODGING

Palermo: **PALAZZO AJUTAMICRISTO**
Via Garibaldi 23
Tel: 091.6161894
www.palazzo-ajutamicristo.com
To fully experience life in Palermo, the ideal solution is to treat oneself to a night at the Palazzo Ajutamicristo, built in the fifteenth century for a Pisan banker who grew rich rapidly and became a baron. On the first floor the palace opens up in a colonnade, followed by a terrace that extends out toward the rooftops of the city.

Castelbuono:
RELAIS SANTA ANASTASIA
Contrada Santa Anastasia
Tel: 0921.672233
A former Benedictine monastery from the twelfth century has been transformed into a luxury hotel that offers twenty-eight rooms, furnished with antiques. The Ruggero parlor is extremely beautiful, with a large hearth and valuable paintings. The restaurant's cuisine is excellent and is based on traditional dishes.

Marsala: **LOCANDA LA FINESTRA SUL SALE**
Cantrada Ettore Infersa
Tel: 0923.966936
www.cilastour.com
The site of the local sailing school has been transformed into this inn, with three elegant and welcoming rooms from which one can enjoy a close-up view of the saltworks. One of them, Room 4, also has a large terrace with a 360-degree view of the Stagnone and Egadi islands and the hills as far as Mount Erice.

DINING

Agrigento: **BAGLIO DELLA LUNA**
Contrada Maddalusa, Valle dei Templi
Tel: 0922.511061
Start with lobster cooked in green pepper and crostini with sesame, then move on to *mezzelune* (crescent-shaped pasta) with a sauce of swordfish, and lobster in basil and mullet roe sauce. Try the fresh grilled tuna with aromatic couscous, the sweet pepper fondue, and the creamy Pachino tomato soup with mint. End with dessert of melted chocolate over a pistachio parfait with two sauces. The wine list is good. There are also rooms available, some with views of the Valley of the Temples.

Erice: **HOTEL ELIMO**
Via Vittorio Emanuele 23
Tel: 0923.869377
www.charmerelax.com
The hotel appears a bit like a house, a bit like a garden, with the rooms laid out in labyrinthine fashion, as in certain African lands. The restaurant offers innovative cuisine and an owner who is also a poet and great storyteller—worth getting to know and listening to.

San Vito Lo Capo: **RISTORANTE DELL' HOTEL CAPO SAN VITO**
Via San Vito 1
Tel: 0923.972122
Behind two rocks that seem carved by hand, a crescent of white sand extends along a warm, transparent sea: San Vito Lo Capo. At the Hotel Capo San Vito, furnished in nautical style with the addition of Arab furniture, an elegant and refined atmosphere reigns, with an excellent restaurant.

the three varieties used to create Marsala. Right in the midst of this—which if it were not for the hot African wind would seem almost more like Monferrato than Sicily—is where Marco De Bartoli retired to an old family farm in **SAMPERI**, just outside of Marsala. He is the person who has been most committed to relaunching Marsala internationally as a high-quality wine. After first making a reservation, one can pay a visit to the winery and attend a tasting, beginning with Vigna la Miccia and ending with the sublime Vecchio Samperi.

Before leaving Marsala, it is worth observing the master coopers at Marsal Botti, a company that has been making oak and chestnut containers for more than two centuries. To see the craftsmen at work bending the staves over a fire, the most spectacular phase of their labor, one has to arrive early in the morning. Entering the large workroom, at first it is impossible to see because of the lack of light. After a moment, one can make out the thin figures of the coopers who, with agile, rapid movements, cut, fold, and beat the wood until, as if by magic, it assumes the desired shape.

GRAND PANORAMAS OF SEA AND HISTORY

The trip resumes, heading toward **TRAPANI**. Beyond the saltworks and just outside the city, one can stop in the agricultural center of **PACECO**. There, at the Casa Vinicola Firriato vineyards an ele-

ABOVE, FROM TOP: Marsala wines in the Cantine Florio, and a view of Azienda Agricola Donnafugata, with barrels of Mille e Una Notte.

OPPOSITE: the bending of the staves over a fire, an old artisan craft still practiced in Marsala at the Marsal Botti establishment.

The Chiesa Matrice in Erice, preceded by a fifteenth-century pronaos and flanked by a bell tower, originally erected in 1322 as a watchtower.

gant, pure Nero d'Avola called Harmonium can be sampled. Other surprises are in store. From Trapani, the road turns toward **ERICE**, already famous in ancient times for the temple dedicated to Venus, known here as Erycina. Silence reigns in the triangular medieval village built entirely from stone and perched on Mount San Giuliano, at an altitude of 2,400 feet (750 meters), on the westernmost point of Sicily. All around are sweeping vistas, from the Egadi Islands to the saltworks, from the curve of Trapani to the Gulf of Bonagia. The town is extremely fascinat-

ing, with close paved streets climbing from the Chiesa Matrice church toward the castle of Venus on the acropolis, crowned with typical well-tended and flowering courtyards. Leaving Erice, the road descends vertiginously toward **SANT'ANDREA BONAGIA**, passing a little town called **PURGATORIO** before arriving at **SAN VITO LO CAPO**, a corner of paradise. The town, Arabic in feel, claims one of the most beautiful beaches in Sicily, chiseled by sea and wind. An ancient Saracene fortress that has often transformed over the cen-

turies, it was built around a sanctuary named for the Mazzarese saint. The barren, wild landscape and the clear line of the mountains recall nearby Africa, as does the typical local dish—couscous with fish—which mixes spices and flavors to pleasantly confound the senses. Traveling along a beautiful coastal road, the next stop is the **ZINGARO NATURE RESERVE**. Cars must be left behind here, but an easy path continues among craggy rocks, wild vegetation, and surprising views, past spectacular small creeks; the silence is interrupted only by the slow noise of the waves. It is difficult to imagine a better ending for such a lovely journey. And yet the return trip to Palermo also includes **SEGESTA**, a Greek theater built into the summit of the hill, so beautiful it takes one's breath away.

The spectacular view from Erice that extends eastward toward the promontory of San Vito Lo Capo, with Sòlanto point in the background.

ABBAZIA SANTA ANASTASIA

Castelbuono
Tel: 0921.671959
www.abbaziasantanastasia.it

Founded: 1980
Production region: Castelbuono
Wines and grape varieties: 70% reds, 30% whites; Inzolia, Chardonnay, Sauvignon Blanc, Nero d'Avola, Merlot, Cabernet Sauvignon, Nerello Mascalese

GREAT WINES

MONTENERO 2000
A blend of 60 percent Nero d'Avola, 20 percent Merlot, and 20 percent Cabernet Sauvignon. Intense ruby-red color, full-bodied, great structure and elegant on the nose, with a complex and structured bouquet. Warm, harmonious, with hints of very ripe wild fruit, soft wood, and preserves. Very long and clean aftertaste. Excellent for aging, and complements red meat, either grilled or roasted.

LITRA 2000
Made from pure Cabernet Sauvignon grapes, this is a wine of superb elegance. Aged for ten to eleven months in new French oak barrels, then refined for about one year in the bottle. Intense ruby-red color, has a complex, fine, persistent perfume with a good presence of red berry and mentholated hints. Dry, powerful, and velvety, with a full-bodied taste. Deserves long aging, and complements red meat.

Visits and tastings: yes, by appointment

TASCA D'ALMERITA

Tenuta di Regaleali, Sclafani Bagni
Tel: 0921.544011
www.tascadalmerita.it

Founded: 1970
Production region: Regaleali
Wines and grape varieties: 50% whites, 50% reds; Inzolia, Varietà Tasca, Cataratto, Chardonnay, Sauvignon Blanc, Nero d'Avola, Merlot, Cabernet Sauvignon, Nerello Mascalese, Perricone

GREAT WINES

Rosso del Conte 2000
Made from Nero d'Avola grapes and some Perricone. Traditional vinification in red and subsequent refinement in 300-liter barrels of French oak. Intense ruby-red color, with purplish-blue reflections. Full and persistent to the nose, with hints of cherry, morello cherry, walnut hull, vanilla, and cinnamon. Dry, powerful, flavorful, and spicy taste, rich in ripe fruit, cherries in brandy, and sweet tannins. Can be aged considerably, and complements red meat, roasts, and game.

Nozze d'Oro 2000
Made from 60 percent Inzolia and 40 percent Sauvignon Blanc grapes, vinified entirely in steel. Straw-yellow color, intense and fragrant perfume with hints of apple, peach, melon, and honey. Dry, elegant, fresh taste with fruity notes and balanced acidity. Can be drunk young as an aperitif, or aged three to five years. Complements white meat or aged cheeses.

Visits and tastings: yes, by appointment

CANTINA PLANETA

Contrada Dispensa
Menfi
Tel: 0925.80009
www.planeta.it

Founded: 1995
Production region: Sambuca di Sicilia, Menfi, Noto, Vittoria
Wines and grape varieties: 50% reds, 50% whites; Chardonnay, Grecanico, Moscato di Noto, Fiano, Sauvignon, Nero d'Avola, Frappato di Vittoria, Merlot, Cabernet Franc, Cabernet Sauvignon, Syrah

GREAT WINES

Cometa 2001
Made from 100 percent Fiano grapes. Intense straw-yellow color with green reflections. Intriguing, aromatic bouquet, with floral hints and white peach, grapefruit, tropical fruit, honey, and thyme. Full-bodied, structured in the mouth, sumptuous but clean thanks to good acidity. Can be drunk in thirteen to fifteen years, and complements fish, vegetable and shellfish soups, chicken à l'orange, and ricotta with honey.

Santa Cecilia 2001
Pure Nero d'Avola. Intense ruby-red color with purplish-blue reflections. Intense, fruity nose with hints of wild fruit and cherries in brandy. Flavorful on the palate, balanced with fresh acidity, and a good presence of soft tannins. Should be aged at least five years, and complements pork roast, red meat, smoked meat, or stewed fish with very well-seasoned sauce.

Visits and tastings: yes

AZIENDE VITIVINICOLE DONNAFUGATA

Via Lipari 18
Marsala
Tel: 0923.7242000
www.donnafugata.it

Founded: 1983
Production region: Contessa Entellina, Pantelleria
Wines and grape varieties: 55% whites, 40% reds, 5% dessert wines; Ansonica, Catarratto, Chardonnay, Zibibbo, Nero d'Avola, Cabernet Sauvignon, Merlot

GREAT WINES

Chiarandà del Merlo 2001
Made from 50 percent Ansonica and 50 percent Chardonnay grapes, vinified separately. Brilliant straw-yellow color. Characterized by a straightforward and persistent perfume, with hints of yellow apple, peach, vanilla, and peanut butter. The taste combines power, complexity, refinement, and balance. Should be aged at least three to five years, and complements smoked fish, Sicilian first courses, and mushroom timbales.

Mille e Una Notte 1999
Made from 90 percent Nero d'Avola grapes and other indigenous varieties for the remaining 10 percent. Dense ruby-red color. Intense and persistent perfume, with fruity, balsamic, and tobacco hints. Great structure, balanced, and complex to the palate, with fine tannins and a long, clean aftertaste. Can be aged for considerable periods. Complements red meat seasoned with spicy sauces and roast mutton.

Visits and tastings: yes, by appointment

CANTINE FLORIO

Via Vincenzo Florio 1
Marsala
Tel: 0923.981111
www.cantineflorio.com

Founded: 1833
Production region: Municipality of Marsala, inland portions of Trapani, Pantelleria
Wines and grape varieties: 100% dessert wines; Catarratto, Inzolia, Grillo

GREAT WINES

Terre Arse 1992
Antique gold color with golden reflections. Intense and persistent perfume, of great refinement, with hints of bitter almond and burnt honey. Dry taste with great harmony, and notes of vanilla and licorice. Should be aged for long periods, and complements smoked fish hors d'oeuvres, aged cheeses, or can be a wine for meditation.

Baglio Florio 1990
Brilliant antique gold color with amber nuances. Intense and ethereal with hints of vanilla, caramelized honey, and toasted hazelnut. Dry, powerful taste, with notes of almond and licorice. A wine for meditation, or excellent as a cold aperitif.

Visits and tastings: yes, by appointment

MARCO DE BARTOLI

Contrada Fornaia Samperi 292
Marsala
Tel: 0923.962093
www.marcodebartoli.com

Founded: 1978
Production region: Samperi
Wines and grape varieties: 17.5% whites, 17.5% reds, 65% dessert wines; Grillo, Merlot, Syrah

GREAT WINES

1986
Vivid amber color with reflections tending to bronze. Complex and persistent bouquet with hints of vanilla, dried fig, toasted almond, and pipe tobacco. Extremely elegant, full and opulent in the mouth, with notes of dry fruit, honey, wood, and citrus. Long and clean aftertaste with notes of dates. Complements medium-aged hard cheeses, or can be drunk as a wine for meditation.

Vecchio Samperi
Every year 20 percent of the content from the solera is bottled, with an average aging of thirty years. Dry, straightforward, and austere, with hints of toasted bread, bitter honey, and candied citrus. Vigorous and balanced in the mouth. A great wine for meditation.

Visits and tastings: yes, by appointment

CANTINA FIRRIATO

Via Trapani 4
Paceco
Tel: 0923.882755

Founded: 1985
Production region: Paceco, Serro district, Soria district, Misiliscemi, Pecoreria
Wines and grape varieties: 60% reds, 40% whites; Catarratto, Grillo, Chardonnay, Inzolia, Nero d'Avola, Syrah, Cabernet Sauvignon, Cabernet Franc, Merlot, Nerello Cappuccio, Nerello Mascalese

GREAT WINES

Camelot 2000
Made from 60 percent Cabernet Sauvignon and 40 percent Merlot grapes. Fermentation in steel, and malolactic fermentation in barrels, where it ages for nine months. Intense ruby color, rich in energy. Intense, full bouquet, with floral hints and recalling licorice, fennel, undergrowth, and spices. Full, structured, elegant, harmonious, and very persistent in the mouth. Should be aged for three to five years, and complements game, such as quail and venison.

Harmonium 2000
Made from pure Nero d'Avola grapes. Aged ten months in small barrels of French and American oak. Intense ruby-red color, complex, long bouquet, with hints of smoke, ripe fruit, cherries in brandy, preserves, and plum. Elegant, harmonious in the mouth, with a presence of wood; extremely graceful, very persistent with fresh acidity that promises longevity. Complements fried grouper.

Visits and tastings: yes, by appointment

DUCA DI SALAPARUTA

Via Nazionale 113
Casteldaccia
Tel: 091.945256
www.vinicorvo.it

Founded: 1824
Production region: Central-western Sicily
Wines and grape varieties: 50% reds, 50% whites; Grillo, Chardonnay, Inzolia, Grecanico, Nero d'Avola, Syrah, Cabernet Sauvignon, Merlot, Nerello Mascalese, Frappato

GREAT WINES

Bianca di Valguarnera 2000
Made from an extremely strict selection of pure Inzolia grapes, harvested by hand. Fermented in wood and aged in small barrels of oak on its own leavens for eight months, then refined in the bottle for another twelve months. Golden yellow color with greenish reflections. Complex and very intense bouquet, with hints of ripe fruit, vanilla, and dry fruit. Dry, full, seductive taste, of great personality and openness. Should be aged about five years, and complements shellfish, tuna, and swordfish.

Duca Enrico 1999
Comes from a selection of the best vineyards of Nero d'Avola and aged for eighteen months in oak drums. Ruby-red color with garnet reflections. Intense perfume, complex and persistent, with hints of ripe fruit and spices. Dry, powerful, full to the palate, with good structure, fine and well-integrated tannins. Can be aged considerably, and complements grilled meat, roasts, and game.

Visits and tastings: yes, by appointment

GERMANY

A JOURNEY INTO the German wine world is a true revelation because of the beauty of the sites and the historical and cultural depth of the viticulture, but above all because of the extraordinary quality and uniqueness of the great German wines. This is particularly true of Riesling, which in regions such as Moselle and the Rhineland has achieved heights of complexity and elegance.

Grapevines have an origin that goes much further back than that of humankind—about 130 million years—and traces of wild vines, descendants of those ancient progenitors, can be found along the course of the upper Rhine. The Romans introduced winegrowing to the regions that make up present-day Germany; even before the birth of Christ, the cultivation of vines was organized and commercially viable along the major German waterway. By the Middle Ages the cultivation of vines, particularly red berry varieties, had reached the borders of the Danish peninsula.

With its ups and downs, geographic shifts, and the evolution of grape varieties, German viticulture has a surprising heritage. German wines are experiencing a period of great renewal today, with a considerable impetus toward new and higher-quality levels. The winegrowing region in Germany is just over 247,00 acres (100,000 hectares, more or less equivalent to the French region of Bordeaux), and its average annual production of approximately 1.3 million bottles represents barely 4 percent of the world output.

Tables set in a room of a winery in Rüdesheim, in the Rhineland.

Close to the fiftieth parallel, German vineyards are some of the northernmost in the world and are somewhat more subject to the rigors of the climate, compared to vines that grow in the Mediterranean region. For this reason, vines are found almost exclusively on south-facing slopes, where they receive the most sun and are protected by forests, which can slow the north winds.

Germany offers some fifty varieties of cultivated grapes, about 80 percent of which are white fruit. The most widespread varieties include Pinot Noir, known as Spätburgunder, Pinot Grigio, Rulander, Müller-Thurgau, Silvaner, and of course Riesling, the king of German wines.

Germany's five great wine regions are subdivided into thirteen districts, almost all arranged along the Rhine valley, which because of its favorable microclimates is an ideal territory for the development of this northern branch of wine production. This is especially true in the Rhineland, the stretch of land where the river, having passed the city of Mainz (near Frankfurt), turns westward, delineating a hilly riverbank with southern exposure. This area is home to many of the oldest and most significant names in the German wine world, such as Kloster Eberbach and Schloss Johannisberg. The Mosel is another river that defines a highly regarded wine region. Because of its winding and spectacular path, the vineyards that overlook the river enjoy excellent exposure, and local winemakers are able to obtain wines of a very high quality.

It is these two regions, the Rhineland and Mosel, that our suggested itinerary explores. It is a journey that combines the best of Germany's history, scenery, and wine flavors.

The bend in the Mosel river at Bernkastel-Kues, with rows of vines in the Doctor vineyard in the foreground.

THE RHINE & MOSEL

ITINERARY LENGTH
160 miles /
260 kilometers

TIME TO SPEND
One week

BEST TIME TO GO
May to late October

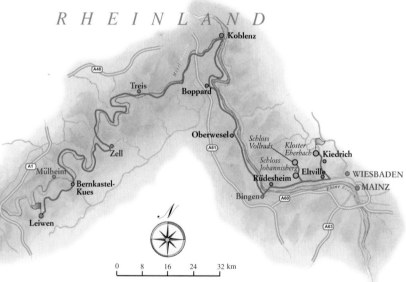

R H E I N L A N D

USEFUL ADDRESSES
German Wine Information
Gutenbergplatz 3/5,
Mainz
Tel. 0049.613128290,
0049.6131282950
www.germanwines.de

THIS JOURNEY BEGINS in the shadows of the great cathedral of Mainz, in the heart of the Rhine palatinate, and follows the course of the Rhine and then its tributary the Mosel almost as far as Trier, Germany's oldest city, situated some 30 miles (50 kilometers) from France. In the Rhineland and along the Mosel, the most important German wine regions, the traveler is immersed in a verdant landscape of soft hills that placidly follow the course of the rivers. The succession of vineyard-covered hills and the consistent climate of this region yield balanced and elegant white wines, which in the eighteenth and nineteenth centuries were as well-known and costly as those of Bordeaux.

THE WINE ROUTE
AMID THE VINEYARDS OF THE RHINELAND

Created by a bend in the river that turns westward for 30 miles (50 kilometers) and grazes the hills that look south, the Rhineland is a climatic paradise within Germany. The slopes of these hills, sheltered from the north winds, were sites of early human settlement, and it has always been an ideal terrain for the cultivation of vines. This landscape is the setting for Kloster Eberbach, the former Cistercian abbey outside of Mainz that was made famous in Umberto Eco's novel *The Name of the Rose* and by the fascinating film of the

261

same name starring Sean Connery. Already known for its wines in the Middle Ages, the abbey has renewed public interest as a winery, producing some of the best Rieslings in the world. The majestic, spectacular structure combines many different styles—including Baroque, Gothic, and Romanesque—which can be admired in the various buildings added over time to the solemn three-nave basilica from the twelfth century. This immense example of medieval architecture contains two spectacular cellars with vaulted ceilings, cen-

turies-old barrels, and suffused light. One, the Cabinet Keller, has been used since the fifteenth century to preserve the most prized wines; the other, the Hospital Cellar, was initially built as a hospital in the thirteenth century but this was immediately abandoned because of its coldness and excessive humidity. Today it holds vintage bottles (from 1853 on). Rhine Riesling has great longevity because of both its high acidity and its considerable sugar levels. A bottle more than twenty years old maintains an intense and persistent perfume, with

hints of rose and a velvety, enchanting taste with notes of tea, tobacco, honey, and even oil. Every thirty years, an important ritual transpires in Kloster Eberbach: Bottles that have aged for long periods are filled up with wine from the same vintage and recorked with new stoppers. If wine from that year is no longer available, glass marbles are placed in the bottle to raise the level of the liquid and to avoid oxidation.

The monastery is located a few miles from **ELTVILLE**, an attractive town overlooking the

WINE *Reading the label*

Reading a German wine label can be rather difficult, in part because of the language, with words that are often long and the meaning of which is not easy to detect (*Trockenbeerenauslese*, for example), but also because of the precise but complex classification system. To find one's way around this maze and choose the wine best suited to every situation, it is necessary to keep a few things in mind. The German wine region is divided into five subregions for the production of table wine, and these in turn are subdivided into thirteen zones from which wines of classified quality are made. Unlike in France, a German vineyard can produce both table wine (Deutscher Tafelwein or Deutscher Landwein) and wine of classified quality. The qualitative classification depends exclusively on the level of ripeness of the grapes when they are harvested. To obtain the best results, frequently there are repeated harvests where only the grapes that have reached ideal sugar concentrations are collected. Wine of classified quality is categorized as follows:

Coming from one of the thirteen specific zones:
Qualitätswein, made from ripe grapes. For all occasions.

Coming from a single district within one of the thirteen zones:
Qualitätswein mit Prädikat, made from completely ripe grapes. For all occasions.

Kabinett, made from grapes that have reached the ideal level of ripeness. A wine of notable concentration, capable of aging well.
Spatlese, made from late-harvested grapes, vinified dry (*trocken*) or semidry (*halbtrocken*). Capable of aging well.
Auslese, made from repeated harvests where only the ripest clusters are collected. A wine of great richness and intensity, this goes well with foie gras and green-veined cheeses. Should be aged.
Beerenauslese, made from repeated harvests during which only the ripest grapes are collected. Sumptuous, rich, with considerable sugar levels, it is a wine that complements foie gras and green-veined cheeses. Should be aged.
Eiswein, made from repeated harvests of only overripe grapes that have been exposed to frost. They are pressed immediately, with the grape still frozen. This is a wine of extremely great concentration, with considerable sugar levels and high acidity. A dessert wine, which can be aged for long periods.
Trockenbeerenauslese, from repeated harvests of only grapes attacked by the *Botrytis cinerea*, the noble rot that gives the wine its unmistakable aroma. A wine of extremely great concentration and high sugar level, it is sumptuous, oily, and sweet. It should be aged for very long periods, and accompany desserts or taken as a wine for meditation.

Rhine. Nearby, a maze of little roads proceeds from the north bank of the river and disappear into the serene order of the rows of vines. The queen of indigenous grapes is the Riesling (and the variety is called Rhine Riesling), which has been cultivated in the Rhineland on choice terrain since being introduced by Benedictine monks from Burgundy in the eleventh century. In **KIEDRICH**, which has the splendid Gothic church of St. Valentin, travelers can visit the cellars and taste the wines from the Robert Weil estate, founded in 1875 (now under Japanese ownership).

The distance between Eltville and **RÜDESHEIM** combines broad landscapes and tempting places to stop to taste great wines accompanied by local dishes such as cheese soup with Riesling, baked ham, or duck filled with figs and plums. At the heart of the Riesling culture there are at least two places that should not be missed: Schloss Vollrads, and Schloss Johannisberg, a former Benedictine monastery founded in 1100, where even in the eighteenth century they were bottling the precious nectar. On the Johannisberg estate, which dominates a sunny slope blanketed with vines, the advantages of a late harvest

ABOVE: The Riesling vineyards at the base of Schloss Vollrads, between Eltville and Rüdesheim.

OPPOSITE: Promises of oenological pleasures at Mulheim (Hotel Richtershof, above) and Oberwesel (Burg Schonburg, below).

OPPOSITE: groomed
vineyard-covered slopes
climb toward a manor
house high above the
Rhine, between
Rüdesheim and Koblenz.

RIGHT: precious volumes
in the library of Schloss
Vollrads.

and exposure to the *Botrytis cinerea* were discovered by chance in 1775. This proved to be truly fortunate for Rhine wine, and is the reason why the original grape variety is often referred to as Johannisberg Riesling.

The two castles are surrounded by estate vineyards, and from their towers or crenellated terraces there is an uninterrupted view of the great river. A visit and tasting at the Vollrads castle begins with a glass of young, fruity wine, served in the vineyard among the rows of grapes. Then visitors continue to the castle itself, with its rooms lined in leather and decorated with arabesques of pure gold, to taste other captivating wines. An unusual tower enclosed by a large moat houses a notable library and historical archive with hundreds of antique volumes.

Rüdesheim is a well-known and rather crowded tourist center facing the river, with typical, narrow paved streets. Excellent Rieslings can be had in the Georg Breuer wine cellar–museum.

ALONG THE RHINE FROM RÜDESHEIM TO KOBLENZ

This is the start of a spectacular stretch of the Rhine valley, where the walls become taller and more imposing and ancient manor houses dominate the bendsof the river. Famous writers such as Johann Wolfgang von Goethe, Mary Shelley, and Lord Byron have celebrated the enchanted atmosphere and beauty of this landscape. This can be the perfect moment to change perspective by boarding one of the many boats that slide smoothly over the water.

There are no bridges between Mainz and **KOBLENZ**. River crossings occur via rapid ferry boats that travel frequently between the two banks. Service is faultless, and it is possible to pass hours on the other shore without losing too much time on long, tiresome transfers. In this region, various extremely beautiful castles have been transformed into luxurious and scenic hotels, set high above the river. Burg Schoenburg is one example—a splendid manor house perched on a crag at **OBERWESEL**. The romantic and refined atmosphere, with the terrace high above the Rhine, makes for an unforgettable stay.

Leaving Oberwesel, the route continues along the west bank, leading to **BOPPARD** a few miles farther on, where there is a chairlift to the most beautiful lookout point in the region: From a clearing in the woods, one can see the narrowest bend in the Rhine, which seems to twist like a snake.

ON THE BANK OF THE MOSEL **KOBLENZ** lies beyond the bend in the river. This former residence of the princes of Trier was built at the convergence of the Mosel and the Rhine, an enviably strategic location. It was formerly a Roman *castrum* (fort), and since time immemorial was a busy commercial crossroads. The road out of the city follows the course of the Mosel—230 miles (545 kilome-

TAKE A BREAK

LODGING

Eltville: **BURG CRASS**
Tel: 0049.6123.69060
www.kellerundkunst.de
This castle just outside Eltville, on the banks of the river, has been transformed into a winery, a restaurant, and a charming hotel. Artistic references to wine are everywhere. The restaurant is in the former cellars of the manor house; in the modern winery, the tabletops are made with wood from crates used for the most prized wines in the world, from Champagne to Sassicaia, a wonderful example of German pragmatism.

Oberwesel: **BURG SCHOENBURG**
Tel: 0049.6744.93930
www.hotel-schoenburg.com
Somewhat intricate, suitable to a castle, with numerous towers, crenellations, and a drawbridge, Burg Schoenburg combines luxury and charm. Meals can be taken on one's own little terrace, or in the austere dining halls. Rooms have canopy beds, and breakfast is served on the terrace as soon as the sun rises, accompanied by birdsong and the distant hum of the barges traveling the river.

DINING

Rüdesheim: **RÜDESHEIMER SCHLOSS**
Steingasse 10
Tel: 0049.6722.90500
Typical cuisine at reasonable prices, with a lovely pergola and music.

Mülheim: **WEINROMANTIK HOTEL RICHTERSHOF**
Tel: 0049.6534.9480
www.richtershof.de
The hotel is a beautiful example of a restored country villa, but it is the restaurant, Culinarium R, that stands out for its elegant, innovative cuisine and attention to regional flavors. Breakfast is served in the old farmyard; visitors can walk in the garden shaded by old trees and rejuvenate at the spa.

Trier: **WEINHAUS BECKER**
OIewiger Strasse 206
Tel: 0049.6519.38080
Young chef Wolfgang Becker, assisted by his wife, Christine, delights the palate with dishes such as millefeuille of foie gras and quail (or venison) crusted in pepper.

ters) of water rising from the southern Vosges mountains in France that marks the boundary between Germany and Luxembourg and flows into the Rhine, passing through intense, shifting landscapes. The valley here is broad, and the landscape is dominated by vineyards; the banks are less rocky and the river's path more winding than that of the Rhine. The itinerary follows the slow progress of the grand barges that travel the river.

The next stop is at **BERNKASTEL-KUES**, a pleasant town cradled in a large bend in the river, surrounded by vineyards and castles. It is considered to be one of the most valuable wine regions in Germany, thanks to the climate, terrain, and ideal slope of the land, which provide grapes with the best exposure to the sun's rays. In the Dr. H. Thanisch winery, in the hamlet of Kues, the charming Sofia Thanisch-Spier produces one of the best wines in Germany. Since 1890 it has been the women of the Thanisch winery who have supervised the vinification: The result is a Riesling, Bernkasteler Doctor, that is considered one of the top hundred wines in the world.

From Bernkastel-Kues, tourist boats depart for excursions on the river, and these are not to be missed. From Mülheim to Leiwen, the boats move along the delightful landscapes of the Mosel. This journey of discovery of great German wines concludes in **LEIWEN**, at the St. Urbanshof winery, where the young Nick Weis continues the family oenological tradition. This is still the world of

Riesling, and it is exciting to visit the room lined with barrels where the white wines are aged.

FROM TOP: Offices of the Dr. H. Thanisch winery in Bernkastel-Kues; precious aging barrels in the St. Urbanshof winery in Leiwen.

KLOSTER EBERBACH

Schwalbacher Strasse 56-62, Eltville,
tel. 0049.6123.92300
www.weingut-kloster-eberbach.de

Founded: Eleventh century
Production region: Rhineland
Wines and grape varieties: 85% whites,
15% reds; Riesling, Pinot Blanc, Pinot
Grigio, Pinot Noir

GREAT WINES

Steinberger Riesling Spätlese 2002
Made from selected grapes collected
from a late harvest in the Steinberg region. Straw-yellow color with golden reflections. Full, intense, and persistent
bouquet, with an opulent, almost oily
taste, and notes of citrus and minerals.
Complements spicy Asian dishes or
creamy desserts.

*Rüdesheim Berg Schlossberg Riesling, Erstes
Gewächs 2002*
A "premier cru" made from a handpicked
selection of overripe grapes. Brilliant
straw-yellow color with golden reflections. Full and persistent bouquet, with
mineral hints and hints of apricot and oil.
A dry, soft, and velvety taste of notable elegance. Great structure and complexity,
and can be aged for long periods. Complements first courses based on fish or
raclette, or, once aged, can be a wine for
meditation.

Visits and tastings: yes, by reservation

SCHLOSS VOLLRADS

Oestrich-Winkel,
tel. 0049.6723.660
www.schloss-vollrads.com

Founded: Eleventh century
Production region: Rhineland
Wines and grape varieties: 100% whites;
Riesling

GREAT WINES

Schloss Vollrads Riesling Spätlese 1993
Made from grapes selected by hand and
gathered at a late harvest. Golden yellow
color, full, complex, and very persistent
bouquet, with hints of ripe fruit, minerals, and oil. Opulent, oily, full taste of notable elegance, with mineral and passion
fruit notes. Can be aged more than fifteen years. Best as an aperitif, or as a wine
for meditation.

*Schloss Vollrads Riesling Erstes Gewächs (Pre-
mier Cru) 1999*
Made from a late harvest of grapes collected by hand in early December 1999.
Intense straw-yellow color and full, very
persistent, and aromatic bouquet. Rich in
notes of minerals and exotic fruit. Full, elegant taste, with notes of apricot and passion fruit. Long, clean aftertaste. Can be
aged for several decades. Should be drunk
on its own, as an aperitif, or with haute
cuisine dishes.

Visits and tastings: yes, by reservation

SCHLOSS JOHANNISBERG

Geisenheim-Johannisberg,
tel. 0049.6722.70090
www.schloss-johannisberg.de

Founded: Eleventh century
Production region: Rhineland
Wines and grape varieties: 100% whites;
Riesling

GREAT WINES

Schloss Johannisberg Riesling Eiswein 2002
Made from hand-selected grapes that
were exposed to the botrytis fungus, harvested in mid-December 2001. This wine
sums up the tradition and character of
Eiswein. Brilliant golden yellow color.
Full, complex, and very persistent bouquet, with mineral hints and hints of
tropical fruit. Sweet, extremely concentrated, and opulent taste. Can be aged for
long periods, and is a dessert wine par excellence.

Visits and tastings: yes, by reservation

WEINGUT ROBERT WEIL

Kiedrich\Rheingau, 5 Mühlberg,
tel. 0049.6123.2308
www.weingut-robert-weil.com

Founded: 1875
Production region: Rhineland
Wines and grape varieties: 98% whites,
2% reds; Riesling, Pinot Noir

GREAT WINES

Kiedrich Gräfenberg Riesling Spätlese 2001
Made from hand-selected grapes collected in a late harvest from the most-prized
vineyard on the property (Kiedrich
Gräfenberg). Delicate straw-yellow color,
fine, elegant, and persistent bouquet,
with notes of apricot and tropical fruit.
Full taste of notable body, very aromatic.
Excellent balance thanks to a fresh acidity that tempers the natural sugar level.
Can be aged at length, and drunk by itself
as an aperitif or as a wine for meditation.

Visits and tastings: yes, by reservation

WIENGUT DR. H. THANISCH

Saarallee 31, Bernkastel-Kues (Mosel),
tel. 0049.6531.2282

Founded: Early nineteenth century
Production region: Bernkastel
Wines and grape varieties: 100% whites;
Riesling

GREAT WINES

Berncasteler Doctor Riesling Auslese 1990
Made from grapes selected and gathered
by hand in a late harvest, from the famous
Doctor vineyard. A wine of excellent elegance and refinement. Straw-yellow color
with greenish reflections, destined to
turn toward gold with time. Full, complex, and very persistent bouquet, with
mineral hints. Rich taste of great balance,
with notes of tropical fruit. Can be aged
considerably, and can complement a wide
range of dishes, from first courses based
on fish to white meat and medium-aged
cheeses.

Baglio Florio 1990
Brilliant antique gold color with amber
nuances. Intense and ethereal, with hints
of vanilla, caramelized honey, and toasted
hazelnut. Dry, powerful taste, with notes
of almond and licorice. A wine for meditation, or, served cold, excellent as an
aperitif.

Visits and tastings: yes, by reservation

WEINGUT ST. URBANSHOF

Leiwen,
tel. 0049.6507.93770
www.urbans-hof.de

Founded: 1947
Production region: Mosel, Saar
Wines and grape varieties: 100% whites;
Riesling

GREAT WINES

Ockfener Bockstein Riesling 2001
A wine of great refinement and elegance,
made from pure Riesling grapes harvested from the Ockfener Bockstein vineyard
on the Saar. Delicate straw-yellow color,
full and persistent to the nose, fruity, with
hints of minerals, slate, and oil. Dry,
clean, balanced taste, with a long aftertaste and mineral notes. Can be drunk
within two to four years, and complements fish, poultry, or spicy dishes.

Ockfener Bockstein Riesling Spätlese 1999
Made from overripe grapes, harvested
and selected by hand. Vinified in steel using only indigenous leavens for the fermentation. Brilliant straw-yellow color.
Full, complex, and very persistent bouquet with hints of tropical fruit, flint, and
oil. Rich, soft taste, with sugar levels balanced by a fresh and elegant acidity. Long
finish with notes of minerals and apricot.
A wine of great refinement, should be
aged at length and drunk by itself.

Visits and tastings: yes, by reservation

AUSTRIA

IT IS DIFFICULT to correlate the origin of wine production in Austria with the present-day reality. It seems certain that in ancient times vines made their way from China to the West, first appearing in Hungary. They then moved in two directions: southward toward the Mediterranean, brought by the Phoenicians as far as the shores of the Empire, and westward, following the barbarian populations that crossed Pannonia, heading toward central and northern Europe. The banks of the Neusiedler See was an obligatory stopping point on this migration, as it was later for Roman troops moving along the "Amber Route" that linked the Mediterranean and the Baltic. And it was along the shores of this lake, which the Romans called *Locus Peiso*, in present-day Burgenland, that the earliest traces of Austrian viticulture are to be found. If the barbarians introduced the vines (around 700 BC), it was once again the Romans who organized their permanent cultivation and above all established the foundations for a wine industry that would last for centuries. Traces of vines and wine emerge intermittently from an analysis of the remains left by the numerous populations that followed in this region (particularly during the Magyar invasion). But written evidence of this does not appear until 1157, in the official documents related to the founding of a monastery in Güssing, which refer to the transfer of some ten vineyards to the Benedictines. A document from 1207 states that the Hungarian king, Imre, made a gift to the Cistercians of a series of vineyards in the area between Lake Neusiedler and the Leitha River (in present-day Hungary). Between the fifteenth and seventeenth centuries the competition between vines from Austrian Burgenland and those from Hungary became so fierce that it led to

RIGHT: the Rhine landscape along the Wachau.
OPPOSITE: the Tement wine cellar in Styria.

the promulgation of numerous laws restricting trade, which in turn led to a widespread traffic in contraband.

Until the nineteenth century wine production in the Burgenland centered on white wines, especially botrytized varieties (Neusiedler See is one of the few regions in the world where *Botrytis cinerea* is found naturally). With the devastating outbreak of phylloxera in France and the resulting scarcity of red wine, local wine producers hurried to increase their own production's, benefiting considerably from the thirty years it took for the disease to reach the shores of the Neusiedler See.

It is worth remembering that it is only since 1919 that Burgenland has belonged to Austria, and of course it was not the only Austrian region to produce wine. Since Roman times the Danube valley has been fertile terrain for vines, and in Styria (close to the border of Slovenia) winemaking has roots that go back to Celtic times. In the Vienna area, noble families possessed vineyards for centuries. These are the regions that the suggested itinerary explores.

The modern history of Austrian wine begins in the late 1980s, with a singular scandal. It was a difficult time, when overproduction of mediocre wines was finding increasingly limited outlets in Germany, traditionally the most important market for Austrian producers. German consumers were increasingly demanding sweet wines of notable structure and concentration, while the Austrian wines were always younger and lighter. Someone discovered that adding diethylene-glycol to wine that was lacking in body had the effect of making it more velvety, full-bodied, and structured. The adulterated wine spread like wildfire, and for years was sold in enormous quantities beyond the Austrian borders. Once the scandal was exposed, the effects threatened the entire wine industry in Austria, but this also created the basis for an extraordinary leap in quality in the past twenty years.

Supported by a series of exceptionally restrictive laws and a system of equally efficient controls, a pool of serious wine producers was quickly able to revolutionize Austrian wine's image. Producers in the Wachau region were the first to react, establishing an association for the safeguarding of high-quality wine (Vinea Wachau Nobilis Districtus), and winemakers from other regions followed. Today the Austrian wine scene has changed radically, thanks to wines that are outstanding in their refinement, their ratio of quality to price, and their distinctive character. These are wines with unique qualities—Riesling or Grüner Veltliner wine from Wachau and Kremstal, robust reds from indigenous vines in Burgenland and Thermenregion, and excellent Sauvignon from Styria. The world of Austrian wine is now filled with surprises that merit careful attention and a place of respect in the cellar of every connoisseur.

WACHAU TO STYRIA

WINE TRAIL *Itinerary*

ITINERARY LENGTH
280 miles / 450 kilometers

BEST TIME TO GO
April to October

TIME TO SPEND
Four to five days

USEFUL ADDRESSES
National Tourism Office
Margaretenstrasse 1,
Vienna,
tel. 0043.1588660
www.austria-tourism.at
Wachau
www.wachau.at
Burgenland
www.burgenland.at
Styria
www.steiermark.com

AUSTRIA IS A surprising country. The astounding scenery changes continually: from the narrow Wachau Gorge, where vineyards scramble up the mountain terraces, to the new Vienna of skyscrapers; from Burgenland, with its Grand Empire style, to Styria, the green prelude to Slovenia. This small corner of Europe produces wines with unique characteristics, wines that long remained anonymous but have now become leading players internationally. For many, they are surprising discoveries. Traveling in Austria is a great pleasure. Every detail is planned to welcome tourists in the finest fashion, and the people are always courteous and open. It is no wonder that in the postwar period this country was able to put together one of the most stable political systems in Europe, establishing itself as an important bridge between different cultures.

THE WINE ROUTE

THE ALLURE OF WACHAU

A combination of Baroque architecture and nature defines Wachau, the valley where the Danube emerges from a wild gorge, northwest of Vienna, delineating one of the most spectacular and seductive

OPPOSITE PAGE, FROM TOP: the Danube in Wachau; a vertiginous ceiling in the abbey in Stift Melk; clusters of Riesling grapes and multicolor squashes in Styria.
RIGHT: a gentle river landscape of tended vineyards in Wachau.

winegrowing landscapes in the world. This birthplace of sublime white wines has harsh rock formations, moderate hills, voluptuous river bends, and woods along the riverbanks. These elements blend harmoniously with those shaped by the human hand: steep, terraced vineyards, monumental castles, imposing fortresses, abbeys, and monasteries. Along the banks of a brief stretch of river, roughly 28 miles out of a total of 1,740 (50 out of 2,800 kilometers), the romantic nature of this slice of Austria emerges. The mutable Danube is enchanting; at some moments it appears like a sheet of silver, reflecting the vineyards, while at others is becomes a golden waterway over which barges slowly glide.

A view of the Wachau region can be had by climbing on foot to the ruins of the Dürnstein fortress (about fifteen minutes along a route accessible to tourists), where Duke Leopold V of Austria imprisoned Richard the Lionheart, king of England. The remaining traces of the building are dominated by the high-pitched red roofs that encircle the blue-and-white bell tower. Jutting out from the rocks, the view stretches as far as the abbey of Göttweig, the Austrian Montecassino. The valley is rocky on one side, plunging straight down to the water, and gently sloped on the other side, in a plain of orderly, serene rows of vines. The scenic road that runs along the Danube celebrates its sinuous course. The origins of wine production here date back to the times of the Celts, although it was the Romans who turned it into

OPPOSITE: the waters of
the Danube and Baroque
elegance in the village of
Dürnstein.

FOLLOWING PAGES:
Weissenkirchen in
Wachau, one of the vil-
lages that dot the valley,
amid hills dense with scenic vineyards.

PERSONALITIES   *Georg J. Riedel*

Georg J. Riedel is the king of crystal wine-glasses made by hand, just like his father and forefathers were. It is a tradition that goes back eleven generations. The company has its roots in Bohemia, and its history is intertwined with events in the Austro-Hungarian empire and Central Europe. They are artists, scientists, technicians, managers, entrepreneurs, and patrons, engaged members of the community, and always innovators, and there is a bit of all this in the character of Riedel glassware. The art—or the science—of glass is their history. But it is only since 1956, when the Riedel family resettled in Austria after a series of moves, that their specialization in wineglasses made the brand a myth. For almost fifty years the Riedels have devoted themselves to the creation of refined tools for celebrating the pleasure of tasting and fully appreciating every type of wine, grasping their every nuance. They are glasses that express a Teutonic precision, coupled with Mediterranean passion and creativity (Georg Reidel's mother is Italian). The Riedels were the first to study wineglasses designed to best transport the aromatic components to the nose and the liquid to the correct points on the tongue and the palate, in order to enhance the bouquet, aftertaste, and balance of the wine. The company creates its wineglasses using an exclusive process, based on repeated tasting workshops. The optimum shape and size is arrived at through the direct involvement of the wine producers—who know the wine better than they do—and Georg, a wine taster of formidable sensitivity, works alongside them. The result: Wineglasses that are perfect for the characteristics of a given wine. Pure, light, subtle—just touching them is a pleasure, just as it is pleasant to chat with Riedel at his beautiful factory in Kufstein, which blends into the mountain landscape of the Austrian Tyrol.

a thriving industry. Rhone Riesling and Grüner Veltliner grapes grow on the rocky, primitive terrain, while the bottom of the valley provides ideal conditions for Neuburger and Müller-Thurgau grapes, the most widespread varieties in the region.

The itinerary begins at the western tip of Wachau, from the abbey of **STIFT MELK**, a colossal Baroque building, bright yellow in color, that played a central, spiritual, and cultural role in the region, first as the residence of the Babenberg family, then, beginning in 1089, as home to Benedictine monks. The historic significance of the complex, whose bulk sits on a rocky spur of land, is immediately apparent from its scale and dominant position overlooking the river. The monks have lived here uninterruptedly for more than 900 years, following the Order of Saint Benedict. In addition to its courtyards, church, and imperial halls, the abbey contains a library, a Baroque masterpiece with frescoes by Paul Troger. The library holds thousands of leather-bound volumes with pure gold spines, many of which are small in size, rather rare for the time, and a seventeenth-century Bible. The terrace offers a wonderful view of the Danube. Along the side of the sacred building, boats leave for brief, scenic cruises to Krems, gliding lazily between vertical walls, past vineyards wedged between woods and drawing on the fertile earth from the mountain, and tiny Baroque villages that extend along the river.

The romantic village of **DÜRNSTEIN** is not to be missed, with its Renaissance courtyards, Baroque

PERSONALITIES   *Arnold Melcher*

Arnold Melcher is quite something. His smiling manners, gentle but decisive, are translated into the Sauvignon Blanc he produces on his 17-acre (7-hectare) vineyard in Gamlitz. In this way he has created a unique white wine, powerful and full of character. It is a golden wine that can cast a spell, above all if accompanied by the fried chicken cooked on the estate for guests. Melcher comes and goes from the cellar with a familiarity inherited from his father, who also made wine (in a more traditional fashion). Despite the youthful energy expressed in his wines, his conversation, his dancerlike dexterity, and in his organization of the jazz and blues Summertimeblues festival (held in Gamlitz in July), he always speaks of his elderly parents with great respect, demonstrating a sensitivity for the past that is striking and perhaps explains the origins of his success.

church, wrought-iron windows, sculptures, and paintings. Just outside the town, on the northern and sunniest slope, are the vineyards of the FX Pichler cellar, one of the most popular in Austria, which produces wines of extreme elegance. At least two other wine cellars should be visited as well in order to appreciate the exceptional refinement and balance of the whites in this region. The Weingut Josef Jamek cellar in **JOCHING** is a name tied to the cultural rebirth of Austrian oenology. It offers wines from the Kellerberg and Nikolaihof vineyards in Mautern, where wine is produced using organic methods and grapes are harvested by hand. Rising on the site is the ancient Roman fortress of Favianis, where in the fifth century one of the first written documents was discovered that attested to wine production in Central Europe.

The cellar has solid Roman walls that survived, undamaged, the catastrophic flood of 2002. The winepress, one of the largest in the world, was used until 1988. In the garden, tables belonging to the tavern are set out beneath an enormous tree, and one can sample typical dishes.

A few miles away is the abbey of **GÖTTWEIG**, an important Benedictine complex that concludes the Wachau part of the trip. Inside the abbey there is another historic library, with volumes from the ninth century.

FROM VIENNA TO BURGENLAND
Following the course of the Danube, the road leads to **VIENNA**, capital city and extremely elegant residence of the Hapsburg emperors. In recent years the

city has courageously introduced new building projects, completely altering its skyline, particularly in the northern section. Glass-and-steel skyscrapers have come to the city of waltzes and historic cafes, and clean, sober lines have prevailed over gold and stuccowork. Yet while experiencing this new Vienna, which surpasses the city's traditional and somewhat faded image, one cannot forget its unusual record: It is the only capital in the world that has vineyards in the city, documented as far back as 1132. Leopoldsberg along the river overlooks the immense (460 square miles) of woods and the vineyards of Nussberg, while the new skyline of the metropolis stands out in the background. This ridge, covered with precise, almost manicured rows of vines, is punctuated by Heuriger-Viennese restaurants set amid the urban vineyards, which open during the harvest and where each place serves only wine of its own production.

In Burgenland, the most eastern and newest region of Austria, the view suddenly changes. Salty pools, steppes, gentle hills, and the Neusiedler See salt lake make this region oenologically superlative. The Alois Kracher is typical of the excellent sweet wines that come from grapes grown along the eastern shore of the lake. The lake functions as a climatic regulator and favors the botrytization of the grapes.

Toward the village of **PURBACK**, typical wine cellars follow one after the other. They are carved into the local tufa stone, a material that allows water to be absorbed and creates ideal conditions for the aging of

TAKE A BREAK

LODGING

Schützen/Gebirge: **TAUBENKOBEL**
Hauptstrasse 27/33
Tel: 0043.2684.2297
www.taubenkobel.at
Three old houses built in 1864 in the heart of this village have been perfectly restored and transformed into one of the best hotels and restaurants in Austria. Walter and Eveline Eselböck have chosen a minimalist, pared-down look. The seven rooms on two floors have canopy beds, are equipped with the most up-to-date technology, and are decorated with works by well-known artists. This is a secret hideaway for many famous people, but their names remain a mystery thanks to the discretion of the hotel personnel. Dishes from the restaurant are an incredible mix of flavors.

Gamlitz: **SCHLOSS GAMLITZ**
Tel: 0043.3453.2363
www.melcher.at
Gamlitz castle was built in the tenth century and then given by the count of Sponheim to the monastery of Sankt Paul im Lavanttal. The monastery owned the property until the arrival of the Melcher family, at the end of the last century. The winegrowing tradition continues, and the vineyards are considered among the best in Styria. There are nine immense rooms,

furnished with antiques and occasional ultra-modern pieces. The manor house drawing rooms host shows the work of contemporary artists, and a wine museum is being installed.

DINING

Joching: **JAMEK WINE ESTATE & RESTAURANT**
Tel: 0043.2715.2235
www.jamekweingut.at
In the pleasant atmosphere of a centuries-old house, wines from the homonymous cellar are served, and in good weather it is possible to eat in the garden, surrounded by terraced hillsides and listening to the simple sounds of nature.

Kapfenstein: **HOTEL RESTAURANT SCHLOSS KAPFENSTEIN**
Tel: 0043.3157.300300
www.schloss-kapfenstein.at
Since 1898 the castle has belonged to the Winkler-Hermaden family. There are two brothers; one oversees the cellar, where he also organizes exhibitions of contemporary artists, and the other takes care of the kitchen. They are both in a class by themselves. Lunch or dinner on the terrace is delightful, with a 360-degree view of the vine-covered slopes.

Roast venison with wild berries.

wine. Elderly winemakers reveal that *weingut* rebuilt using cement are not up to par with the traditional ones. A visit to taste the wines of Birgit Braunstein, one of the female faces in the Austrian wine world, presents an occasion to see the inside of one. Wine has always been her passion, and she has succeeded in transmitting her personality to her Chardonnay Oxhoft, which has won many awards. The most prized area is thought to be that around the village of **RUST**, birthplace of the noble Ruster Ausbruch, a wine that has been famous since the sixteenth century. Some important names to note are the Feiler-Artinger winery, and Ernst Triebaumer, who heads a winery with his son Herbert. Arriving in Rust is extremely pleasant. The road runs among rows of vines that droop down in an arc , following the slope of the terrain, and in the background one can glimpse the lake as far as the Hungarian shore. Properties are very fragmented, and as a result the vineyards have bizarre shapes.

The historic center of Rust is a picturesque collection of modest, bourgeois houses. Built in the sixteenth and seventeenth centuries and painted in delicate colors, they frame a Gothic-style fishermen's church, the town hall, and a tower. Many of the houses have storks' nests on the chimneys. In 1524, during the reign of Marie of Hungary, the citizens of Rust received the privilege of marking their barrels with a crowned "R," to protect their wine from counterfeiting, and the symbol is still often found today on

LEFT: the ferris wheel in Vienna.

OPPOSITE: Der Insel in der Mur, a spectacular island of steel in Graz.

the corks of the principal wine cellars. The specificity of Ruster Ausbruch is tied to the mold, the *Botrytis cinerea*, which regulates the delicate and subtle sweetness of the wine. Another historical event helped make this town unique: In 1681 Leopold I was sent 60,000 gold denari and 500 buckets (30,000 liters) of Ruster Ausbruch—the entire harvest for a year. As a sign of his appreciation, the monarch elevated Rust to the rank of a free town at the imperial parliament in Odenburg. The town's widespread prosperity is attested by the beautiful building façades.

The charm of **EISENSTADT** is quite different. While only a few dozen miles from Rust, it was a free town under the Hungarian crown, beginning in 1648. The sumptuous palace of the princes of the Esterházy family, Hungarian aristocrats who built the residence in the seventeenth century, has become the symbol of Burgenland. Under the influence of the noble family during Hungary's reign, the castle of Eisenstadt transformed and expanded, adding both classical rigor and Austrian Biedermeier style to the structure's Baroque splendor; it eventually became the center of court life and provided a theater for the compositions of Joseph Haydn. The frescoed hall dedicated to the composer boasts extraordinary acoustics, still among the best in the world.

THROUGH STYRIA, TOWARD SLOVENIA

In terms of the landscape, southern Styria also numbers among the most interesting wine-producing regions. **GRAZ**, once the royal residence of the Hapsburgs in the Middle Ages and the Renaissance, has been able to transform itself into a modern city, with an ultramodern technology hub and an important university center (including Europe's only university department of jazz), while still showing appreciation for its past. The historic center is one of the best preserved in Central Europe. Credit goes to the town's citizens, who love it and care for it with an almost filial affection. The admirable outcome, easily visible while walking through the city streets, resulted in Graz being named European Capital of Culture in 2003. The tranquil and relaxed atmosphere of this city rich in art, culture, light, color, and flavors is echoed in the grand architectural innovations that celebrated the event: The placid waters of the Mur, which divides the city in two, come up against a futur-

istic island of steel, lattice, and glass built in the middle of the river. It may look like a ship without sails, or a large clam, but in reality it houses an open-air amphitheater with seating for 250 people, a children's playground, and a café from which one can observe Graz from a new perspective. And there is no ignoring the Kunsthaus, the new museum of modern art, spectacularly designed by English architects Peter Cook and Colin Fournier—a sort of gigantic blue bubble on which are reflected the river and beautiful palace façades .

The romantic nature of this land gradually blends with the characteristics of nearby Slovenia, with its vineyards planted on gentle slopes. Small hollows alternate with valleys covered in orderly vines and dotted with lively colored houses topped by steeply pitched wooden roofs. The *klapotec* are ever present sentinels—rudimentary scarecrows that keep away the birds with the noise they produce when the wind moves them. Amid expanses of sunflowers, squash, and tall woods, the road arrives at the castle in

KAPFENSTEIN that houses the Winkler Hermaden winery, where the excellent Olivin is produced, a red wine made from highly select Zweigelt grapes—a masterpiece. The itinerary continues along a picturesque route to **GAMLITZ**. There, in the summer and autumn one can see carts laden with squash of the most unusual shapes and colors. The gourds are for sale and can be purchased by leaving some coins in the containers left out for that purpose; neighbors here trust each other. In Gamlitz the Sauvignon Blanc of Arnold Melcher excels above others. An artist of wine, imaginative and creative, he lives in a villa—a castle surrounded by a large, flower-filled garden. Slovenia is only a few steps away.

A panoramic view of Vienna, both an old and contemporary capital, from the top of the Prater ferris wheel.

F.X. PICHLER

Oberloiben 27, Dürnstein
Tel. 0043.2732.85375
www.fx-pichler.at

Founded: 1900
Production region: Dürnstein, Loiben
Wines and grape varieties: 100% whites;
Grüner Veltliner, Riesling, Sauvignon
Blanc

GREAT WINES

*Pichler Grüner Veltliner Smaragd
Dürnsteiner Kellerberg 2002*
Made from grapes harvested by hand
between mid-November and early
December, on the terraces of the finest
vineyard in the region (Kellerberg). Straw-
yellow color. Intense, persistent, and elegant bouquet, with hints of mineral and
exotic fruit. Full taste, with hints of
smoke and peach. Long and clean aftertaste. Should be aged at least three to four
years. Complements fish in sauce or can
be a wine for meditation.

FX Unendlich, 2002
A special selection of Riesling grapes
from the terraces of the Kellerberg vineyard and produced only in specific years.
Brilliant straw-yellow color. Complex, elegant, very aromatic and persistent bouquet, with mineral, hints of mango, and
melon. Dry, full, complex taste, with great
balance between body and acidity. Long
aftertaste of apricot and green melon.
Should be aged at least three to four years,
and complements spicy dishes or can be a
wine for meditation.

Visits and tastings: no

WEINGUT JOSEF JAMEK

Joching 45
Tel. 0043.2715.2235
www.jamek.cc
Anno di fondazione 1912

Founded: 1912
Production region: Joching,
Weissenkirchen, Dürnstein, Wösendorf
Wines and grape varieties: 90% whites,
10% reds; Grüner Veltliner, Riesling,
Pinot Blanc, Chardonnay, Muskateller,
Zweigeit, Sankt Laurent

GREAT WINES

*Grüner Veltliner Ried Liebenberg
Smaragd 2002*
Made from grapes selected and harvested
by hand in the Liebenberg vineyard in mid-
November. Brilliant straw-yellow color.
Full, aromatic, and persistent bouquet,
with mineral and spicy hints. Dry, aromatic, balanced, and elegant taste, with
notes of pepper and exotic fruit. Long and
clean aftertaste. Should be aged at least
three to four years, and complements
white meat or fish dishes without sauce.

Riesling Ried Klaus Smaragd 2002
Made from pure Riesling grapes from the
Klaus vineyard and harvested by hand over
a period of three weeks. Vinified in steel
and aged for eight months in large oak barrels. Brilliant straw-yellow color. Intense,
complex, and fruity bouquet, with hints of
exotic fruit and apricot. Dry, harmonious,
and balanced taste, with notes of apricot
and peach. Should be aged at least three to
four years, and complements fish in sauce,
or, when aged up to ten to fifteen years, can
be a wine for meditation.

Visits and tastings: yes

WEINGUT NIKOLAIHOF

Nikolaigasse 3, Mautern/Wachau,
Tel. 0043.2732.82901
www.nikolaihof.at

Founded: 1894
Production region: Mauten
Wines and grape varieties: 100% whites;
Grüner Veltliner, Riesling, Pinot Blanc,
Chardonnay

GREAT WINES

*Nikolaihof Grüner Veltliner im Weingebirge
Smaragd 2001*
A completely organic wine, made from
grapes gathered by hand in the
Weingebirge vineyard and aged for six
months in large oak barrels. Straw-yellow
color with greenish reflections. Bouquet
perfumed with spices and pepper. Dry, full
taste, important and spicy. Long and cool
aftertaste. Should be aged up to twenty-
five years, and complements lamb and
hard, medium-aged cheeses.

Nikolaihof Riesling Vom Stein Smaragd 2001
A completely organic wine, made from
grapes gathered by hand in the Vom Stein
vineyard. Straw-yellow color with greenish reflections. Elegant and floral bouquet
with notes of apricot and peach. Dry,
structured, fine taste, with a long, clean
aftertaste. Can be aged at length, up to
twenty-five years, and complements mollusks, smoked salmon, and roast veal.

Visits and tastings: yes

WEINGUT FEILER-ARTINGER

Hauptstrasse 3, Rust
Tel. 0043.2685.237
www.feiler-artinger.at

Founded: 1936
Production region: Rust
Wines and grape varieties: 30% whites, 70%
reds; Chardonnay, Pinot Grigio, Pinot
Blanc, Sauvignon Blanc, Welschriesling,
Neuburger, Blaufränkisch, Pinot Noir,
Zweigelt, Cabernet Sauvignon, Cabernet
Franc, Merlot

GREAT WINES

Solitaire 2001
A blend of Blaufränkisch and Merlot
Franc, elevated in large oak casks for the
first five months and then in barrels for
twelve months. Ruby-red color with
purplish-blue reflections. Slightly volatile
and not very persistent bouquet, with
hints of new wood, spices, and red berry.
Should be aged and complements large
roasts and stewed lamb.

Ruster Ausbruch Pinot Cuvée 1998
A blend of Pinot Blanc with Pinot Grigio
and Neuburger (an indigenous variety
called Pinot Giallo), the result of a manual
selection of botrytized grapes. Fermented
and aged for eighteen months in new barrels. Brilliant golden yellow color, with
amber reflections. Full, sumptuous, and
elegant bouquet, with hints of exotic
fruit, vanilla, coffee, and bread crust.
Should be aged for decades, and complements green-veined cheeses or foie gras.

Visits and tastings: yes

WEINGUT ERNST TRIEBAUMER

Raiffeisenstrasse 9, Rust
Tel. 0043.2685.528
www.triebaumer.com

Founded: 1953
Production region: Rust
Wines and grape varieties: 25 % whites, 75% reds; Pinot Blanc, Sauvignon Blanc, Chardonnay, Welschriesling, Cabernet Sauvignon, Blaufränkisch, Zweigelt, Merlot

GREAT WINES

Blaufränkisch Ried Mariental 2000
Probably the finest expression of Blaufränkisch. Made from grapes from the oldest vines in the most-prized vineyard on the Triebaumer estate (the Mariental vineyard). Full, complex, and persistent bouquet, with hints of red fruit, ripe banana, and rare wood. Can be aged at length, and complements game.

E. T. 1995 Ruster Ausbruch
A blend of Welschriesling, Pinot Blanc, and Chardonnay, exclusively from grapes botrytized and harvested by hand in late October. Sweet, oily, complex, elegant, and buttery taste, with notes of ripe fruit, honey, and spices. Should be aged, and complements veined cheeses and foie gras, or a wine for meditation.

Visits and tastings: yes

WEINLAUBENHOF KRACHER

Apetlonerstrasse 37, Illmitz
Tel. 0043.2175.3377
www.kracher.at

Founded: 1960
Production region: Illmitz
Wines and grape varieties: 95% whites, 5% reds; Welschriesling, Chardonnay, Traminer, Muskat Ottonel, Scheurebe, Zweigelt, Blaufränkisch.

GREAT WINES

Traminer TBA N° 1 "Nouvelle Vague" 2000
Made from pure Traminer grapes, fermented and matured in barrels of new French oak for twenty-four months. Brilliant golden yellow color. Hints of mango, peach, rose, and spices. Should be aged at least ten years, and complements seared foie gras.

Welschriesling TBA N° 4 "Zwischen den Seen" 2000
Made from pure Welschriesling grapes. Fermented and aged for twenty-two months in large oak barrels. Intense golden yellow color. Hints of citrus, candied fruit, green tea, spice, and tobacco. Can be aged, and complements strong cheeses, or can be a wine for meditation.

Visits and tastings: no

WEINGUT SCHLOSS GAMLITZ

Gamlitz, Styria
Tel. 0043.3453.2363
www.melcher.at

Founded: 1904
Production region: Gamlitz
Wines and grape varieties: 100% whites; Sauvignon Blanc, Chardonnay, Muscat

GREAT WINES

Schloss Gamlitz Sauvignon Blanc Spatlese 1993
Straw-yellow color with golden reflections. Full, complex, and persistent bouquet, with hints of ripe fruit and nuances of oil. Dry, intense, deep taste, with notes of fruit preserves and elderberry. Should be drunk after its first ten years. Can be an aperitif, but above all goes well with fried chicken.

Schloss Gamlitz Sonneck Alte Reben ("old vines") 1997
Made from pure Sauvignon Blanc grapes from a vineyard planted in 1947. Fermented and aged for twenty-four months in barrels. Straw-yellow color with golden reflections. Dry, powerful taste, with great body and hints of vanilla, honey, and cinnamon. Should be aged at least ten years, and complements stewed game, or can be a wine for meditation.

Visits and tastings: yes

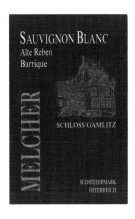

WEINGUT WINKLER-HERMADEN SCHLOSS KAPFENSTEIN

Kapfenstein
Tel. 0043.3157.2322
www.winkler-hermaden.at

Founded: 1898
Production region: Kapfenstein
Wines and grape varieties: 40% whites, 60% reds; Pinot Grigio, Pinot Blanc, Morillon, Traminer, Sauvignon Blanc, Pinot Noir, Zweigelt, Cabernet Sauvignon

GREAT WINES

Grauburgunder Reserve 2001
Pure Pinot Grigio, fermented and aged on its own leaves in barrels for over one year. Golden yellow color with amber reflections. Full and persistent bouquet, with mineral notes and notes of ripe fruit. Full, mature, slightly pungent taste, with hints of exotic fruit, caramel, and smoke. Should be aged up to five years, and complements cream of lobster soup and shellfish in general.

Olivin 2001
Made from grapes selected and gathered by hand, fermented in steel and then aged twelve to fifteen months in the barrel. Complex and persistent bouquet, with notes of spices, wild fruit, and cherries in brandy. Powerful, velvety taste, with fine tannins and hints of new wood. Should be aged at least eight to ten years, and complements red meat and game.

Visits and tastings: yes

SLOVENIA

 SLOVENIA'S OENOLOGICAL HISTORY has distant roots. Vines were cultivated first by the Illiri and the Celts and flourished in Roman times. Medieval monks then expanded the vineyards and improved winemaking techniques.

In the nineteenth century the most advanced local winemakers began publishing technical manuals. Until the end of World War II, wine was produced mainly by farmers and tenant farmers working on behalf of noble families; after the war, large state cooperatives took over. This was a difficult period in terms of quality, with wine production geared toward markets where quantity was the dominant force.

In recent years (Slovenia did not become an independent republic until 1991) there has been a return to private bottling, which has encouraged the birth of a great number of small- to medium-size wineries, resulting in improvements to quality and grape varieties and creating a veritable revival of Slovenian oenology.

Slovenia is a country with considerable wine potential, thanks to its geographic and climatic diversity. The hills, close to the sea and the Alps, the Pannonic plain and the Collio region produce a variety of microclimates and terrains suited to the cultivation of numerous older indigenous grape varieties, such as Ribolla and Refosco, as well as international varieties.

The country has three winegrowing regions, and they in turn are subdivided into fourteen districts, each with specific characteristics. Two of these regions are located in eastern Slovenia, east of Ljubljana, in the direction of Maribor.

The Drava region, influenced by the pannonic climate, produces wines of considerable elegance, closer to German and Austrian wines than to those of southern Europe. Some of the well-known wines include Rhine Riesling,

An olfactory analysis of a Slovenian wine.

Rulander, Sauvignon, and Traminer, as well as many indigenous varieties such as Ranina and Sipon, and sparkling wines. The Sava valley, with brown, calcareous, and dolomitic soil, produces characteristic wines such as Cvicek and Metliska, but also others made from the Franconia Blu grape; there are also some wines that result from late harvests.

The itinerary covers the third Slovenian wine region, Primorska, near the Italian border, traveling from the Adriatic to the Alps and passing through Carso and Collio. In addition to the area's natural beauty (including the grottoes of San Canziano and the Isonzo gorges) and splendid towns and villages (Piran above all), there are a variety of surprising oenological treasures, from the dry, decisive wines of Carso to the wonderfully elegant ones of Vipava and Collio. And the journey will not fail to take a detour into the Italian Collio region, which deserves a place of honor in the European oenological panorama for its great wineries and splendid wines, both reds and whites.

A pedestrian bridge over the ravines of the Tolminka, a spectacular hollow carved by the Isonzo River, near Tolmin.

ISTRIA, CARSO, COLLIO

WINE TRAIL *Itinerary*

ITINERARY LENGTH
130 miles / 210 kilometers

BEST TIME TO GO
April to November

TIME TO SPEND
One week

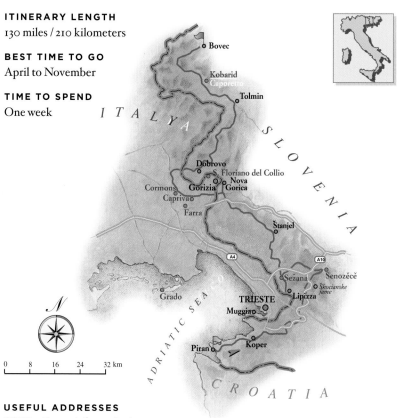

USEFUL ADDRESSES
*STIC—Centro informazioni
turistiche Sloveno*, Krekov trg 10, Ljubljana,
Tel. 00386.1064575, 00386.13064576
www.ljubljana-tourism.si
Movimento turismo del vino Friuli Venezia Giulia, via Manin 12/3,
33100 Udine
Tel/fax: 0432534040
www.mtvfriulivg.it

MINUTE, INDUSTRIOUS, BEAUTIFUL:

After centuries of invisibility Slovenia, a young republic of two million inhabitants wedged between western and eastern Europe, is now one of the most advanced of former Communist bloc countries. Yet even in the time of Tito it was considered the "Switzerland of Yugoslavia."

More than half the region is green, covered with woods, meadows, vineyards, pastures, and rivers— after Finland, it is the greenest country on the continent. And that isn't all. Despite its size (it is similar to Wales), in just a few miles its landscape changes from the Venetian climate of the coast to the gentle hills of the interior, characterized by rows of vines and tilled fields, and then the jagged rocks of the Isonzo valley.

THE WINE ROUTE
FROM ISTRIA TO CARSO

A strip of land jutting into the Adriatic, **PIRAN** is a fascinating seaside village, medieval in feel, that was long ruled by Venice. It should be experienced at dusk, walking along the harbor, when the fading light

OPPOSITE PAGE, FROM THE TOP: a view of the marina in Piran; Spessa castle, in the vicinity of Capriva del Friuli; horses from the renowned stables in Lipica; an old barrel used as a sign in Slovenian Collio.
RIGHT: an image of the Tolminka gorges, near Tolmin (Tolmino); they look idyllic, but it seems Dante drew inspiration from them for images of his *Inferno*.

caresses the immobile boats. The streetlights then come on in the scenic Piazza Giuseppe Tartini, named for the famous violinist and composer who was born here in 1692. Narrow paved streets lead up to a small hill dominated by the Gothic church of San Giorgio. The bell tower is reminiscent of the one at the piazza of San Marco in Venice. From the churchyard the view stretches out along the entire Slovenian coast, to Trieste and the Julian Alps.

The first wine cellar on the itinerary is in **KOPER**, just a short walk from the old city. With 4 million liters of wine produced every year, Vinakoper is one of the biggest wineries in Slovenia. The city is surrounded by an orderly landscape of vines that delineate the terraces and hills overlooking the Adriatic.

Leaving Koper, the route cuts inland toward Kras, an immense plateau of caverns, sinkholes, depressions, and wells. A spectacular example of the limestone terrain can be seen at Škocjanske jame, the grottoes of San Canziano, which require about an hour and a half on foot to explore. The tracery of stalactites and stalagmites creates a splendid picture; Slovenia boasts 7,000 grottoes, but these are the wildest. Less frequented than those in nearby **POSTOJNA**, they offer the visitor unexpected moments of intimacy. Lovely country roads separate the grottoes from **LIPICA**. Surrounded by a park of linden, oak, and maple trees, it seems like an enchanted wood (in Slovenian *lipica* means small lin-

OPPOSITE: a view of the Jazbec wine cellar in Štanjel, which produces great wines, and even sparkling ones.

RIGHT: barrels of the large Vinicola Vinakoper winery in Koper.

FOLLOWING PAGES: the scenic Tartini piazza by night, in Piran.

PERSONALITIES *Ivan Batič*

Ivan Batič is a farmer. His ancestors have worked this land and these vineyards in the heart of Vipava since the late sixteenth century. His gestures are those of the earth, his words reflect the tranquil security of one who has always known nature and its products. In the courtyard of his farm, seated at the stone table beneath the pergola, chatting with the elderly locals, you can sample wines made in accordance with simple and traditional methods, far from the electronic whir of modern technologies. But these are great wines, rich in the strong personality that comes from the region. They are organic, made with respect

and humility, and they transmit the true tastes of this corner of Slovenia. Ham, homemade bread, and grilled mushrooms and horse meat accompany surprising white wines made from indigenous grapes such as Pinela, or from international varieties such as Chardonnay; there are also full-bodied wines, like the red Batič, a blend of Merlot and Cabernet, which can be aged for very long periods. Batič smiles. While he cuts another slice of ham he tells how his wines are exported to the United States, France, and Germany, but his world is here, among his vines or in the old cellar, excavated by hand.

den). The town owes its fame to the breeding of Lipizzaner horses for the Hapsburg dynasty, beginning in 1580. The stables can be visited, where there are riding exhibitions, excursions in horse-drawn carts, and lessons in dressage.

In the Slovenian region of Kras, the traditional wine is Teran (Terano), a clone of Refosco with a green peduncle (berry stem)—the version that is popular in Italy, in Friuli, has a red peduncle. It owes its organoleptic characteristics to the red earth, typical of Kras, and the unusual climate, the result of an encounter between the mountain winds and the sea breezes, which in the period preceding the harvest portends cool nights and hot days. It is a medium-bodied wine, meant to be drunk young. It conveys the power of the cold north wind and the sun, and the perseverance of the local wine growers. It has a fresh, fruity flavor, quite acidic in terms of international taste. It complements game, spicy dishes, and the local cured ham. A good Teran can be sampled at the Cantina Vinakras in **SEŽANA**, a few kilometers from Lipica.

The road to **ŠTANJEL** passes through woods, vineyards, and little stone towns until it arrives at the slopes of the fortified village. At the foot of the homonymous castle, hidden behind a door in the shape of a barrel, carved into the old railroad water cistern, is the wine cellar of Jožef Jazbec, the first Slovenian winemaker to make spumante. He makes Refosco using the Champagne method. The red spumante is unique, exemplary in its harmony and elegance. The philosophy of this *vigneron* is simple: make wine for love, and don't be in a hurry to market it. And if the spumante stays in the cellar for six years, the Cabernet Sauvignon spends at least as much time in the barrel and then stays longer in the bottle, until he deems it ready. Only then does he sell it. The result is a wine of incredible elegance and great structure, a complement to roasts or to be sipped by itself for meditation.

The route then points toward the Vipava valley, beyond **NOVA GORICA**, another wine-growing region in Slovenia. The ultimate in this region's wine

production is found at the Agricola Batič winery, whose roots date back to 1592 (for more on Ivan Batič, who leads the tour, see inset).

SLOVENIAN COLLIO

Just beyond the border the view opens up amid gentle hills punctuated with infrequent farms and villages. It is an enchanted valley, forgotten by time, with no recent or devastating traces of man. Slovenian Collio opens out around the town of **DOBROVO**. It has the same geological and climatic system, the same terrain, the same grape varieties as in Italy—the border is purely political. The only difference is the higher alti-

OPPOSITE: wines from the Erzetic cellar, one of the main producers in Slovenian Collio.

ABOVE: barrels for aging wine from the Novia winery, another important Slovenian producer.

ACROSS THE BORDER   *Friulian Collio*

Crossing the Slovenian border near Gorizia, one arrives in the hills of Friulian Collio. Formentini castle in **SAN FLORIANO DEL COLLIO** is surrounded by vineyards. High on a hill, it is an excellent base for an exploration of the region. A glance takes in both Friulian and Slovenian Collio, a region divided by a political border but homogeneous from a geographic and climatic standpoint. These are gentle, green hills, marked by labor and covered in vines.

A lovely road among the rows of vines descends toward the highway that links **GORIZIA** to **GRADISCA**. The town of **FARRA** is home to Cantina Jermann, winemakers since 1881. Their specialties are blends of grapes, as Silvio Jermann, the current proprietor, explains. "During hard times in Collio, it was a tradition to mix the grapes, because the farmers bought and planted what they could find and what they could afford. It happened that they had some Tokay vines, a bit of Sauvignon, and a bit of Ribolla. At harvest time it would have been unthinkable to make a wine from only one variety because there wouldn't have been enough grapes of a single type, and this was how the blends came into being." Today Jermann tempts us once again. With different resources, he suggests great blends that respond to today's tastes and high standards.

Some of the best wineries in the region are located in the vicinity of **CAPRIVA DEL FRIULI**, a village in the foothills. One of these is Villa Russiz, founded in 1869 by the French count Teodoro de La Tour and his Austrian wife Elvine Ritter. Together they chose the Capriva estate, then in Austrian territory, as an ideal place to live. Count La Tour, who was passionate about wine-growing, was the first to understand Collio's extraordinary potential. The proximity to the Adriatic Sea and the Julian Alps, the gentleness of the climate between sea and hills, and the composition of the soil make this corner of Friuli an oenological paradise. The estate comprises several buildings, including the castle, a villa, and a building for winemaking, beneath which is the historic cellar with its barrel-vaulted ceilings. Count La Tour's tomb is located on a hillside, surrounded by rows of vines. Nearby, on a gentle rise, stands Spessa castle. Connected to a noble family who hosted audacious guests such as Giacomo Casanova, it offers a bucolic view, and concealed inside is a unique wine cellar. In 1939 the Italian army built a reinforced concrete bunker, almost 60 feet down in the heart of the hill, which turned out to be a stroke of fortune for the winery. With a constant temperature of 57.2°F (14°C and absolute darkness, the old subterranean blockhouse became the ideal aging room for the present-day winery. The historical cellar between the castle foundation and the bunker is also beautiful. Before crossing the border, visit the Angoris estate in **CORMONS**, one of the oldest winemaking houses in the region.

BELOW: vineyards in Friulian Collio. *OPPOSITE PAGE:* above, barrels from the Villa Russiz estate, near Capriva del Friuli; below, left, a view of Formentini castle in San Floriano del Collio and right, Angelo Jermann, winemaker extraordinaire, in Farra.

tude of the Slovenian slope that, according to some, makes it more suitable for Sauvignon. Today the drive for high-quality wine comes from the Italian slope; the wine of Slovenian Collio is potentially excellent, but high-quality producers are still few in number. Under Communism most farmers were forced to take their wine to cooperatives, with certain exceptions including the Vinicola Erzetic, which has been bottling their wine autonomously since the eighties.

On the western border of Slovenia the roads traverse vineyards surrounded by cherry, plum, and peach trees, and the rather poor terrain (stratified marl and sandstone, *ponca* in the local dialect) creates the ideal habitat for Ribolla, which seems to have been created right here. There is a nearly 5,000-acre (2,000-hectare) expanse of vineyards between the two rivers, the Soca and the Idrija. They produce one-quarter of the Slovenian wines that come with a guarantee of origin. The Movia winery, which has been in production since 1820, offers a prime example of high-quality wine and warm hospitality. Seated on the terrace, looking out over an endless expanse of vineyards, one can taste wines accompanied by cold cuts and cheeses made in-house. Meanwhile Ales, heir to the dynasty, recounts his family's history. The wines of Edi Simcic, near Movia, are equally exceptional and are known for their strength and structure.

Moving on toward **TOLMIN**, the vineyards become more dispersed and the altitude increases, along with the magnificence of the natural surround-

---

TAKE A BREAK

LODGING

San Floriano del Collio: **CASTELLO FORMENTINI**
Tel: 0481.884051
www.golfhotelcastelloformentini.it
On a hill surrounded by vineyards, two of the seventeenth-century houses in the village that encircled the Formentini family castle have been transformed into a hotel, furnished with period pieces and prints. Amid the estate vineyards and orchards, there is also a nine-hole golf course.

Capriva del Friuli: **CASTELLO DI SPESSA**
via Spessa 1
Tel: 0481.808124
0481.808228
www.castellospessa.com
Five suites have the true atmosphere of a nineteenth-century castle—exclusivity, elegance, and legends—surrounded by nearly fifty acres (twenty hectares) of green parkland and vineyards. The Tavernetta al Castello restaurant is also excellent and serves traditional dishes accompanied by a splendid wine list.

DINING

Štanjel: **TRATTORIA JAZBEC**
Tupelče 12
Tel: 00386.5.7691060
intanto@volja.net
Stopping at the Jazbec trattoria in Štanjel is an occasion for tasting their wines. They also offer excellent traditional home cooking, with careful attention paid to the quality of the ingredients. Reservations required.

Zemono: **PRI LOJZETU**
5271 Vipava
Tel: 00386.5.3687007
www.prilojzetu.com
Located in the cellars of an old wine cooperative with seventeenth-century origins, the restaurant has been run by the Kaucic family for four generations. The cellar offers a selection of both Slovenian and international wines.

Staro Selo: **HIŠA FRANKO**
Staro Selo 1, Kobarid
Tel: 00386.5.3894120
www.hisafranko.com
In the elegant Hiša Franko restaurant, nothing is left to chance, from the cuisine to the decoration of the dishes, and the flavors are refined but tied to the region. It has an excellent wine list, and there are also a small number of very welcoming rooms.

ings. This is the valley of the Soca, an emerald river that descends from the Triglav National Park in the north, carving out a path among the impenetrable rocks and brush. There is an incessant murmuring of waterfalls and rapids, through breathtaking gorges and canyons, followed by stretches of tranquil waters. The road winds gently along the bottom of the valley. The most enchanting spots are well marked, and it is advisable to heed the signs so as not to miss the rickety little bridges from which one can admire the eruption of the river, compressed between narrow rocks, or its placid waters that form small, lazy waterfalls and ponds. The river creates natural spectacles like the Boka Falls, which has a drop of over 340 feet (100 meters), outside **BOVEC**, or the Tolminka gorges above Tolmin, which could have inspired certain scenes in Dante's *Inferno*.

RIGHT: The promise of good wine, good food, and delightful nature at the Hiša Franco restaurant in Staro Selo.
OPPOSITE: Detail of a dish at the Pri Lojzetu restaurant, in Vipana.

VINAKOPER

Smarska 1, Koper
Tel. 00386.5.6630100
www.vinakoper.si

Founded: 1947
Production region: Koper (Capodistria)
Wines and grape varieties: 30% whites, 70% reds; Malvasia Istriana, Chardonnay, Pinot Grigio, Moscato Giallo, Sauvignon, Pinot Bianco, Refosco (Terano), Cabernet Sauvignon, Cabernet Franc, Merlot, Syrah

GREAT WINES

Chardonnay Labor 2001
Comes from a vineyard 980 feet (300 meters) farther above sea level than the others. Vinified in steel, it maintains a freshness and fullness of bouquet now rare in Chardonnay. Straw-yellow color, intense and persistent perfume with notes of yellow apple, wild flowers, and honey. Fresh, balanced, and elegant in the mouth. Should be drunk within four to five years, and goes well with shellfish and fish in sauce.

Capris Plemenito Rdece (Nobile Rosso) 1999
A blend of 35 percent Merlot, 30 percent Cabernet Franc, 30 percent Cabernet Sauvignon, and 5 percent Refosco Terano. The result of a great selection in the vineyard, it is an intense ruby red. Profound and persistent to the nose, it is harmonious and complex with hints of wild fruit, ripe fruit, wood, and leather. Full and enveloping in the mouth, and rich in fine tannins. It has body that balances its marked acidity. Should be aged at least ten years, and goes well with roasts, roast lamb, and game.

Visits and tastings: yes, by appointment

AZIENDA VINICOLA E TRATTORIA JAZBEC

Tupelce 12, StanjeI
Tel. 00386.5.7691060
intanto@volja.net

Founded: 1980
Production region: Tupelce
Wines and grape varieties: 20% whites, 80% reds; Malvasia Istriana, Pinot Grigio, Refosco (Terano), Cabernet Sauvignon, Merlot

GREAT WINES

Chateau Intanto 1996
Spumante wine created using the traditional method, starting with Terano (Refosco) grapes. Stays in the bottle on its own leavens for at least five years. Brilliant ruby-red color. Fine and persistent periage with fruity notes against an elegant background of yeast. Dry, decisive taste, with hints of blackberry and cassis. Should be aged in the bottle for at least another five years, and goes well with cold cuts or can be drunk as an aperitif.

Intanto 1998
Made from pure Cabernet Sauvignon grapes, fermented and aged in small barrels of French oak, where it remains for four years. Intense ruby-red color with violet reflections. Full, fruity, and persistent bouquet, with hints of blackberry and cherry. Dry, full, powerful taste, with notes of red berry and cherries in brandy. Should be aged for ten years or so, and goes well with roasts.

Visits and tastings: yes, by appointment

AZIENDA AGRICOLA BATIČ

Sempas 130
Tel. 00386.5.3088676

Founded: 1980
Production region: Sempas, in the Vipava valley
Wines and grape varieties: 70% whites, 30% reds; Ribolla, Pinela, Chardonnay, Pinot Grigio, Sauvignon Blanc, Tokay Friulano, Malvasia, Cabernet Sauvignon, Cabernet Franc, Merlot

GREAT WINES

Chardonnay 2001
Fermented with its own leavens and aged in small barrels of Slovenian oak for one year. Straw-yellow color with golden reflections. Full, complex, and persistent bouquet with hints of bread crust, tobacco, sandalwood, and caramel. Dry, full, sumptuous, and velvety taste with notes of tropical fruit, honey, and rare wood. Should be aged five to three years and goes well with grilled mushrooms, carpaccio, and white meat.

Rosso Batič 1999
A blend of 70 percent Merlot, 20 percent Cabernet Franc, and 10 percent Cabernet Sauvignon. Intense ruby-red color tending toward garnet. Full and persistent bouquet with hints of animal, red berry, cherry, and sandalwood. Dry, powerful, and fine taste with mentholated notes and notes of sour cherry, pepper, leather, wood, and coffee. Long and clean aftertaste of licorice and anise. Should be aged at least ten years, and goes well with meat.

Visits and tastings: yes, by appointment

AZIENDA AGRICOLA ERZETIČ

Visnjevlk 25, Dobrovo
tel. 00386.5.3959460
erzetic.visnjevik@voija.net

Founded: 1725
Production region: Visnjevik
Wines and grape varieties: 60% whites, 40% reds; Ribolla, Chardonnay, Pinot Grigio and Bianco, Sauvignon, Cabernet Sauvignon, Merlot

GREAT WINES

Ribolla 2002
Vinified completely in steel. Light straw-yellow color with greenish reflections. Fine, elegant, and correctly persistent, with hints of green grass, dry fruit, and chestnut. Fresh and flavorful in the mouth, leaves the mouth clean. Should be drunk one year after the harvest, as an aperitif or with fish hors d'oeuvres, either hot or cold.

Pinot Grigio 2002
Traditional vinification in steel, rests on its dregs until January. Brilliant straw-yellow color, intense and persistent to the nose, with hints of dog rose. Flavorful and fresh to the taste, with memories of walnut hull, wild flowers, cut grass, and spices. An elegant and harmonious wine. Can be drunk young, but also after two or three years. Goes well with fish soup, Dalmatian prawns, and first courses such as orzo soup.

Visits and tastings: yes, by appointment

AZIENDA AGRICOLA MOVIA

Ceglo 18, Dobrovo
Tel. 00386.5.3959510
www.movia.si

Founded: 1820
Production region: Ceglo
Wines and grape varieties: 60% whites, 40% reds; Ribolla, Chardonnay, Pinot Grigio and Bianco, Sauvignon, Tokay Friulano, Cabernet Sauvignon, Merlot, Pinot Nero

GREAT WINES

Veliko Belo 1998
A blend of Ribolla, Pinot Grigio, Sauvignon, and Chardonnay. Intense straw-yellow color with golden reflections. Persistent, fruity perfume, with hints of peach, butter, vanilla, and ripe fruit. Full, rich, and elegant in the mouth. Should be drunk after five years. Goes well with white meat, river fish, or can be drunk as a wine for meditation.

Veliko Rdece 1996
A blend of Merlot, Cabernet Sauvignon, and Pinot Nero. Aged in barrels of Slovenian wood for six years. Intense ruby-red color, bouquet of ripe fruit, wild fruit, and leather. Harmonious and full in the mouth, with an aftertaste of licorice. Can be aged for long periods, goes well with traditional grilled meats and roasts.

Visits and tastings: yes, by appointment

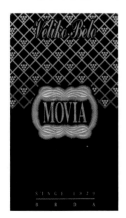

AZIENDA AGRICOLA VILLA RUSSIZ

Capriva dei Friuli
Tel. 0481.80047
www.villarussiz.it

Founded: 1869
Production region: Capriva del Friuli and San Floriano
Wines and grape varieties: 80% whites, 20% reds; Pinot Grigio, Pinot Bianco, Tokay, Sauvignon Blanc, Malvasia, Riesling, Ribolla, Chardonnay, Merlot, Cabernet Sauvignon

GREAT WINES

Sauvignon de La Tour 2002
A great Sauvignon that stands out for the fragrance of its fruity aromas and its perfumes of aromatic grasses. Straw-yellow color with greenish reflections, with a delicate and aromatic perfume and hints of yellow pepper, peach, grapefruit, and sage. Elegant and velvety, and full-bodied in the mouth. Can be aged for long periods, and goes well with ham and with fish in sauce.

Graf de La Tour 2000
A pure Merlot rich in nuances, aged twenty-four months in the barrel. Intense ruby-red color, full and robust in perfume. Full, enveloping, powerful to the taste, rich in fine and soft tannins. Can be aged for long periods, and goes well with large roasts, fine poultry, venison, and game.

Visits and tastings: yes, by appointment

CASTELLO DI SPESSA

Via Spessa 1, Capriva del Friuli
Tel. 0481.639914
www.castellospessa.com

Founded: 1881
Production region: Capriva del Friuli
Wines and grape varieties: 70% whites, 30% reds; Pinot Grigio, Pinot Bianco, Tokay, Sauvignon Blanc, Ribolla Gialla, Merlot and Cabernet Sauvignon, Cabernet Franc, Pinot Nero

GREAT WINES

Segrè 2001
Made from Sauvignon grapes harvested by hand in two phases to obtain the ideal ripening conditions, and subsequent passage on selection tables. Straw-yellow color and fresh perfume, with hints of elderberry, sage, and rosemary. Olfactory sensations present on the palate. Great balance between acidity and body. A wine of notable elegance, should be aged for five to six years, and goes well with prawns, lobster, and sardines.

Conte di Spessa 2000
Made from very ripe 75 percent Merlot, 20 percent Cabernet Sauvignon, and 5 percent Cabernet Franc grapes. Aged twenty-four months in barrels of French oak. Deep ruby-red color, complex, fine, and persistent to the nose, with hints of ripe fruit and spices. Full, straightforward, and enveloping to the palate. Ages well, and is an excellent complement to game.

Visits and tastings: yes

VINNAIOLI JERMANN

Via Monte Fortino 21, Villanova di Farra
tel. 0481.888080
info@jermannvinnaioli.it

Founded: 1881
Production region: Isonzo (Farra, San Lorenzo, Mossa, Lucinico), Collio (Farra and Dolegna).
Wines and grape varieties: 80% whites, 20% reds; Tokay Friulano, Chardonnay, Pinot Grigio, Pinot Bianco, Sauvignon, Ribolla Gialla, Malvasia, Traminer, Riesling, Müller-Thurgau, Piccolit, Cabernet Sauvignon, Cabernet Franc, Pinot Nero, Pignolo

GREAT WINES

Vintage Tunina 2001
A blend of Sauvignon, Chardonnay, Malvasia, Ribolla, and Piccolit. Late harvest of grapes that are worked together, fermented and purified in steel with a brief passage in wood. Brilliant straw-yellow color. The taste is soft, dry, very aromatic, and full-bodied. Should be aged. Goes well with baked fish or fish in sauce, or with delicately prepared white meat.

Capo Martino 2001
A blend of Sauvignon, Pinot Bianco, Malvasia, Ribolla, and Picolit. Late harvest, fermentation, and aging in barrels of Slovenian oak for eleven months. Intense straw-yellow color, full and complex perfume, with floral hints and exotic fruit, honey, and citrus. Taste is rich in personality with an evolution in the mouth that ranges from citrus to ripe fruit to vanilla. Should be aged, and goes well with shellfish, white meat, or risotto with asparagus.

Visits and tastings: yes, by appointment

HUNGARY

 WITH AVERAGE ANNUAL per capita wine consumption at 30 liters (one of the top fifteen in the world) and twenty-two wine regions defined by law in 1997 covering 230,000 acres (over 93,000 hectares, putting it among the top twenty-five producers in the world), Hungary represents the most significant wine realm east of Vienna.

Hungary's wine history dates back approximately 5,000 years, to the heart of Asia. The vines, which started out in a region now known as the Turfan depression, in the Taklimakan area of China, spread to the rest of the world, with present-day Hungary being only one major stop in this evolution. The earliest evidence is provided by grape seeds discovered in Celtic funerary urns in the vicinity of Sopron, near the Hungarian side of the Neusiedler See, which date to the fifth century BC; but the linguistic root of the names tied to the culture of wine is Turkish and related to tribes that arrived in the region in pre-Roman times. As in so many other parts of Europe, the Romans were decisive in developing viticulture, when the Pannonic plain fell under their control in the years just prior to the birth of Christ. In the first century AD, the diffusion of vines in the region was so extensive that Emperor Domitian promulgated an edict to slow their spread and contain the competition that Hungarian wine was presenting to production from other parts of the Roman Empire.

Around 1000 AD, after the region's conversion to Christianity, Hungarian viticulture began to follow other European models. Monks contributed most to the diffusion of cultivation and vinification techniques, and their work had great impact. Indeed, in 1031, Stephan, the first king of Hungary, invited his son to drink wine to keep his mind lucid. Beginning in the thirteenth century, the Italians, Germans, and

RIGHT: the Tokaj-Oremus cellar in Tolcsva.
OPPOSITE: vineyards and cellars at the Hétszóló winery, in the Tokay region.

Walloons, and then the Serbs around 1400, introduced new vinification techniques and tools. By the mid-seventeenth century Tokay wine was already famous throughout the world. The Hungarian wine industry experienced two centuries of glory and fortune before the arrival of phylloxera in 1875; subsequently, as a result of World War I and the Versailles Treaty, Hungary lost one third of its vineyards.

Hungarian wine went through another dark period under Communist rule at the end of World War II. Almost all wine production was forced into cooperatives, with centralized sales; wine was exported principally within the Soviet bloc, and qualitative improvements came to a halt.

After 1990 Hungarian wine experienced a rebirth, as small private enterprises resumed production (sometimes with the help of foreign capital), and many oenologists became involved in the revival of Hungary's rich, indigenous varietal heritage. These experiments have borne wonderful results, which include Furmint, Juhfark, Hárslevelü, Keknyelvu, Kadarka, and Kéfrankos grapes.

The climate in the Carpathian basin is essentially continental, with cold winters and hot, dry summers, but the region is also affected by the Atlantic Ocean and the Mediterranean. This combination generates a series of varied microclimates, depending on the area's

geographic position and the year. In general the Hungarian climate is more suitable to white grapes, which represent three-quarters of the production.

The diversity of the soil is also considerable, decisively contributing to the different types of wine. For example, volcanic soil characterizes the highlands of the northern coast of Lake Balaton, and löss is typical of the Szekszard region, resulting in wines of a specific mineral nature. Moving eastward, the Egar region has subsoil permeated with thermal springs, and the result is the famous "Bull's Blood," a potent, full-bodied red wine. Finally, along the country's eastern border, not far from Ukraine, is the Tokay region, home of the Hungarian wine par excellence. Here, the unique combination of elevation, terrain, climate, and oenological tradition has helped to produce one of the most unusual and famous wines in the world. Tokay owes its uniqueness to the development of *Botrytis cinerea*, a "noble rot" that attacks the grapes and brings them to exceptionally high levels of sugar concentration. Even the cellars here are unusual—humid labyrinths whose walls are covered in mold, with hundreds of small barrels where the wine is fermented for years instead of months, and where it ages for decades instead of years.

The itinerary for the discovery of Hungarian wine focuses on the country's eastern part. Departing from Budapest, splendid capital along both sides of the Danube and a fundamental stop for understanding Hungary's complexity (including its wine and food), the route continues eastward, crossing over the large central plain to the Baroque city of Eger and its impressive cellars. Finally, the route arrives in Tokay, where it is possible to taste the golden-flecked wine that was enchanting royalty throughout Europe as far back as the seventeenth century.

BUDAPEST & TOKAY

WINE TRAIL *Itinerary*

ITINERARY LENGTH
220 miles / 350 kilometers

BEST TIME TO GO
May to late November

TIME TO SPEND
One week

USEFUL ADDRESSES
Ufficio Nazionale del Turismo Ungherese,
Suto utca 2, Budapest
Tel. 0036.13179800
0036.14388080
www.hungary.com

Ufficio del Turismo Tokaj,
Serház u. 1, Tokaj
Tel. 0036.47552070

ALTHOUGH HUNGARY COVERS an area of just 35,000 square miles (92,000 square kilometers), it expresses a seductive diversity. Its language is not spoken in any other part of the world; its landscapes, ranging from cold and bare to warm and abundant, are unsurpassed, and its popular music is unlike any other. The country's boundless national pride would also be difficult to match, and the inventive talent of its people is unequaled. There are more than ten Hungarian Nobel Prize winners—not bad for a small, enchanting country at the crossroads between East and West. The terrain is likewise varied. The mountains are not tall, but rather of average height, and the hills, woods, and forests are rich in game. Then there are splendid vineyards, sun-drenched highlands that herald the Russian steppes, Lake Balaton (the largest lake in Europe), ancient cities, historic monasteries, castles, and, after Iceland, the world's largest reserve of thermal waters. Hungary's bucolic landscapes have inspired poets of all eras, and its wine, Tokay (or *Tokaj*, in Hungarian), has been appreciated at royal courts since the fifteenth century.

OPPOSITE PAGE, FROM TOP: Budapest and the Danube; a harvest scene on the Eger; various sauces for goulash; the public hot springs in Eger.

ABOVE: one of the bridges that links Buda and Pest.

309

THE WINE ROUTE
BUDAPEST'S DELIGHTS

On a clear sunny day, **BUDAPEST** is the most beautiful city on the Danube. It lovingly embraces the river and makes it its own, causing it to "snake between its breasts with pleasure," according to Péter Esterhàzy, a novelist and descendant of one of the most important noble Hungarian families. Not even elegant Vienna matches up. Looking out from the fishermen's rampart, the Halászbástya, one can see gorgeous palaces, evidence of different historical eras reflected in the water that slowly drifts by. It is a clear, powerful, unique image of the sensual relationship between city and river.

The wealth of monuments and Budapest's extraordinary intellectual vitality are strongly tied to the city's anguished, late-nineteenth-century race to catch up with and exceed the opulence of Vienna, twin capital of the Hapsburg empire. Óbuda, Buda and Pest, three separate towns, now comprise the capital, the first two on hilly terrain and the latter on a plain. They remained separate until the construction of the first stone bridge, in 1849. The Széchenyi Lánchíd, the chain bridge, permanently joined the two shores and contributed to the unification of the city—although even today, Buda and Pest maintain their differences and their separate attractions.

In old, aristocratic Buda, developed around the hill of Várhegy, one can admire the impressive royal palace, the church of Matthius (Mátyás-templom),

and the fortress, first built in the thirteenth century by King Béla IV and then renovated numerous times in different styles including Gothic, Renaissance, and Baroque. But perhaps the strongest memories will be of the quiet streets in the neighborhood of the castle (Várnegyed and Vár), which can be traveled by horse-drawn carriage. That suspended atmosphere recalls Paris in the period between the two world wars, punctuated by the pounding of horseshoes on the cobbled pavements, the succession of noble palaces, their façades washed in warm pastel colors, and by the villas in the residential district of Rózsadomb. Because of the abundance of hot springs—every day tens of millions of cubic feet gush forth—bathing establishments can be found throughout the city, but the mosaic-lined pools and Art Deco windows of the Hotel Gellert are the high points, an unforgettable plunge into the grandeur of the Magyar capital.

On the opposite side of the river, Pest combines elegance, modernity, and business. The Parliament building, with its pinnacles and spires, is nearly 880 feet long (270 meters); there are Hungarian Art Deco works by artist Odön Lechner, and the Ferenc Liszt Music Academy. For strolling, head to the pedestrian zone (Váci street) and the "iron cathedral," as the Central Market is known—a spectrum of colors, goods, and aromas that reflect the country's gastronomic diversity.

During the early years of the last century, Budapest was known as the "city of five hundred cafes"; today, after numerous vicissitudes of history and regime changes, and after surviving the iron curtain of Soviet rule, it once again shines like a star in the night. Social life no longer centers around the legendary Cafe New York, the sumptuous historic haunt of Hungarian intelligentsia, decorated with stuccowork and columns, silk and velvet. Instead a growing number of night spots, cafes, and bars have opened in recent years, in the squares and in beautiful palaces. For gourmands, Gerbeaud's pastry shop

OPPOSITE: vineyards as far as the eye can see in the land of Tokay.

ABOVE: the colors of Budapest: a tram in front of the covered market, and an old Trabant.

OPPOSITE: Sárospatak castle, long a center of culture and fine wines.

remains an unforgettable stop, while a few minutes'
walk away Liszt Ferenc tér is alive with the excite-
ment of the city.

The number of things to do and see can be bewil-
dering for the first-time visitor to Budapest and it can
be difficult to think about wine, but connoisseurs and
wine devotees will not be discouraged for long. Since
the 1990s, the growing interest in wine has encouraged producers to focus on quality, and specialized
wine shops and cellars have opened on almost every
city block. The House of Hungarian Wines
(Szentháromság tér 6), in the Citadel, next to
Matthius church, offers a broad selection of the best
labels from Hungary's twenty-two wine producing
regions.

WINES AND THERMAL SPRINGS

After leaving the capital, the journey turns eastward
to a landscape punctuated by the Cserhát, Mátra, and
Bükk massifs (although none of these is much more
than 3,200 feet [1,000 meters] above sea level). The
mountains slope from the north toward the endless
central plains. Almost immediately, one begins to see
planted fields and vineyards lined up on the less steep
hills, alternating with forests and woods. Here and
there one can glimpse bell towers of old churches and
castle ruins perched on mountaintops, or the occasional aristocratic palace adorning a village. About 60
miles (100 kilometers) north of Budapest, in the
Cserhát mountains, lies the village of **HOLLOKO**,

where travelers will feel that they have stepped back
in time. The town's history dates back to 1200, when,
following the invasion of the Tartars, a castle was built
at the summit of Szár-hegy mountain; now only the
ruins remain. The complex—which has burned on
numerous occasions because until the early twentieth
century the roofs were made of straw—is made up of
tiny one-story cottages. On holidays and Sundays, the
local women wear colorful costumes when they
attend mass in the delightful little wooden church.
The town's inhabitants are Palóc, and they have maintained their dialect, traditions, and characteristic
dress. During local festivals flat bread cooked over a
wood fire can be sampled; at one time, these pieces of
bread dough were slipped into the oven just to test its
temperature.

Some 60 miles (100 kilometers) farther, amid
expanses of planted fields, is the first important wine
stop: **EGER**, one of the most beautiful Baroque cities
in Hungary. Here, in 1552, a group of Magyar soldiers,
aided by their heroic women, stopped the aggressive
Turkish army—a glorious event that is commemo-
rated by the statue in Dobó Square, across from the
church of Saint Anthony of Padua. The church is a
wonderful example of late-Baroque, central European
architecture, not to be confused with the Eger basilica, the second largest in the country, located in
another square across from the Lyceum. This is the
land of Egri Bikavér, the "bull's blood of Eger," a wine
known for its intense aroma and full body. Previously

it was made from Kadarka grapes, which probably originated in the Balkans, but today it is made from Kékfrankos grapes (Bläufrankisch in Germany) and other international varieties. The wine's name also is tied to the courageous defense of the Hungarian soldiers. It is said that during the decisive battle of the Turkish siege, Dobó, the valiant captain of the fortress, opened up the cellar to provide courage to his exhausted soldiers, and the men, drinking hurriedly from their helmets, bathed their faces and shirts with the intense ruby color of the wine. The Turks, seeing their enemy's red beards, fled, believing they were covered in bull's blood, drunken to fortify themselves for battle.

Just outside the town are wine cellars excavated from the rock where it is possible to sample the wines, which are preserved at a constant temperature and humidity. The most typical labels include those from the Pók-Polónyi cellar and those of Tibor Gál, who returned to Hungary after a long period in Tuscany. The wines of Vilmos and Katalin Thummerer merit a separate discussion. Aged in centuries-old cellars carved into the volcanic stone, they include not only an excellent red, the Vili Papa Cuvée, but also the Cuvée Polett, which will not easily be forgotten. Leaving Eger and heading toward **EGERSZALÓK**, the road cuts through a dense and extremely green forest. Suddenly, in a clearing, an unexpected vision appears that looks like something from Dante's *Inferno:* Hidden in the mist is a small

LEFT: work in a cellar in Tokay, conducted with the concentration of a ritual.

OPPOSITE: Tokay being harvested; right, historic bottles.

WINES   *The various styles of Tokay*

Only white wines are produced in this region. Ninety percent of the territory is planted with Furmint and Hárslevelü grapes, and only a very small area is planted with Moscato Lunel and Oremus, two local varieties that are used to fortify the aroma of the wine. Tokay is made from overripe grapes attacked by *Botrytis cinerea*. These raisin grapes, called *aszú,* traditionally selected earlier during the harvest, are placed in baskets (*puttony,* singular, *puttonyos,* plural, in Hungarian) for 678 days. Each basket contains 48 to 55 pounds (22 to 25 kilos) of grapes and produces 2 liters of *eszencia,* the extremely concentrated juice that collects on the bottom. Removing the *eszencia,* the remaining grapes are remixed in the baskets and then poured into a 136-liter cask known as a *gönc,* along with a dry white wine made from Furmint and Hárslevelü grapes and traditionally vinified. The sweetness of the wine depends on how many baskets are added, in any case no fewer than three.

Eszencia. Extremely rare and prized *eszencia* is the juice from botrytized grapes that collects in the barrels under the weight of the clusters contained in the *gönc.* One liter of *eszencia* contains up to 800 grams of sugar residue. It becomes refined, aging slowly in wooden barrels to develop its unmistakable taste and aroma.

Tokay Aszù. One of the most refined sweet wines in the world, it has a high sugar residue. It is drunk as an aperitif or as a dessert wine, ideally at a temperature of 57 to 61°F (14 to 16°C).

Tokay Szamorodni. This name, Polish in origin, indicates a wine made from mixing botrytized grapes with other grapes that have not been attacked by the noble rot. There are two types:
Èdes (sweet), sweet but elegant because of its acidity. To taste its qualities, it should be drunk at a temperature of 54 to 57°F (12 to 14°C).
Száraz (dry), amber in color, the taste of which develops during aging for years. Should be drunk at a temperature of 50 to 54° F (10 to 12 °C).

Of the wines made from a single vineyard, Tokay Furmint Száraz is full-bodied and harmonious; Tokay Hárslevelü is dry, potent, and very aromatic; and Tokay Lunel Muscat is smooth.

Wines in the rock: Tarcal, the sixteenth-century cellar of the István Szepsy winery.

hill, white with layers of limestone, that is home to the public baths of Egerszalók. The hot water spills down the walls of the hill, creating natural steaming pools. Some of it is then collected in two large tanks, while the rest descends, wild, forming small water-falls. The locals come here early in the morning to get their day off to a good start and not only to cure various illnesses. The baths in Hungary are like cafes, and people go there in part to pass the time and con-verse.

THE LAND OF TOKAY

The journey continues toward the easternmost part of the country, legendary land of Tokay, the historic fortified wine of Eastern Europe, famous throughout the world for its golden color and great aromatic com-plexity. It is no accident that when democracy was established in 1989, this region became a focus for numerous foreign investors.

From Eger to the wine region of Tokay-Hegyalja the road is flat and tranquil, embellished by fields,

large expanses of green, and sunny vineyards, located on the southern slopes of the Zemplén mountains. The slopes are covered by chestnut groves, whose wood is used to produce the barrels in which the prized sweet wine is aged. A short distance from the town of **TOKAY**, at the foot of the Kopaszhegy mountains, stands solitary Monte Calvo. This is where the hills begin, covered by an orderly patch-work of vineyards, and also site of the first designed wine cellar built in Hungary. The curious construc-tion, built in an organic style and designed by archi-tect Dezsó Ekler, is the new symbol of the Disnókó winery, owned by the French company AXA Millésimes. It is totally surrounded by vineyards, in a strategic position between the slopes of the Zemplén and the *puszta*, the legendary Hungarian steppes, land of horses and Gypsies.

The uniqueness of this wine—named *vinum regum, rex vinorum* ("wine of kings, king of wines") by the courts of Louis XIV and Louis XV—is due in part to the Furmint and Hárslevelü grapes, and to a lesser

316

degree the Lunel and Oremus Muscat. But other factors play a part, including the volcanic origins of the soil, covered by layers of sand accumulated over the centuries, the morphology of the terrain, and the microclimate linked to the dry summers and long, mild autumns. The proximity of the Bodrog and Tisza rivers creates a fine veil of humidity, favorable to the development of *botrytis cinerea*, the mold that creates the wine's sweetness. Tokay wine is so important to Hungary that it is even mentioned in the national anthem as one of the country's most significant natural gifts. It was long believed that Tokay's incredible color was due to gold that originated from the depths of the volcanic soil, reaching the grapes and finally the bottle. Even in the eighteenth century the royal Hapsburg family had research conducted to verify this belief. It finally was recognized that the wine's golden shadows were only the effect of the juice that becomes resinous due to the sun's heat.

Near the tiny village of **TARCAL** are the luxurious castle-hotel and the age-old cellars of the refur-bished Degenfeld winery. Their Tokay Hárslevelü is excellent. From the village, the journey takes a detour up Monte Calvo for a fine panoramic view of the expanses of vines, as orderly and precise as lines in a Piet Mondrian canvas. Back in Tarcal, visit the István Szepsy winery, recognized as one of the pillars of the Tokay revival after 1989. The sixteenth-century cellars are beautiful, but the best places to taste the renowned nectar are the cellars, excavated dozens of yards into the volcanic rock creating a maze with walls covered by a thick layer of *Cladosporium cellare*. This mold is nourished by the alcohol that evaporates from the barrels and, mixed with the air, penetrates the wood of those same barrels, creating Tokay's unique and distinctive aroma. Every descent into the cellar is a ritual, with every gesture enveloped in calm and respect. One has the impression of entering a sacred place.

Tokay wine takes its name from its locale. Located at the confluence of two rivers, the Bodrog and the Tisza, it once was a dynamic town. Today life

Bottles spread out to age in the cellars of the Thummerer winery in Eger.

ABOVE: in Eger, the Pók-Polónyi winery, and an ancient wine cellar tool.

OPPOSITE PAGE, RIGHT: the vines (and atmosphere) of Tokay.

is much more tranquil, and what remains of the glorious past is now in a museum devoted to the royal wine, in a modest, late-Baroque building, where the most important displays are located on the second floor. The beautiful main square has an obelisk erected to celebrate the 100-year anniversary of the founding of the Hungarian state; there are also small palaces with elegant façades, shops, and a church. The streets are filled with the ever-present Trabant, minicars built in the former East Germany, painted absurd colors and with a distinctive, incongruous shape. At the end of the Tokay wine region, on the old royal lands, are the splendid Hétszóló vineyards, replanted in the early 1990s. They are considered some of the most beautiful in the world. The rows of vines, with a southern exposure, fan out as they climb up a hillside that is tinged with green in spring and red in autumn. The löss terrain gives Hétszóló Aszù its special character, and the wine has won numerous international awards.

The renowned Oremus Tokay is produced in Tolcsva, a very successful winery that is attempting to look to the future, but always with a nod to tradition. The 6 Puttonyos Aszù is excellent.

Our journey concludes at **SÁROSPATAK**, the most important spiritual center in the region. This is the site of the Calvinist college that shaped much of the thought of the Magyar intelligentsia from the sixteenth to the early twentieth century, and the marvelous Gothic-Renaissance castle has just been restored. Tasting the illustrious Pajzos and Megyer wines in the old Rákóczi cellars that extend up to the castle garden, it is easy to conjure the leading characters from Hungary's beleaguered past.

TAKE A BREAK

LODGING

Budapest: **CORINTHIA GRAND HOTEL ROYAL**
Erzsébet Krt. 43-49
Tel: 0036.1.4794000
In an elegant play of stuccowork and stained glass, marble, and crystal, this hotel was recently renovated and restored to its opulence of old. The building is one of the finest expressions of Hungarian style, refurbished according to contemporary architectural standards, resulting in a judicious and pleasing mix.

Tarcal: **CASTELLO HOTEL DEGENFELD**
Terézia kert 9
Tel: 0036.1.47580400
The family of the counts of Degenfeld was once important in the Tokay-Hegyalja region as the owner of enormous vineyards, and they lived in this castle that has now been transformed into a luxury hotel, surrounded by greenery and located next to the prestigious wine cellars.

DINING

Budapest: **GUNDEL**
Állatkerti körút 2
Tel: 0036.1.4684040
Class, refinement, and style coexist in the best of fashion in this restaurant. The gentle tones of live Gypsy music, silver tableware, fine linen tablecloths, crystal glassware, and impeccable service create a distinctive atmosphere. Károly Gundel's triumph has been to refine Hungarian cuisine, enhancing every individual ingredient, which he personally chooses each day at the market. The restaurant is located in a small house with a garden, in the small woods of Budapest, next to the zoo.

Tokay: **DEGENFELD RESTAURANT AND WINE PUB**
Kossuth tèr 1
Tel: 0036.47.553050
www.tokajtc.com
In this restaurant, located in Tokay's main square, diners can taste traditional dishes. The marhapörkölt (goulash), a national dish, is excellent. It is a stew of mixed meats accompanied by dot-shaped pasta, while a true gulyás is a rather spicy beef soup, quite popular throughout the country.

TIBOR GAL

Verószala 22, Eger
Tel. 0036.36.429800
Anno di fondazione 1993

Founded: 1993
Production region: Eger, Ostoros
Wines and grape varieties: 35% whites,
65% reds; Chardonnay, Leanyká,
Traminer, Pinot Grigio, Sauvignon Blanc,
Viognier, Merlot, Kékfrankos, Cabernet
Sauvignon, Cabernet Franc, Syrah,
Kadarka, Pinot Noir, Oporto Blu

GREAT WINES

Chardonnay 2000
Fermented and aged for one year in barrels of Hungarian oak. Intense straw-
yellow color. Full and persistent bouquet,
and the wood, well-integrated and elegant. Dry, oily taste, with hints of vanilla
and bread crust. Complements salmon,
meat soups, or smoked cheeses. Should be
aged at least three years.

Bull's Blood 2000 Reserve
Made from a blend of 40 percent
Kékfrankos and the rest Merlot, Cabernet
Franc, Syrah, and Kadarka. Aged for two
years in barrels of Hungarian oak. Intense
ruby-red color, with purplish-blue reflections. Full and persistent bouquet, with
hints of cherries in brandy, wild fruit,
smoke, and spices. Dry taste, good body,
harmonious, with soft tannins. Should be
aged up to fifteen to twenty years.
Complements large roasts or game, particularly venison paprika.

Visits and tastings: yes

THUMMERER

Noszvaj, Eger
Tel. 0036.36.463269
www.thummerer-pince.com

Founded: 1984
Production region: Nosvaj, Jovaj, Eger
Wines and grape varieties: 15% whites,
85% reds; Chardonnay, Leanyká, Kiraly
Leanyká, Pinot Grigio, Muscat Ottonel,
Sauvignon Blanc, Zenital, Merlot,
Kékfrankos, Cabernet Sauvignon,
Cabernet Franc, Kadarka, Pinot Noir,
Oporto Blu, Blauburger

GREAT WINES

Polett Cuvée 2000
A blend of 60 percent Chardonnay, 30 percent Zenit, and 10 percent Sauvignon
Blanc, fermented and aged for seven
months in barrels of Hungarian oak.
Intense straw-yellow color, with golden
reflections. Notes of bread crust, yeast,
and citrus. Should be aged three to ten
years, and drunk as an aperitif or as a complement to goose liver.

Vili Papa 2000
A blend of 40 percent Cabernet Franc, 30
percent Merlot, and 30 percent Cabernet
Sauvignon, aged for eighteen months in
new barrels of Hungarian oak. Dark
garnet-red color, with purplish-blue
reflections. Full, complex, and persistent
bouquet, with notes of wild fruit, ripe
banana, fruit preserves, and leather. Full
body and dry taste, elegant, harmonious,
with soft tannins and a long aftertaste of
licorice. Should be aged five to twenty
years, and complements large game.

Visits and tastings: yes

CHATEAU PAJZOS

Szt. Erzsebet U, Sárospatak
Tel. 0036.47.311902
www.wineplanet.com

Founded: 1991
Production region: Sárospatak,
Bodrogolaszi
Wines and grape varieties: 100% whites;
Furmint, Hárslevelü, Muscat Lunel, Zeta

GREAT WINES

Chateau Pajzos Tokay Aszù 1993 5 Puttonyos
Made from the vinification of Muscat
grapes with the addition of botrytized
Muscat and Furmint. Fermented and aged
for a minimum of two years in small barrels of Hungarian oak. Golden straw-
yellow color, with amber reflections. Full,
complex, and very persistent bouquet,
with notes of spices and caramel. Sweet,
sumptuous taste, with hints of green tea,
tobacco, and caramel. Long and clean
aftertaste. Should be aged ten to thirty
years, and complements foie gras.

Chateau Pajzos Eszencia 1993
Made only in exceptional years from the
extremely slow, spontaneous fermentation of completely botrytized Furmint
grapes. Aged three years in small barrels
of Hungarian oak. Amber color, and
intense, complex, and persistent bouquet,
with notes of fig, date, and raisin. Sweet
taste (the sugar residue exceeds 400
grams per liter), oily, with hints of dry
fruit and oil. Should be aged up to fifty
years, and complements a good cigar.

Visits and tastings: yes

TOKAJ-OREMUS

Tolcsva Bajcsy-Zsilinszky, Tokaj
Tel. 0036.47.384520
www.tokajoremus.com

Founded: 1993
Production region: Sàtoraljaùjhely, Tokaj-
Tarcal, Bodrogkeresztùr, Tolcsva,
Solaszliska
Wines and grape varieties: 100% whites;
Furmint, Hárslevelü, Sàrga Muskotaly (a
yellow Muscat different from the French,
which is smaller), Zéta

GREAT WINES

Tokay Aszù 1999 5 puttonyos
A passito wine made from the addition of
five *puttonyos* (baskets) of botrytized
grapes to the must of Furmint grapes, and
aged two and a half years in small barrels
of Hungarian oak. Golden yellow color.
Complex and persistent bouquet, with
hints of apricot, quince, chamomile,
honey, and raisin. Sweet, oily, full taste,
with hints of citrus, honey, and tobacco.
Can be aged at length, and complements
caramelized sweets.

Tokay Aszù 1999 6 puttonyos
A passito wine made from the addition of
six *puttonyos* of botrytized grapes (highly
select, from all four vineyards in the
region) to the must of Furmint grapes.
Aged two and a half years in small barrels
(136 liters) of Hungarian oak. Intense
golden yellow color, with amber reflections. Full, complex bouquet, with notes
of elderberry, mint, pineapple, and honey.
Sweet, sumptuous, elegant taste, with
hints of exotic fruit, citrus, apricot, and
dry fig. Can be aged at great length, a wine
for meditation.

Visits and tastings: yes

GROF DEGENFELD

Tarcal
Tel. 0036.47.380173
www.grofdegenfeld.com

Founded: 1994
Production region: Tarcal, Mad
Wines and grape varieties: 100% whites;
Furmint, Hárslevelü, Sàrga Muskotaly (or
Muscat Lunel, a yellow Muscat different
from the French, which is smaller), Zeta

GREAT WINES

Tokayi Hárslevelü 1999 Late Harvest
Made from a late harvest of overripe
Hárslevelü grapes. Fermented in steel and
aged directly in the bottle. Brilliant
golden yellow color, and full and persistent
perfume, with floral notes and notes of
exotic fruit and green tea. Sweet, fine, and
elegant taste. Good structure with cool,
clean aftertaste. Should be drunk young or
aged eight to ten years. Complements foie
gras or sweet and sour dishes.

Tokay Furmint 1999 Noble Late Harvest
Made from a late harvest of botrytized,
hand-selected Furmint grapes. Vinified
entirely in steel. Brilliant golden yellow
color, with amber reflections. Intense, persistent, and fruity perfume, with notes of
raisin, dry apricot, peach, and exotic fruit.
Sweet, balanced, and elegant taste, with
hints of honey, must, and green tea. Long,
clean aftertaste. Complements dry pastries.

Visits and tastings: yes, by appointment

ISTVÁN SZEPSY

Màd
Tel. 0036.47.348349

Founded: 1987
Production region: Tarcal, Màd, Ratka,
Bodro
Wines and grape varieties: 100% whites;
Furmint, Hárslevelü, Yellow Muscat

GREAT WINES

Tokay Cuvée 2000
Made from a late harvest of partially
botrytized Furmint, Hárslevelü, and
Yellow Muscat grapes. Fermented and
aged for eleven months in small barrels of
Hungarian oak. Golden yellow color.
Complex and persistent bouquet of great
refinement. Notes of tropical fruit, ripe
banana, and peach. Sweet, oily, sumptuous, velvety, and elegant taste. Long aftertaste of honey. Should be aged up to thirty
years and drunk by itself, in place of
dessert.

Tokay Aszù 1998 6 puttonyos
A sweet wine made from the addition of
six *puttonyos* of botrytized grapes to a fermentation of Furmint and Hárslevelü
grapes, aged for two years in small barrels
(220 liters) of Hungarian oak. Amber-
yellow color, complex, intense, and persistent bouquet, with notes of orange
peel, honey, tobacco, and caramel. Sweet,
oily, velvety taste of great balance and
structure, with notes of honey, strawberry
tree fruit, and caramelized sugar. Can be
aged at very great length, and drunk as a
wine for meditation.

Visits and tastings: yes, by appointment

KIRÁLYUDVAR

Tarcal
Tel. 0036.47.380111
www.kiralyudvar.com

Founded: 1997
Production region: Tarcal, Màd
Wines and grape varieties: 100% whites;
Furmint, Hárslevelü, Sàrga Muskotaly

GREAT WINES

Tokay Cuvée 1999
Made from a late harvest of partially
botrytized Furmint and Hárslevelü
grapes. Fermented and aged for eleven
months in small barrels of Hungarian oak.
Golden yellow color, complex and persistent bouquet of great refinement. Notes of
tropical fruit, ripe banana, peach, and linden flowers. Sweet, balanced, velvety, and
elegant taste, with hints of grapefruit,
honey, and raisin. Should be aged up to
thirty years. Complements dry fruit.

Tokay Aszù 1999 6 puttonyos
A sweet wine made from the addition of
six *puttonyos* of botrytized grapes to a fermentation of Furmint and Hárslevelü
grapes, aged for two years in small barrels
(220 liters) of Hungarian oak. Brilliant
golden yellow color. Intense and persistent bouquet, with notes of orange peel,
honey, and tobacco. Sweet, oily, velvety
taste of great balance and structure. Can
be aged at very great length, and drunk as
a wine for meditation.

Visits and tastings: yes, by appointment

DISZNOKO SZOLOBIRTOK ÉS PINCÉSZET

Tokaj
Tel. 0036.47.569410
www.disznoko.hu

Founded: 1992
Production region: Mezozombor
Wines and grape varieties: 100% whites;
Furmint, Hárslevelü, Zeta, Sàrga
Muskotaly

GREAT WINES

Szamorodni Edes 99
A wine of 90 percent Furmint and 10 percent Hárslevelü. Made from four harvests,
the first three grape by grape and the
fourth for the best clusters. Fermented in
steel and aged for eighteen months in small
barrels of Hungarian and French oak.
Intense straw-yellow color with golden
reflections. Complex and persistent bouquet with hints of minerals, green plum,
and dry fruit. Sweet, balanced taste, with
notes of honey, green tea, and tobacco.
Complements foie gras, duck with dry
fruit, and medium-aged cheeses.

Tokay Aszù 1995 5 puttonyos
A sweet wine made from the addition of
five *puttonyos* of botrytized grapes to wine
made from Furmint and Hárslevelü grapes,
aged for two and a half years in barrels of
Hungarian oak. Golden yellow color, with
amber reflections. Menthol, spices, fruit
preserves, and dry fruit. Sweet, potent
taste of great balance, with notes of orange
rind and honey. Can be aged at great
length, and drunk as a wine for meditation.

Visits and tastings: yes, every day from May
to late October; the rest of the year by
appointment

INDEX

AUTHORS' ACKNOWLEDGMENTS

WE WOULD LIKE to express our infinite thanks to Piero and Angelo Solci of Enoteca Solci in Milan for their invaluable suggestions. Our thanks also go to the associations and organizations that helped us create the itineraries in Europe: the German National Tourism Board, the Austrian National Tourism Board, the Portuguese Tourism Office, the Slovenian Tourism Office, Spanish Tourism, the Hungarian National Tourism Board, and the French National Tourism Board, with special thanks to Barbara Lovato for her constant support in the creation of six chapters. We are also extremely grateful to the various people, boards, organizations, tourism agencies, consortia, and associations that helped us to finalize the wine trails we created in the following Italian regions: Chianti, Maremma, Langhe, Sicily, Umbria, Collio, and Alto Adige.

Heartfelt thanks also go to: Massimo Sagna, Attilio Capurro, Marcello Giuntini, the wonderful Angelo Marrucci who passed away prematurely, Ana Ros and Valter Kramar, Graziano Piccardi, Paolo Valdastri, Elio Altare, Marco De Bartoli, Angelo Gaia, Umberto D'Alessio, Henri Bourgeois, Christian Etienne, Arnold Melcher, Fabrizio Niccolaini, Giorgio Pinchiorri, Boris Bajzelj, Pétér Horvàth, Peter Righi, Luigi Alfieri, Paolo Derchi, Uta Radakovich, Ivan Bati, Toni Gomiscek, Alberto Dragoni, and all those whose names will inevitably fall through the cracks of these acknowledgments, but who believed in us and helped us from the beginning.

No author can claim a lineup of supporters more wonderful than our respective children: Eric, Marianna, and Pietro, who sustained us with their affection and encouragement during two years of intense effort to create this book.